About The Author

Richard Prosser was born in West Auckland in 1967 and grew up on the Hauraki Plains. He has traveled extensively overseas, living in Britain for several years before returning to New Zealand in 1990.

Richard is an initiated Reiki Master and has had a long association with natural health and complementary therapies. He is a qualified winemaker and viticulturist, and has worked in a variety of industries in New Zealand and abroad; everything from building anti-tank missiles to running London pubs, from driving trucks to selling tractors to designing farm irrigation systems, from labouring on building sites to installing vineyards to manufacturing fruit schnapps, and helping to craft a Gold medal-winning Central Otago Pinot Noir along the way.

Richard is a proud and patriotic New Zealand nationalist, and has long been a vocal advocate for individual rights and freedoms. He has always been a country boy, and by his own admission has an uncomplicated agricultural approach to many of life's issues.

Richard moved to Central Otago in 1994 and now lives near Rangiora in Canterbury, with his partner Mel, and their daughters Olivia and (can't tell you what Bubs' name is until she's born!). Mel is originally English, and does a good job of keeping him in line.

Richard is a passionate believer in democracy, the rights of the citizen, and the security and sovereignty of the New Zealand nation. He wants nothing more than to serve his country and to make the world a better place for his children and their children.

To Mum and Dad, with love
Thanks for everything,
And just because.

Uncommon Dissent

Richard Prosser

HOWLING AT THE MOON PUBLISHING LTD

First edition published 2012
Howling At The Moon Publishing Ltd
PO Box 188, Kaukapakapa
Auckland 0843, NEW ZEALAND

www.howlingatthemoon.com
email: editorial@investigatemagazine.com
Copyright © Richard Prosser & HATM Magazines Ltd
Copyright © Howling At The Moon Publishing Ltd, 2012

ISBN 978-0-9876573-4-3

Typeset in Adobe Garamond Pro and Ronnia
Cover concept: Ian Wishart, Heidi Wishart, Bozidar Jokanovic
Book Design: Bozidar Jokanovic

To get another copy of this book airmailed to you anywhere in the world, or to
purchase a fully text-searchable digital edition, visit our website:
WWW.HOWLINGATTHEMOON.COM

LEGAL NOTICE: Criticisms of individuals in this book reflect the author's honest
opinion, for reasons outlined in the text or generally known at the time of writing

Contents

Foreword

Richard Prosser first came on board as an *Investigate* columnist in 2002, and quickly established himself as one of our most outspoken writers.

With his election to Parliament on the NZ First list last November, and the news media and talk radio managing to get a week's worth of headlines from his *Investigate* column that month, it became obvious that if people were going to trawl through old *Investigate* collections looking for something to beat Richard Prosser with, the least we could do was make their job easier – after all, it's already in the public domain.

The beauty of a book, however, is that it provides an easy-access contextual reference so that you can quickly measure what is being said about Prosser's opinion pieces, against what he actually wrote.

Because he's written more than a hundred columns at nearly two thousand words each, it would take a book of around 600 pages to exhaustively reproduce them all. What's here is the best of Prosser: a hard hitting collection of essays reflecting issues facing New Zealand and New Zealanders.

One of the things I've always enjoyed about Prosser's writing is how well he makes his points. The second thing I enjoyed as an editor was how I almost never had to apply a sub-editor's pencil to his copy.

The issues he raises are important, and provoke meaningful public debate.

– Ian Wishart, Editor, InvestigateDaily, January 2012

Introduction

"Eyes Right" came about ten years ago thanks to Helen Clark, who also deserves the ultimate credit – or perhaps that should be blame – for my becoming an MP a decade later.

Our second woman Prime Minister's scrapping of the combat wing of New Zealand's Air Force was the catalyst for a simple winemaker from Central Otago being transformed first into an outraged writer of Letters to Editors, then a columnist for *Investigate* Magazine, and finally a candidate for the New Zealand First Party.

I grew up in a house that was filled with politics, and swore never to get involved in it myself; genetics and destiny, however, had other ideas.

The articles in this book reflect a diary of my life of sorts, as much as an evolution of thinking, over what has been something of a decade-long roller coaster ride. I have had two career changes over the course of my writing for Ian and Heidi's magazine, started a business and closed it down again, been married and divorced, met my soulmate, and become a father, as well as watching my stepkids grow into adults.

Because these essays span ten years, and I'm a thinking New Zealander, not a statue, it's possible my views on some issues have been fine-tuned or altered according to newly-emergent evidence since I first wrote them. I stand today by what I said then in the context of what was known then. I'm not embarking on a mass rewrite because there's no need, nor would it be appropriate to sanitise history. Instead, sharp-eyed readers will detect an evolution of thought in some cases when comparing essays from 2002 or 2003 with those of 2010 and 2011 on the same subjects. In other cases, my opinions will remain the same.

On a few issues, and with regards to one or two individuals, my thinking has come around by a full 180 degrees; but as John Maynard Keynes remarked, when the facts change, I change my mind.

That said I have always been something of a non-conformist. I have always questioned authority and I have always challenged orthodoxy to justify itself, not for the sake of it, but because too often I see laws and policies being crafted and implemented in ways which are the polar opposite of what logic indicates as being required.

— Richard Prosser, January 2012

Chapter One

The Right To Pump Buckshot Into Vagrants

"A good and honest Government has nothing to fear from an armed population. Those who might bristle or rankle at this observation would perhaps be well advised to very objectively examine their motivations for wanting to be involved in Government at all"

— Prosser, Investigate, January 2003

My Home, My Castle

Several years ago when the Government reneged on yet another contract with the people, I was required to renew my "life-time" firearms licence. The local sheriff visited my home, to review the security provisions I had installed to prevent my arsenal (a .22 rifle and the slug gun I was given for my thirteenth birthday) from falling into criminal hands, and to inquire of my then partner as to my suitability to be entrusted with the responsibility of owning guns.

He left, impressed with my safe, and leaving my good lady impressed with the image of a handsome young man in uniform.

My next task was to present myself at the local Constabulary to fill out some forms, pay some money (of course) and answer a few questions.

Amongst them was a simple one-liner: "Would you use a firearm in self-defence?"

"That's a tricky one isn't it?" I inquired of the constable reading the questions from a list.

"That's why we put it in," she replied.

After a moment's contemplation I answered; "In all honesty, I have to say yes."

"So would I," said she, and stamped the form.

Now it would seem that a Northland farmer is to be prosecuted by the same Police force, ostensibly for doing just that.

Police have announced that they will, after all, be laying charges against a Kawakawa farmer, in relation to his shooting of one of three men involved in the attempted theft of a $20,000 four wheel farm bike from his remote Northland farm.

The charges are that the farmer "caused injury with reckless disregard for the safety of others", and that he "discharged a firearm without reasonable cause."

In shooting at the tyres of the would-be thieves' vehicle, rather than at the men themselves, as will probably be argued in court, the farmer was presumably attempting quite deliberately to avoid harming anyone, which can hardly be called *reckless* disregard.

As for the second matter, much depends on what society is prepared to class as "reasonable cause".

Put yourself generally in any farmer's shoes for a moment. A group of intruders arrive at your farm in the dead of night. They are intent on violating the sanctuary of your home and stealing your property. They are armed. Who knows what else may be on their minds?

Your family is inside; you and your firearm are all that stands between them and violence.

Is it reasonable to expect you to do nothing?

The nearest Police Station is probably forty-five minutes distant over gravel roads, and it isn't manned at night. By the time your emergency call rouses the duty officer, help is at least an hour away. Faced by armed criminals, is it reasonable to expect you to wait this long?

They outnumber you by three to one, and they have the means and the intent to take your property, doing you harm in order to facilitate this if necessary. Is it reasonable to expect you to remain passive?

If you sit back and allow your property to be stolen, taking a chance that you and your family will be unharmed, you will still suffer loss; true, insurance will cover the cost of your stolen farm bike, but you will still have to front up with the excess, and your premiums will rise as well, not just now, but through all the future to come. If you want cover in the future you will have to increase your security, with better locks and more alarms, all at a direct cost to yourself. Is it reasonable to expect you to simply pay out for this because some criminals decide to break both the law and society's code of conduct?

Is it reasonable for society to expect you to allow yourself to be violated because that same society is uneasy about people "taking the law into their own hands"?

The Police, in remote rural New Zealand, are quite simply not capable of protecting people. They have not the manpower, resources or budget. Is it reasonable, under these circumstances, that they insist you do nothing, and leave it all up to them? No, it most certainly is not.

If you, as an honest and law-abiding citizen, take the only action you can in order to protect your life, your home, family, and possessions, against those who have no regard for the law or for the rights and property of others, can this be called unreasonable? I think not.

If one of those intending criminals is injured as a result of your actions in defending yourself, can he claim that he has been treated unfairly? No, he damned well can't, and neither can society nor the Police claim that.

Honest citizens have a right to be protected. This right over-rides any that those who would violate that right may have. If society and its Police force are not capable of offering you protection, then they do not have the right to prevent you from protecting yourself. If criminals are injured in the course of committing crime, well, that's just tough. No-one forced them to be there.

The hand-wringers and the bleeding hearts can say what they like; until society abandons its liberal guilt mentality and demonstrates that it is prepared to get tough, until we are prepared to put the rights of decent folk above those of thieves and low-lifes, the criminal menace will remain. The wholly contemptible "better red than dead" approach of wets and pacifists contributes nothing to the building of a better society.

A man's home is his castle, and it is his right to defend it; and to defend his family and his possessions, and to offer his protection to his neighbour.

First published December 2002, this was Richard Prosser's first column for Investigate magazine.[1]

Weapons of Choice

Driving home from work one afternoon last week, I spied a bumper sticker which gave me cause to reminisce. It read "Take My Gun, Lose My Vote."

Time was, that such stickers, and others with similar slogans, adorned many a vehicle on New Zealand's roads.

There are not so many now, and those still on display are largely fading; their demise a testament to the successful campaign waged by legitimate, law-abiding gun owners, the last time the control freaks of the self-important academic left tried to convince New Zealanders that we were all rabid criminals hell-bent on mass murder.

We won that time, and for a few years the gun-control Nazis have been relatively quiet. But there have been stirrings in the jungle of late, signs and sounds that they are on the move again. Compulsory firearms registration lurks just beneath the surface of the parties of the Left, and in this election year, it is a fairly safe bet that this pointless and discredited theory will rear its ugly head yet again.

Whatever the colour of their politics, the proponents of firearms registration appear to suffer from some form of collective learning disability. They can't seem to get it through their heads that gun registration doesn't work.

The reason behind this is quite simple; for compulsory registration to be effective, gun owners have to register their guns. Law-abiding citizens will of course do this, because by definition, they abide by the law. But criminals will not – that's what makes them criminals, y'know?

---

1   For statistical validation of the claim that personal gun ownership leads to a drop in violent crime, see http://www.thebriefingroom.com/archives/2007/08/the_gun_debate.html

New Zealand knows this better than most nations. Up until 1983, all firearms owned by New Zealanders were required to be registered. But in that sensible year the firearms register was finally axed, to the great relief of the Police Force, who had long since given up pretending that it was accurate enough to be of any use. The registration of individual guns was replaced by the licensing of individual users, and that far more practical system has worked well to this day.

1983 was also the year that this writer, then aged 16, purchased his first firearm. I was one of the last people to be issued with the old "Permit to Procure" a firearm, and one of the first to receive the new "lifetime" firearms license.

That same .22 rifle, lovingly maintained, is still in my collection, and still has regular workouts against bunnies on the vineyard. And in the twenty-two years that I have owned it, and many other firearms, I've never used any of them to commit a crime. This is not because I haven't had means or opportunity; it's because I haven't had the inclination. Guns do not commit crimes. People commit crimes. And I am not a criminal.

But just as being required to register my guns individually won't affect my behaviour with regard to the law, neither will it affect the behaviour of my hypothetical criminal neighbour up the road. He'll carry on being a criminal, he won't be applying for a license, and he most certainly won't be registering his sawn-off shotgun with the Police. Why the control freaks have difficulty understanding this, is quite beyond me.

But fail to understand it they do, and they still clamour for registration. Some firearms in this country do still have to be registered, of course, and so they should; pistols and military-style semi-automatics, and a few other categories of restricted weapons, accounting in total for around three or four percent of the estimated 1.2 million guns owned legally by New Zealand citizens.

The anti-gun nuts, however, would like to see registration for all weapons, and it is this desire which gives cause to question their motivation.

Registration is an essential precursor to confiscation, and there are many amongst those who hold power in this country – and those who would like to – who would very much prefer ordinary New Zealanders to be unarmed, and thereby weak and vulnerable.

Their stock standard argument is that fewer guns in the hands of citizens equates to fewer gun-related crimes, and a safer and more caring society, and blah blah blah. The reality, born out by statistics from all over the world, is quite the opposite. Those nations whose people are denied the right to own firearms have rates of violent crime far higher than those who permit their citizens to possess The Great Equaliser.

Luxembourg, for example, where private firearms ownership is banned outright, has twice the murder rate of Israel, where it is virtually compulsory. Sweden and Switzerland, where citizens are required by law to keep and maintain their national service-issue rifles at home, have lower rates of murder, rape, and armed robbery, than do Britain or Germany, where firearms ownership laws are most restrictive.

The story from Australia is even more telling. Following the Port Arthur shootings in Tasmania in 1996, Australia's knee-jerk reaction was to drastically re-write its firearms laws, placing draconian restrictions on who could own guns, and on what type of firearms they could own. During the amnesty period which followed, the Australian Government bought back, and destroyed, at a cost of around AUD500 million, some 600,000 of Australia's estimated four million rifles and shotguns.

Predictably, it was only law-abiding gun owners who made use of the voluntary disarmament scheme. In the twelve months from the end of the amnesty, across Australia, homicides increased by 3.2%, assaults by 8.6%, and armed robberies by a staggering and tragic 44%. In the State of Victoria, homicides by firearm rose by a sickening 300%. Criminals, it would appear, much like control freaks, prefer their victims to be unarmed.

The similarity between the mentality of armed criminals, and that of anti-gun politicians, is unsettlingly obvious.

Why is there, I cannot help but wonder, such a fervour amongst so many who would seek to govern, to ensure that the citizenry is denied the most fundamental tool enabling resistance against the worst excesses of the usurpers of authority? What do these wannabe-rulers have to fear from a population which is able to resist the illegitimate and unconstitutional misuse of power?

Perhaps the answer lies in some stark and telling statistics from the turbid history of the twentieth century. Many regimes from our recent past have succeeded in taking the right and the ability of self-defence away from their populace, and the results have followed a grim and disturbing pattern.

- In 1929, the Soviet Union established gun control. From 1929 to 1953, about 20 million dissidents, unable to defend themselves, were rounded up and exterminated.
- In 1911, Turkey established gun control. From 1915 to 1917, 1.5 million Armenians, unable to defend themselves, were rounded up and exterminated.
- Germany established gun control in 1938. From 1939 to 1945, 13 million Jews and others, who were unable to defend themselves, were rounded up and exterminated.
- China established gun control in 1935. From 1948 to 1952, 20 million political dissidents, unable to defend themselves, were rounded up and exterminated.
- Guatemala established gun control in 1964. From 1964 to 1981, 100,000 Mayan Indians, unable to defend themselves, were rounded up and exterminated.
- Uganda established gun control in 1970. From 1971 to 1979, 300,000 Christians, unable to defend themselves, were rounded up and exterminated.
- Cambodia established gun control in 1956. From 1975 to 1977, one million "educated" people, unable to defend themselves, were rounded up and exterminated.

Defenceless people rounded up and exterminated during the 20th Century because of gun control: 56 million. Is it intended, somehow, that Australians and New Zealanders should be amongst the next to suffer?

I enjoy hunting and shooting. I always have. As a teenager, my mates and I shot possums, rabbits, and goats, as much for fun, as for the skins and the bounties. We were taught gun safety by responsible parents who had experienced military service, and who regarded a rifle as being as much of a natural and wholesome accessory for a young man, as was a bicycle or a dog.

Today, I still shoot as much for recreation, as to fill the freezer. Like a third of a million other New Zealand farmers, hunters, and good ol' boys and girls, I don't subscribe to *Soldier of Fortune* magazine, or stalk the hills in camouflage pants and face paint. I don't regard myself as being a criminal, a radical, a red-necked vigilante, or a subversive-in-waiting.

But at the same time, in this day and age where a home invasion 111 call in the middle of the night, from a small South Island town named Alexandra, is quite likely to result in a Wellington-based Police operator dispatching a car to an Auckland trotting park – and probably a taxi, at that – it's reassuring to know that the means of protecting my home and family is only as far away as the gun safe in the wardrobe, and that I know where the key is and the intruder doesn't.

And I regard with great suspicion, the motives of any self-professed do-gooder who wants to take that protection away from me. Law-abiding folk like me giving up our guns, or providing the Government with a list of them, won't make a shred of positive difference to the crime statistics; and in all honesty, I have to say that I simply don't trust the self-appointed gun control freaks, or their plans for the future of my democracy.

So to those who claim that the innocent have nothing to fear from the law, I can only say that I agree wholeheartedly. After all, innocent Governments have nothing to fear from people like me owning firearms.

Perhaps that bumper sticker of a decade ago needs to be revised and updated for a changing world. Maybe nowadays, it should say "I'll Keep My Gun, So That You Can't Take Away My Vote."

Investigate, April 2005

Canvassing the need for a written constitution

The Second Amendment to the Constitution of the United States of America affords the citizens of that nation the right to bear arms. It does so for one express, if little-known purpose. The founding fathers of America, visionaries and patriots, included this provision in the Constitution to ensure that the free peoples of the States of the United States would have at their disposal the means to resist the Federal Government, in the event that it should attempt to over-ride the Constitution and gain excessive power over the individual States.

Power, to these state-smiths of old, was the inseparable companion of freedom. Freedom was the inalienable, God-given right of every man, and power was something vested solely, and rightly, in the expressed collective will of the people.

To ensure that this power and freedom could never be usurped, the Government and Nation of the United States of America were structured in such a way that no part of the hierarchy held absolute dominion The House of Representatives is answerable to the Senate, the Senate is answerable to the President, the President is answerable to the whole of Congress, and all of the above are answerable to the Supreme Court, who are in turn answerable to the electorate. And the Electorate, the Supreme Court, Congress and the President are all answerable to the Constitution, which is written down in black and white, signed in honour, and many times defended in blood.

In a sense, the Constitution embodies the Nation in much the same way that the Queen represents the nation in Britain's constitutional monarchy. In the purest form, the Monarch ceases to be a human individual, and becomes the embodiment of the People, the Nation itself; the proclaimer and protector of the common good, the collective will, of freedom and justice.

In Britain's constitutional monarchy, and by association New Zealand's, there are no written rules to follow. The actions of the State, or Government, which gain authority ultimately by the grace of the Sovereign, are dictated by convention, tradition, and a host of unconnected laws. Adherence to the principles of freedom and justice rests largely on the courage and conviction of the individual fulfilling the role of Monarch, and on their ability and willingness to determine right from wrong, and more importantly, to stamp the authority of right on those who would seek to usurp that authority to their own ends.

When the individual Sovereign fails in this function, constitutional freedom and justice fail with them. The relativity of such failings are open to interpretation, to question, to redefinition. Always, in such debates, something of the intended essence of freedom is lost. The authority of the Sovereign, alone under God, embodying the collective will of the People, is the sole defender of the rights and freedoms of the Nation against the machinations of the State. In the absence of written rules to govern this defence, human weakness or disinclination to act will almost always, ultimately, lead to the denigration and degradation of accepted constitutional freedoms by those who, following their own motivations, continuously redefine and question such freedoms.

Against this creeping assault on their freedoms and birthrights, in the absence of lawfully enacted rules, and faced with a Sovereign or Sovereign's representative lacking in courage or determination, the People find themselves with little or no recourse to remedy the situation within the laws prescribed by the very State from which they require defending. That this situation is intolerable, is a truth which may be considered self-evident.

Some might argue that Government is benign, and that no such protection is needed. However human nature and the lessons of history remind us that this is very seldom the case. That there is debate on the subject at all serves to illustrate that many do not share this viewpoint. When government is structured without checks and balances, power tends to accumulate ultimately around one individual. As is known, power tends to corrupt, and absolute power tends to corrupt absolutely. That it is unacceptable to have absolute power vested in one single, absolutely corrupt individual, is a truth which may be considered self-evident.

In history there are numerous examples of what happens when the People, faced with corrupt and totalitarian government, and left without recourse to lawful means to remedy the situation, elect to restore freedom and justice by means which are not lawful. Whether the State which results from this restoration is itself legal is a matter for some contention.

By contrast, in a state governed by a written constitution, and where the dictates of one tier of Government must pass scrutiny by two or more others, the tendency for absolutely corrupting power to accumulate around a single individual is negated.

When the common good, and the authority of the collective will of the people, is vested in a written Constitution, it cannot be usurped by anyone motivated by self-interest. The Constitution spells out in plain language precisely what authority the Government does and does not have.

Furthermore, when, as is the case with the United States example, the Constitution affords the People not only the right but also the means with which to defend it, it is ever less likely that those who would seek unconstitutional power should find also the motivation to challenge the rights and freedoms of the nation directly. It would seem that the very threat contained within the actual power to defend the Constitution, provides the People with sufficient confidence that it is never likely to be tested.

Perhaps it could be argued that such ultimate reliance on barbaric means to protect the rights and freedoms of a higher ideal, may negate the moral justification for having such rights in the first place. Conversely one might contend that a direct response to a threat is more honest than an insidious, creeping attempt to undermine the well-intentioned foundation on which a civilised society is built. Perhaps dishonesty, of intention, word, or action, and the stealthy corruption of thought which accompanies it, breeding self-justification as it goes, is more sinister and barbaric than the use of force of arms, particularly when the resort to arms is in response to an action which is itself illegal, unwarranted, and unconstitutional.

The relative honesty of Governments may perhaps be judged against their opposition to, or ambivalence towards, the bearing of arms by the People. It could be argued that the only Government which opposes its people carrying arms is a Government which is afraid that the People might use those arms to rise against it. The only Government to have this fear will be a Government which is not doing right by its People, and knows this to be the case. A good and honest Government has nothing to fear from an armed population. Those who might bristle or rankle at this observation would perhaps be well advised to very objectively examine their motivations for wanting to be involved in Government at all.

To focus on the lowest common denominator as a means of defending a Constitution is not a digression from the argument in favour of needing one; rather, it highlights both the depth of emotion, and the frustration of a well-formed rationale, behind the debate in favour of the adoption of such a document for New Zealand – a debate which, regardless of the direction from which it is approached, always and with ever increasing frequency manages to arrive at the same conclusion. The actions of Governments in recent decades, and the inaction of Governors-General, the incompetence of the Executive and the impotence of Parliament, the failure of two separate electoral systems to deliver a representative democracy and the failure of the Judiciary to either deliver justice, or be accountable to the electorate all serve to illustrate the same thing.

New Zealand needs, right now, a set of written rules to govern those who govern the country.

In addition, in order to ensure the success of a Constitutional democracy in New Zealand, and given the parlous state of our institutions of Government and the degree of contempt and mistrust in which they are held by the public, it is probably necessary to create a second tier of Government at the same time. Whether this is in the form of a Senate or Upper House, or in the form of regionalised Government based on the old provincial structure, remains a matter for debate itself. Some have suggested that a federal structure similar to the models employed in Switzerland, Canada and Australia may serve New Zealand better than the two-tier system such as is used in Britain and the United States. Under such a system, local and regional issues would be decided at a regional level, with central Government being responsible primarily for external considerations, such as Foreign Affairs, Overseas Trade, Defence and Immigration. Major policy concerns such as arming the Police, entering or exiting military alliances, and the signing of treaties affecting sovereignty, would be subject to support from, and possible veto by, a majority of regional Governments.

Whether New Zealand chooses to become a republic — or even

a number of republics – is a separate issue; it is not relevant to the need for a written Constitution. However, as it is probably inevitable that in the fullness of time such a course of action will probably be followed, for better or worse, the creation of the Constitution and its related additional governmental structures needs to incorporate the possibility of this occurring.

Just as republicanism is irrelevant to this pressing question, so the Treaty of Waitangi has no part to play here. A written Constitution is about ensuring the rights and freedoms of all New Zealanders. It is not about separateness or division, or about the real or imagined injustices of the past. Indeed, the principles of the Treaty may continue within the confines of the Constitution; but they may not override it. Such is the essence of democracy, equality, and liberty.

The signing of the Treaty of Waitangi may well have been the conception of the New Zealand nation, but it was most certainly not its birth. That splendid occasion may have occurred in South Africa, or with the granting of Dominion; in the Dardanelles, the Somme, El Alamein or Crete; perhaps even with the emancipation of women or the declaration of the nuclear free zone. Or perhaps what we have witnessed thus far has been a particularly difficult and tumultuous gestation, and the delivery of a modern democratic New Zealand nation is a responsibility which rests with us.

But one thing is certain, and that is that birth did not occur in 1840; and equally certain is the reality that we cannot hope to build a free, fair, and just future on the basis of a myth from the past, and a myth which is, at best, contentious and incomplete.

A written Constitution is more than simply a document. It is the living embodiment of the wishes, hopes and dreams of a people, a nation. It is the unassailable fortress of truth, justice and freedom, the protector of the common good. It is the proclamation of the God-given birthright of Man, as if carved in stone, that none may dare oppose. It is the Law, the Will of the People, that all must obey, including and especially the holders and seekers of high office. It is The Rules.

In the example of the United States we have not seen a nation hamstrung by the requirement for its Government to adhere to a set of rules intended to preserve honesty, freedom, justice and democracy. Rather, we see a nation grown strong and proud, a nation which leads the free world, and which has twice come to rescue that world from tyranny and oppression.

Even now, as we in New Zealand debate the need for a written Constitution, the President of the United States is seeking to wage extended war against a man and a nation whom many consider to be his enemy. Yet he has not the authority to initiate such action unilaterally; he must gain the approval of Congress, and do so within the framework of the Constitution.

In New Zealand, a Prime Minister suffers under no such constraints. His or her authority is effectively absolute, without checks, balances, or rules. He or she is greater than all others, and he or she makes the rules.

In the United States of America, the Rules are greater than all others, and all must abide by them.

If we seek to build as strong a nation, then we must build it upon equally solid a foundation. We must determine the aims and ideals that are of importance to us; the values and principles to which we aspire and which we hold dear, and to which we shall compel our leaders to adhere. We must identify the rights, freedoms and truths which we consider self-evident, which we regard as being the gift of a Universal Law that goes by many names.

We must enshrine these truths in written form, for all to see, for all time, as the law under which all are equal, and above which there can be no man or woman. This then must be the foundation on which our nation is built.

Such a nation will be strong and true, with a heartfelt conviction of the rights and freedoms of everyman. It will be a nation healthy in mind, vigorous in body, robust in thought and action; a nation, indeed, of sound constitution.

Investigate, January 2003

Chapter Two

Nanny State

"I cannot possibly know best. I must not be allowed to observe, comprehend, decide, and act, without the permission of Nanny State. I must be regulated. I must be legislated, qualified, registered, inspected, recorded, audited, instructed, and approved, at every turn and in every endeavour"

– Prosser, Investigate, March 2007

Man's Best Friend

There is a similarity, it is said, between slow-witted people and computers; you have to punch the information into both of them. Now I'm not of a mind to advocate violence, but y'know, some people just don't get it.

And whether it's compulsory gun registration, or fart taxes, or the current Idiotic Suggestion Flavour of the Month, dog micro-chipping, it seems to be the same people who just don't get it.

Worse still, they're frequently people who occupy positions of public office, tasked with responsibility, and granted the power to impose their stupidity on the rest of us.

I struggle to understand what motivates these types. Are they mentally compromised in some way, I find myself asking; have they suffered accident or trauma, is it perhaps a genetic flaw, or are they simply burdened with hopeless naiveté coupled with a lack of capacity for self-analysis?

I have the same gripes and reservations about micro-chipping dogs, and the same opposition to it, as I have about gun registration, and for the same reasons. It is unnecessary. It is expensive. It is intrusive. And most importantly, it just won't work; and this is the bit which the proponents of this insidious and pointless scheme just don't get.

We are told that we must insert microchips into our dogs in the interests of public safety. The chips are no bigger than a grain of rice, we are told; they can be injected painlessly and without distressing one's faithful mutt, and once in place, being able to be read by a hand-held scanner, our children will never have to fear the dog's bite again. Quite how this is supposed to work, escapes me.

Apparently, if I, as a law-abiding dog-owner, have a microchip inserted in my elderly, arthritic, blunt-toothed, Border Collie bitch with failing eyesight, in rural Central Otago, this will somehow prevent an unregistered mongrel pit bull-cross, owned by an unemployed gang associate, from biting someone in South Auckland. Hmm. Perhaps these aren't really microchips; they sound more like magic beans.

But the somewhat challenged individuals who make policy in this country appear to believe it, and microchipping is to become compulsory for dogs newly registered from the first of July. I have a nice brochure from the Department of Internal Affairs, proclaiming that this will lead to "Better Dog Control." "Better control", in the minds of some, is apparently a euphemism for "more control". I can't help but wonder whether it would be cheaper for the nation to just pay for these sorry souls to have some proper therapy, than to let them vent their fixations on the rest of us.

Dogs registered prior to July 1st 2006 will, presumably, not bite anyone anymore. What an amazing piece of legislation!

See, it's the whole registration thing which is at the crux of this matter. People will microchip their dogs when they register them, one process, all nice and simple, a bit like checking the batteries in your smoke alarm at daylight saving time. Pay your money, stamp the form, inject the chip, collect the tags, all done, thank you Sir, next please. No problem – unless, of course, you don't register your dogs.

And the fly in the ointment, which the air-heads in their fantasy land don't appear to be able to understand, is that the people who are the worst owners, who own the most dangerous dogs, who don't look after, or train, or control those dogs, and who's dogs are most likely to offend against society, are also the ones who just simply don't register them in the first place.

"But it's compulsory!" wail the idealists disbelievingly. At this point you have to take them aside, and pat their hands, and speak slowly and comfortingly, because this is one of the things they just don't get. Maybe they had a sheltered upbringing. Maybe they couldn't see the blackboard properly. Maybe they're just thick. Whatever the reason, some people in authority, and policy-setting authority at that, appear genuinely unable to grasp the reality that there are people out there who ignore the law. You can make something as compulsory as you like, and it will still only be the law-abiding who take any notice.

"But with microchips, we'll be able to identify the offending owners!" trumpet the naïve. Yes dear, but only if the dog HAS a microchip. And if it has a microchip, it's also registered. And if you look at a registered dog, you'll see some distinct features. Around its neck is a bit of leather with a buckle. That's called a collar. On the collar is a wee plastic ring, proudly displayed in this year's fashion colour. The ring has a number on it, and the name of the issuing local authority. It's called a registration tag. The number matches another number in the local authority's data base, which contains all the identifying details about the dog and its owner. So we don't need to reinvent the wheel; it's already here, it's round, and it works.

"But what if the tag comes off, or the dog loses its collar?" they ask smugly. Yeah, what if? What if the sky falls, come to that? I wonder if any of these people have ever actually owned dogs. I wonder because I currently have six dogs (actually twelve if you count the puppies, but their registration won't be my responsibility), and over the last thirteen years and a total of ten faithful mutts, I can't recall a single occasion where a registration tag has broken off, and while I've had two particularly energetic hounds who were capable of crafty Houdini tricks with their collars, I've found the problem is easily overcome by putting them in a cage rather than tying them up. I suppose that comes back to looking after them properly once again.

"But microchips will help to identify pets that have been lost or stolen," they will suggest. Maybe so, and as such, some owners may choose to avail themselves of the technology, but it is not sufficient excuse to impose the mandatory cost and intrusion of it on the rest of us.

Dogs do stray from time to time. On most of those occasions, they are found again, hopefully alive, still with their identifying collars and tags. But pets which are stolen are stolen for a purpose, and criminals are adept at finding ways around the law. In general, the sillier the law, the more easily it is circumvented. A late-night visit to a local vet clinic via the back door will swiftly avail a criminal of a scanner, and once found, a microchip can be removed by an effective if unsanctioned operation, allowing the unfortunate mutt to be sold to an unscrupulous buyer – who can, of course, have it re-chipped – or make a fist of it in the dog fighting ring.

By a similar token, VIN plates were supposed to prevent stolen or rebuilt cars from being re-sold to unsuspecting buyers….but shortly after their inception, it didn't take a well-known gang very long to pinch a supply of blank plates, complete with an impressing machine for same.

Now good citizens and law-abiding folk don't go around stealing cars and cutting them up, but they do warrant and register and insure them. Crims don't. Why do the powers that be have such difficulty understanding this?

Good citizens and law-abiding folk don't go around shooting people and committing crimes with their guns, either. They get licensed, and lock their firearms up in approved gun safes. Crims don't.

And good citizens and law-abiding folk don't keep savage, uncontrolled, aggressive dogs. They keep registered pets and working dogs, look after them, and keep them under control.

Crims on the other hand, or the plain unpleasant, obnoxious, or uncaring, keep undisciplined mutts, let them roam free, breed at will, and become a menace to society. They are no more going to register their dogs than their cars or their guns, and so the microchipping exercise quite simply won't reach them.

No microchip is going to prevent a dog from biting anyone, and no microchip is going to identify an unregistered dog. And as the cost of microchipping is added to the cost of registration, so more and more otherwise law-abiding dog owners will tend towards non-registration. Is this reality really so hard to understand?

Or are we suffering this insane regime for another reason? Could dog control be merely an excuse to perfect the technology of micro-chipping, to allow its future use on some other animal…say, as a for example, people maybe? Unthinkable? Conspiracy rubbish? Maybe; or maybe not. Britons are having identity cards forced upon them, a process one would have regarded as impossible even ten years ago. A great deal has happened over the last few decades which was once considered unthinkable. The Berlin Wall came down. Nelson Mandela became President of South Africa. We have photos on our driver's licences. Wouldn't a microchip be, well, so much more convenient than a passport or an identity card? Safer? More tamper-proof? Unstealable, unforgettable, unloseable?

Hmm. Good arguments, and as these sorts of changes are brought about by a process of gradualism, you can bet your bottom dollar that sometime in the next few years, someone in authority will tentatively but seriously suggest it, as a first gauge of public opinion or opposition.

Naturally, of course, the crims would find a way around it, as would the authorities themselves; and once again, the only people to suffer from it would be those who were law-abiding anyway.

The slow learners are of course free to follow the dictates of their political masters, who obviously have a different way of thinking on their home planet. They can chip their dogs in sheepish adherence to a foolish, unnecessary, costly, invasive, and unworkable law. Personally, I've half a mind to join with my farming neighbours in ignoring it.

Maybe they'll think again when they realise that the pounds, the vans, and the army of dog control officers who will inevitably be needed to enforce non-compliance with this new law will have to be paid for by someone, and that someone will be them, the taxpayer.

This is a dog of an idea, and we haven't got a dog's show of making it work.

You'd like to think they could figure that out for themselves, before it happens; but as we know, they're not very bright.

Investigate, April 2006

The Law of Rules

I had a birthday last week. This isn't necessarily a big deal; it happens every summer at about this time of year. This time however, it was the Big One. It's finally happened. I'm forty. That's 40. Four Zero. My wife bought me a new office chair to mark the occasion. It has wheels, it swivels, it goes up and down, it's a vast improvement on the old clunky thing I acquired at a garage sale several aeons ago, and reupholstered with an elderly car seat cover. If her choice of present was a subtle attempt to suggest that I spend too much time out here, in my cave at the end of the workshop off the side of the garage, then it may have backfired, because it's a whole lot more comfortable than the old one was, as well.

But I digress. My passing of this milestone is obviously significant for a number of reasons. I'm not having a crisis; I've already done that in bite-sized pieces over the last eighteen months. But I am now officially allowed to be a Grumpy Old Man. Furthermore, I am entitled to have my opinions taken seriously. The frivolous thirties are behind me. Time will now be measured in decades, rather than insignificant and fleeting mere years. In the same way, I suppose, according to several commentators (and not just the kids, either) that any temperature below minus ten Celsius is just cold, any age over 40 is apparently just old.

Thus I am now a grown-up. I am responsible. I am ready to take my place amongst the pillars of society, to steady the foundations of conservative civilisation, to lead the next generation by example, to promote common sense and uphold the rule of law.

Or, at least, so sayeth the tradition of our British colonial culture – though this is not, apparently, a view shared by our dear Labour Government.

No, according to the academics, and the intellectuals, and the unionists, and the feminists, and the "educators" (not necessarily grouped in mutually exclusive categories, by the way), and all the other assorted elitist socialist control freaks who comprise the New Zealand Government, there is no room in this country for the recognition of common sense, no place for the discretion of the individual. I cannot possibly know best. I must not be allowed to observe, comprehend, decide, and act, without the permission of Nanny State. I must be regulated. I must be legislated, qualified, registered, inspected, recorded, audited, instructed, and approved, at every turn and in every endeavour. Preferably in triplicate.

What the Government has done in terms of increasing the number of useless pen-pushers and interfering seat-polishers since being elected in 1999 is a matter of public record. Quite why they have taken this course is perhaps more a matter for concern. Policy and administrative staff numbers have swelled by 95% in seven years. Health sector bureaucrats are up by 23%. Across the board, the Government payroll has increased by more than 50,000. Why? What for? What do these people do?

Nothing useful, in this writer's now respectable opinion; but worse than that, they are actually having a destructive effect on New Zealand, both economically and socially. It would be bad enough if all they were doing was wasting their lives, our money, and the Government's time. But they're not. Administrators by definition have to have something to administer, and that means regulations are required. New regulations. Lots of new regulations, to match the lots of new regulators.

What are they regulating? Well, everything, it would seem – and above all, common sense and experience. These two things are obviously dangerous, and must be regulated away forthwith. Ten years of safe and qualified chemical handling and pesticide application have gone down the drain for Yours Truly. I now need a new bit of paper – obtainable after attending a two-day course, and naturally, paying the appropriate fee. Ditto twenty years of driving forklifts, fifteen of them with the requisite heavy licence; now, for some reason, I won't know what I'm doing unless I obtain an OSH endorsement to that same licence. My old man, who did his time in the RAF and taught me everything I know about firearms, isn't allowed to borrow my .22 to shoot blackbirds out of his fruit trees, unless I supervise him – because he doesn't have the right licence. Does any of this make sense?

A local contractor of my acquaintance has had to hire, at not inconsiderable expense, a compliance manager, who is employed full-time (and kept very busy) purely in ensuring that the contractor's systems and procedures are in line with the systems and procedures of the firms and Government agencies with which he deals, and who in turn must hire compliance managers to ensure that their own systems and procedures (which naturally they must have, in writing, logged, recorded, and constructed within an appropriate template) adhere to the requirements of various regulations which, quite frequently, are administered by another division of the same Government agency for which the work in question is being done. This is paperwork for its own sake, and it would be funny if it wasn't such an utterly unnecessary waste of time and money.

Much of what we now endure in the way of Government interference is done in the name of safety. It's a serious buzzword and primary excuse for many control freaks in this Brave New PC World. Health and Safety. Food Safety. Road Safety. Cultural Safety (whatever that is). Everyone must now, apparently, be wrapped up in cotton wool. The rot set in with the likes of seatbelts and bike helmets being made compulsory. Good ideas, yes, and worthy of promotion; but mandatory, regulated, and enforced? I mean if I want to kill myself through stupidity, is it the taxpayer's responsibility to stop me? Likewise the fencing of swimming pools; time was, we taught water safety, and made kids learn how to swim whether they liked it or not. Now, because we don't do that anymore – presumably because it violates some United Nations human right or another – their safety has become the responsibility of every complete stranger with a fishpond. Don't get me wrong, we certainly need to protect people from unnecessary risks and from the exploitation of unscrupulous employers; but at the same time, anyone dumb enough to climb a power pylon, or poke their head into a stump grinder, probably shouldn't be in the gene pool anyway.

Whatever the motivation, over the last few years we have created a veritable army of busybodies in New Zealand, who are, now, quite literally, running out of things to stick their noses into. Naturally, they are turning to that reliable old standby, the motorist. Don't speed! Don't cross the centerline! Don't take Party Pills! You're an idiot at intersections! We're going to regulate you!

Yesss. In the absence of a breath test for party pills, I will soon be able to demonstrate my relative ability to drive under their influence by walking a straight line and touching my nose – assuming that I was silly enough to want to eat a pill made out of cattle drench in the first place, though if I was, my days of buying them legally are probably numbered. Regulations are on the way. There is, incidentally, no law at the moment preventing me from nipping down to Wrightsons and buying a whole bottle of cattle drench to quaff at my leisure, though doubtless this will change when someone in Government realises that here is something else which they haven't regulated yet.

But party pills are not the only evil available over the counter in a bottle, it would seem. Vitamins and herbal supplements are next for the legislative lasso, with restrictions in the pipeline as to their composition and strength; this, we are told, is to "bring their sale into line with regulations in Australia" (why? I don't live in Australia...?) – and presumably, in order to justify hiring even more inspectors, administrators, and managers.

Misinformed Government and Police fixation with road safety has, I believe, made me a less safe driver. Time was, during the two million-odd kilometres I clocked as a sales rep and truck driver, my focus was on the road, fifty and a hundred yards in front of me; I gave not a second thought to pruning the inside off a badly-shaped corner. Now, in the age of demerits and ticket quotas, I drive with half an eye on the speedo, and force my vehicle to stay on the inside of a line painted on a road which was never designed for the automobile. A tarmac coating doesn't change the reality that most of our roads were carved from the bush for the horses and carts of a century ago, and that picking the straightest course through their winding centre is often the safest option. Do the Government regulators and the traffic division really not know this?

So why is the Government doing all this? Partly, I would guess, to ensure their ongoing electoral support; every new pointless job is a potential guaranteed vote. Partly, to hide the true extent of unemployment, because most of these new pencil necks are actually beneficiaries in all but name. But mostly, I would guess, because they're socialists, and all socialists are control freaks – and because control freaks, like other bullies, have self-esteem issues which they attempt to exorcise by dominating others. That, of course, and the Nanny-Knows-Best attitude which typifies people whose experience of real life is somewhat limited, as demonstrated by everything from dog microchips to fireworks to smoking in pubs.

And why are we putting up with it? This is not how the Empire was forged. The West was not won by men who needed a permit to break wind.

New Zealand is drowning in a sea of red tape. The time and cost of compliance with ever more pointless bureaucracy and regulation is strangling small businesses and sapping the spirit of enterprise and innovation. This, as much as any monetary factor, is why we have a brain drain, and this, as much as issues of law and order, defence, and entrenched welfarism, is what the next Government must prioritise and deal with.

The youth of a bygone age lived by but one edict, which was that A Breach of Common Sense is a Breach of the Rules. I suggest we go back to it, assuming we still trust ourselves to know the difference. That, at least, is what this grumpy old grown-up thinks.

Investigate, March 2007

Chapter Three

A Political Journey

"Winston Peters also had a pleasing come-from-behind performance, as remarkable to his many opponents and detractors as it was irksome to them; and not predicted, it would seem, by anyone other than the man himself"

– Prosser, Investigate, March 2007

The Decline and Fall of Helen Clark

Helen Clark is on a roll.

Her personal and party support is riding high in the polls, she has a record second term in Government in the bag, an internationally vaunted social programme and the apparent support of the business community. It would seem that New Zealand's self-proclaimed 'first elected woman Prime Minister' can do no wrong.

Why then would anyone think that what appears to be the finest hour of Clark's presidency – that being, in effect, what it amounts to – in fact masks the beginning of the end for the political career of the woman herself, and also for the party and the parliamentary system she represents?

Election night 2002 produced some remarkable, and in some quarters, unexpected results.

In retrospect however the actual result was perhaps more predictable than might have at first appeared to be the case, and is of interest less for the way the votes were counted than for the make up of the Government to which this lead; and for what this means, and what it tells us, about the reality of present and future government in New Zealand, in the brave new world of MMP.

Remarkably for a party in New Zealand returning for a second term in Government, Labour increased its share of the vote.

Very remarkably, on a political tide following the world-wide trend back to the right of the spectrum, National returned its worst-ever election performance.

Unexpectedly, the Greens failed to capitalise on their pre-election poll indicators; United Future on the other hand made a quite remarkable come-from-nowhere showing.

Winston Peters also had a pleasing come-from-behind performance, as remarkable to his many opponents and detractors as it was irksome to them; and not predicted, it would seem, by anyone other than the man himself.

Perhaps the most remarkable feature of ACT's performance was that in a time of turmoil its support remained virtually unchanged.

But the most telling feature of the election result is the Parliament which has been delivered by it; in this MMP environment, we still have a first-past-the-post Government.

It is this paradox which will be the undoing of the system as we know it. The environment is changing, and those who would survive must change with it. The dinosaurs of the past are doomed. Just as the National party in its present configuration appears to be in the death throes, so Labour, the adversarial Westminster Parliament, and indeed Helen Clark herself, have been mortally wounded.

Democracy is the ideal to which our society aspires, as do those of the Free West with which we identify. Democracy is what the People wanted when we voted in the referendum on electoral reform, and democracy is what MMP was supposed to deliver.

And yet, despite all this, the Government which New Zealand received is an FPP government.

And you can dress it up any way you like, but the reality is the same: First Past the Post is not democracy. It is minority dictatorship.

Indeed, New Zealand has not had a democratic majority Government since 1951, the first and only administration in this country's history to enjoy the support of better than 50% of the electorate.

Ultimately, Helen Clark's downfall centres on this one fact. As a politician and as a parliamentarian, she has built her career on the promotion of democratic values; and yet she herself knows only too well that the absolute power she enjoys under the regime legitimised by this country's faulty electoral system is anything but democratic, and by association, anything but legitimate.

Many holders of public office before her have claimed some kind of moral right under the same circumstances; most however have not deluded themselves, even if they have passively participated in the deception of the public, that their tenure was anything other than a turn at the wheel brought about by the fortuitous fall of some fairly dubious numbers.

And these numbers, as they fell on election night last year, indicated that the nation desired a Government very different from that which they received. History tells us that the nation will not be forgiving of this difference.

Just as the People were subsequently unforgiving when, in 1981, a greater number of voters opted for Labour than for National and yet the electoral system delivered a National Government, so the People will prove unforgiving of the fact that, in 2002, the mood of the nation desired a right-wing Government, yet we have been delivered a second helping of Labour.

In 1999 Labour gained absolute dominion despite 62% of the population not wanting them to be in Government at all. This year the proportion absolutely opposed was a mere 59%; circumstances under which the terms "elected" and "mandate" take on a particularly hollow tone.

This delusion is what separates Helen Clark from those who have gone before her. The reality is that Helen Clark is not an elected Prime Minister, first woman or not. The office of Prime Minister has never appeared on any ballot paper in New Zealand's history. To claim such an endorsement is an egotistical fantasy of quite dangerous proportions.

Almost six of every ten New Zealand voters oppose Labour's inclusion in the Government. This is fact, reality, truth; the Labour Government has no mandate to govern. It is an undemocratic regime, and an illegitimate one.

The electorate will be equally unforgiving towards the United Future party. Given the support of an unprecedented number of voters, and the opportunity to make a difference and to strike a blow for common sense, it has instead supplicated itself before Labour and disappeared from view. The hopes and dreams of a couple of hundred thousand New Zealand voters have evaporated into the void of our one-person Government.

The simple truth of politics is that if you are given power and fail to use it, the People will take it away again. Social Credit discovered this to their cost when they failed to stop the construction of the Clyde Dam. Whether the building of it was a good thing or not is irrelevant, although this writer happens to think it was; the point is that they failed to use the power given them, and so it was taken away again.

United Future were given the power to make a difference. They have failed to grasp that opportunity; it will not be afforded them again.

MMP itself will be a loser because of the same frustration felt by the People before its adoption. Had the last election been carried out under either PV or STV, the result would have been a right-of-centre coalition, with no single party, or individual, able to command absolute authority. Such is what the People want; the sensible, representative, consensus Government typical of the mature democracies of Europe.

Labour will be a loser because it has relied too heavily in recent years on the image of its leader. Parties which allow themselves to become personality cults discover, when that personality departs, that the lack of policy or substance behind them means that the People no longer have reason or motivation to give their support.

Not since the late Sir Robert Muldoon has New Zealand had a Prime Minister who ruled in the same manner as Helen Clark has become accustomed to do. And just as pride comes before a fall, so those who exercise high office with arrogance, and with a greater regard for their own opinions than for the wishes and concerns of those whose obedient servant they are supposed to be, tend to end their political careers in ignominious defeat.

Perhaps the greatest irony of Helen Clark's tenure will be the legacy for which she is remembered.

Making policy on the hoof, and basing that policy on the shallow and uninformed ideology of one's youth, is not always a good idea. Yet this has become the Prime Minister's style, and it has been allowed to prevail by the unconstitutional nature of New Zealand's government. The destruction and demilitarisation of the Armed Forces, amongst other changes, has been a policy created in precisely this manner.

When circumstances dictate, as they shortly will, that the urgency for the nation to rebuild its military capabilities becomes apparent even to the most head-in-the-sand Clark supporters, the folly of allowing such a course of events to have been followed will be starkly illustrated by the price we will have to pay to regain it.

The monetary cost is a secondary concern; this will be happily subsidised by the only two nations capable of assisting us to restore this capability, Britain and the United States.

The real cost will be the intangible price demanded by our Allies, for saving us from our own foolishness, intransigence, and naiveté. The cost will be something dear to New Zealand's heart, and its loss will hang heavy.

Helen Clark will be remembered in New Zealand's history as the Prime Minister whose ego cost us our nuclear-free status.

Investigate March 2003

Flights of Fancy

Abraham Lincoln said, "It is the purpose of Government to do *for* the people, those things which the people cannot do for themselves."

If I were of a mind to make addition to the words of the great man, it would be to mention that it is not the purpose of Government to do *to* the People, those things which the people do not wish to have done.

Nor, it may be said, do Governments have any business involving themselves in things which, while they may not be to the detriment of the People, are simply not necessary, especially if this means that the resources of Government are directed away from matters of essential concern to the People.

It goes without saying, of course, that Governments must on no account busy themselves with agendas which work against the interests of the People.

In short, the business of Government should be boring. Mundane, basic, day-to-day fundamentals, and nothing else, unless such else is specifically requested and authorised by the People.

Raising Armies, commissioning Police, planning and building roads; these are the concerns of Government. Promoting particular lifestyle choices, scolding certain others, and actively pursuing non-inclusive ideologies, are not.

Setting and maintaining the standards for achievement in education, is the concern of the Government. Dictating to individual parents as to how that standard should be achieved, which schools should be attended, what subjects chosen, is not.

Likewise, Governments must regulate the training and practise of the medical profession, but they have no business in telling the People in whom they should place their medical trust.

All too often, however, Governments find their own passions, priorities, and pet projects far more interesting than the dull business of Governance. They concern themselves with the personal lives and private choices of the People, with bizarre economic doctrines and experiments, with fanatical dogma, curious scientific theories, and disturbing programmes of social engineering.

Little, if any, of this type of activity can legitimately be described as part of a Government's core business. Much of it is undesirable, and almost none of it is mandated.

Yet over the past twenty or more years, New Zealand has been subjected to a veritable maelstrom of unrequested, unnecessary, potentially and actually damaging, not to mention expensive, flights of fancy by successive Governments.

We have seen the fabric and structure of New Zealand society ripped up, and replaced with somebody's idea of a brave new world;

the family silver sold off, national institutions such as the Railways, the Ministry of Works, Telecom, Air New Zealand, and much of the old Electricity Department, passed into private hands, without so much as a by-your-leave, and on the back of some flimsy – and as yet to be realised – promise of a better deal all round.

We have seen our traditional Allies pushed rudely away, our old friends and family told they are no longer welcome, while at the same time our political "representatives" are seen hobnobbing with Communists and holding hands with terrorists.

We have been pulled out of long standing alliances and signed up to new treaties and conventions, many of which pass into law in the dead of night, little known and less well explained. More than a few of such agreements have far-reaching ramifications, affecting our national sovereignty, and locking us, and our future generations, into agreements which will hold in perpetuity.

Smoking in bars, the Kyoto Protocol, the seabed and foreshore, anti-smacking legislation, peacekeeping, gay marriages, the TVNZ charter, and the Americas' Cup, are all symptoms of this malaise of irrelevancy in the application of the energies of Government.

And all the while, the bricks and mortar of society are being neglected. The health system is in decay, with psychiatric patients disgorged into mainstream society while the wards and hospitals close behind them, oncology patients sent to Australia for treatment, doctors and nurses heading offshore in search of the real salaries they require in order to repay their nonsensical student loans, and genuinely needy people dying on the waiting lists. Even as this happens, our Government pours fifty million dollars a year, of taxpayers' money, into the (obviously) vitally important Maori Television channel, which is yet to broadcast anything more than a test pattern.

Our schools are in disarray, as underpaid teachers flee the insanity of Tomorrow's Schools and the NCEA, for the better pay, better teacher-pupil ratios, and the actually sensible (read: boring, conservative, and effective) curricula of Britain and Australia.

New Zealand fixates over political correctness in the classroom and produces a generation which is well schooled in the pre-European history of the Maori, but who cannot read or write about it in English.

Meantime, the Government allows "artists" who are unable to produce "art" of sufficient quality for anyone to want to buy it, to languish on the dole instead, at an annual cost of $320 million.

The arts have always required patronage. This is not the responsibility of Government; especially not when our children, through basic lack of resourcing to schools, are unable to master the three 'R's.

The state of the Defence Forces is at an all-time low, chronically under-resourced, and facing bloc obsolescence of much major equipment. Morale, already low following New Zealand's withdrawal from ANZUS and after decades of inadequate funding and poor pay, has been dealt a further body blow by the axing of the Air Combat Force and the downsizing of the Navy, to the point where recruitment and retention of quality people across all three services is becoming almost impossible.

Effectively New Zealand is now without defence, while the present Government pursues its own naïve, irresponsible, and unlawful agenda of pacifism and disarmament, claiming that military forces are not only unnecessary, but also unaffordable. At the same time, the same administration spends – for a population of just four million people – nearly thirteen billion dollars, per annum, on Social Welfare. That's around 1.4 million dollars an hour, 24 hours a day, 365 days a year, or over twenty-three thousand dollars *per minute,* on the dole and the DPB – any wonder we can't afford a Navy or an Air Force?

Defence is a fundamental responsibility of Government; old fashioned armed services, doing the military thing, providing security, preparing to meet the threats, both present and future. This is a part of Government's core business. Making up fairy stories about Benign Strategic Environments to suit some peacenik fantasy, and justifying them with lies, fiction, and propaganda regarding costs, is not.

Most parties in Parliament today are tarred, to some degree, with the fanciful notions brush. Labour's woeful record speaks for itself, and it is getting worse. A Supreme Court which was unnecessary, and given life in altogether too much of a hurry, masks a republican agenda for which there exists no public demand.

National's last Government was as guilty as any previous administration of needless and unhelpful tinkering, with everything from broadcasting to education, while hospital waiting lists grew ever longer and New Zealand's standard of living steadily declined. Even today, in opposition, National has plans to resurrect that greatest socially and economically destructive doctrine of them all, Rogernomics. As if the country hadn't suffered enough already – and just when we need them most, the Nats seem set to shoot their electoral chances in the foot.

For the Greens to want a low-brow subsistence economy for themselves personally, is fine. But to proclaim the supposed virtues of such a way of life whilst in Parliament is irresponsible. Parliamentarians, of whatever hue, are tasked with ensuring the material security of the nation. Good jobs, solid housing, affordable services, effective infrastructures. Money. Boring stuff like that.

The claimed benefits of smoking cannabis or eating vegan, or the spiritual superiority of living without material goods, are not germane to the business of Governance. They are irrelevant and distracting.

The Progressive Coalition – whatever that now means – would perhaps have earned more friends and contributed more to the good of the nation, by putting its energies into achieving adequate funding for Pharmac, or fixing leaky homes, than by spending $80 million to re-invent the Post Office Savings Bank.

Winston has some very clearly defined views, and I have to confess a liking for certain of them; but for the life of me, I have no idea what his economic policies are. Is this a deliberate and clever strategy on his part, or a failure to ask the right questions on mine? Are the three major planks of NZ First's election platform truly essential to the health and wealth of New Zealand, or are they merely more whims on the wing?

Governments in this country tend not to be voted in; rather, they are voted out, when the electorate grows tired of listening to the same half –truths, excuses, and meaningless waffle, rehashed over and over, and of waiting for the promised benefits of change and suffering to trickle down.

In this pre-election year, Parties aspiring to Government could do themselves a favour by remembering the KISS principle: Keep It Simple, Stupid.

They could all do with taking a leaf out of Honest Abe Lincoln's book. Perhaps they may even discover that a Government which can be boring, un-intrusive, straightforward, honest, and above all effective, might just be rewarded with a longer term in office.

Investigate, March 2004

Cradle of the Republic

I'm quite tempted to not pass any further comment on the makeup of our new Government. In a sense, it's a bit like shooting fish in a barrel; safe, predictable, and everyone's doing it. But I'm going to anyway. It's my stock in trade. To not put my two penny-worth in would be remiss of me.

Perhaps this Government can be defined less well by what it is, than by what will come after it. What it is, plainly, is unashamed expediency on the part of all involved. What may come after it, could be all the more predictable because of this.

One of the historical quirks of the New Zealand psyche is our disinclination towards revolution, civil disobedience, or any other form of violent opposition to those acts or directions of inept or corrupted Government which we find unpalatable. Rather, we respond to such dictates by ignoring them. It is not in our nature to rant or rave about the desires and designs of Government which are demonstrably foolish, unworkable, or draconian, or even a com-bination of all three. We don't (at least not anymore) join unions, and protest loudly, like the Australians. We don't fire guns in the street like the Arabs. We don't wave placards, and throw potatoes, and get water-cannoned by the Police, like the Europeans; we don't burn books, or lynch people, or block the motorways with tractors (even if we may occasionally drive them up Parliament's steps), or leave severed horses' heads in the beds of politicians' mistresses. Instead, we are more inclined to simply shake our collective heads, and walk away. With such disregard comes, inevitably, a diminution of respect for, or regard to the relevance of, Government in general.

I believe that the shallow and expedient nature of the Government we have been delivered will be reflected in just such a response from much of the electorate. Many New Zealanders already felt disenfranchised before the election, and the numerous, and inevitable, post-poll machinations and Machiavellianisms have done little if anything to dampen their cynicism.

That National should attempt to cuddle up to the Maori Party is hardly surprising, and I was one of those who suggested just such a liaison, long before the 17th of September. But that they should offer to abandon so much of the policy and rhetoric of Orewa One, without so much as a batted eyelid, in pursuit of the Ninth Floor of the Beehive, left even me with raised eyebrows.

That Winston should hop into bed with Helen, after vehemently denying that he had any such intention, will surprise few, but please even fewer.

That Labour should so comprehensively, and so unashamedly, shaft the Greens, after such a rosy, cosy, joint election campaign, will surprise no-one outside the naïve, and poorly informed, if well-intentioned, Green core vote.

That Peter Dunne should shoot himself in one foot before the election, and appears to have shot himself in the other following it, is quite bizarre; clinging to the Ministerial salary which is all that remains of his once-proud ship of public respect, he will almost certainly go down with the wreckage of this Last Labour Government.

That the Deputy Leader of the National Party should be openly critical of the Governor General is a little surprising; but quite frankly, I don't blame Gerry Brownlee for his comments, nor do I disagree with him. We have arrived at a crux in our nation's history. The position of Governor-General has become corrupted. It has become a political rubber stamp, along with such appointments as the Commissioner of Police and the Chief of the Defence Force. Ordinary people no longer take such high offices, or their temporal holders, seriously. They are seen as being little more than mouth-pieces of the Government of the Day, in no way independent, and certainly not able – or even intended – to protect the rights of the citizenry against the excesses of the State.

It is inevitable, as time goes by, that New Zealanders will feel less and less regard for both the monarchy, and its constitutional position, if both our Queen's representative, and the Government which appoints that person, continue to display open and blatant disregard for both the principles of democracy, and the essential apolitical posture of the Head of State.

Indeed, it is perhaps time that we as a nation gave serious consideration to the manner in which the holder of such office is selected. At this time, several contenders have been suggested as possible successors to Dame Sylvia Cartwright – who, as a former Judge, may be seen as a political appointee herself. They include a former rugby player, and a self-confessed Republican former Prime Minister. I would contend that both such suggestions are ridiculous.

If New Zealand is to have even itself, take itself seriously, as a nation where State and Government are independent, we need to look very closely, and honestly, at the constitutional position of the Vice-Regal, and at the motivations of the person who fills that role.

I would suggest that a patsy appointment of some politically acceptable, and politically correct, placeholder, is not acceptable. Our Queen's representative needs to be an unbiased statesperson; someone unaffected by the political machinations of the day, and someone who will, by compunction of duty, be possessed of the courage and moral fortitude, and just as importantly, the support of the people, to sack the Government of the Day, should such become necessary.

I would suggest that perhaps only a very few people, from only a very few walks of life, are possessed of such necessary attributes, in New Zealand at this time.

My first choice, and I have suggested it more than a few times now, would be the Maori Queen.

Alternatively, a distinguished retired career military officer, holder of the Queen's Commission, could be expected to execute the office of Viceroy with honour and distinction. Perhaps such officers and gentlemen as Air Marshal Carey Adamson, or Vice Admiral Sir Somerford Teagle, or men of their ilk, may be available to fill this vital position.

The only other option I see as viable, in terms of both public acceptability, independence, and effectiveness, is the direct appointment of a Royal Vice Regal; and in this, the only figure to spring immediately to this writer's mind, is HRH Prince Andrew – an accomplished former military officer himself, and without question, Her Majesty's representative.

But if our elected representatives do choose to ignore the fundamental importance of constitutional Governance, they would be foolish to presume that the public's apathy towards the subject will automatically translate itself into support for the not-very-well-hidden Republican agenda which pervades not only the core of the Government, but the upper levels of the Opposition as well. I believe there is a fork in the road to Republicanism, which the secret planners and back-room dealers, blinded by their own ideology and arrogance, have failed to see.

The signpost to this fork may be found in the way in which rural New Zealand voted this year. Overwhelmingly, the provinces swung to National, and the pundits, Left, Right, and Media, have all assumed that this is because they had tired of the direction in which the Labour Government has been leading New Zealand. They are only partially right. Provincial New Zealand swung to the right because they are tired of being ignored. The roughly one-third of New Zealanders who don't live in big cities, think differently from the roughly two-thirds who do. They have different value systems, a different work ethic, they are inherently conservative, quite patriotic, and, perhaps because of the necessity born of isolation, they are resiliently independent-minded. They have flocked to National this past election because they see the National Party as the most obvious saviour to deliver them from the evils of urban liberalism. When they eventually realise that National is just as subservient to the clamour of the city vote as is Labour, they will, in all likelihood, and in true Kiwi fashion, simply walk away, both from the two major parties, and from that same urban liberal New Zealand society.

Why is this important? After all, in any democracy, reality is that minorities will be subject to the will of majorities; and so it should ever remain. But there is a difference in this case, and it is an important one. That Provincial one-third of New Zealand, just happens to produce about three-quarters of its national wealth. And if conservative, patriotic, Monarchist, rural New Zealand is bullied into abandoning their nation as they know and love it, they are quite likely to take the cities out at the knees, by abandoning them as well. Urban economic activity is largely consumed internally. But export dollars come from farming, fishing, mining, and forestry, and these things don't happen in cities – and the Provinces know it. Faced with the prospect of enforced Republicanism, the Heartland may up and decide that it is better off without an unproductive urban millstone around its neck. The South Island, brimming with tourists, bursting with sheep, and floating on a sea of untapped oil, has had a simmering pro-independence undercurrent for more than a century. The Provincial North, equally marginalized, under-appreciated, and contributing magnitudinally more than its demographic fair share, may well feel the same way.

How ironic it may prove, that the strongest proponents of Republicanism may be those who ultimately fail to benefit from it. Clinging to power at any cost, for the sake of pushing an agenda for which there is little public support, may well be the undoing of this Government and its various several factions. What may come after them, then, could be very interesting indeed.

There is already grumbling discontent in the hinterland. Motorists have taken to flashing their headlights to warn other drivers of impending speed traps, in numbers this writer has not seen these past twenty years; and as we know, this sort of behaviour is about as close to civil revolt as New Zealand ever gets. Mayhap these beacons of danger, also serve to indicate trouble on the highway ahead.

Perhaps in this cauldron of social engineering which we call New Zealand, we are destined to witness the conception and birth of not one, but maybe two, or even three, Brave New Republics.

Investigate, December 2005

Lest We Forget

Adolph Hitler, apparently, once stated "It is a fortunate thing for Governments that men do not think."

Herr Schicklgruber, for all his faults (you know, being an insane, xenophobic, genocidal psychopath, that sort of thing) may have had a point; but I think, in this case, that it would be more correct to say that men do not remember, so much as do not think at all.

We're quite good at forgetting things in New Zealand, and strangely enough, particularly so when an election is imminent. We forget – and forgive – the sins and the slip-ups of the Parties of Previous Governments, we push their track records to one side, cast their past indiscretions from our minds, and happily give them another go.

On current polling, we're about to do just exactly this, yet again. Come October, or November at the latest, Labour are toast. I think this is pretty much a foregone conclusion. The nation has had enough of Labour, enough of Helen Clark, enough of the so-called "coalition" Government we have suffered these past nine years; this strange amalgam of backstabbers and turncoats cobbled together out of expedience and foisted upon us without means of protest or redress. Yep, they're about to be hoist from their own petard, and may it serve them right.

National will be our saviours now; the real old Natural Party of Government, with their shiny new Leader and the promise of excitingly different policies to carry us all into the glorious dawn of the new millennium.

Curiously, we seem to have forgotten that this is the very same National Party which, only six years ago, we similarly toasted, delivering them barely a fifth of the popular vote, and their worst election placing ever. This year, that result is likely to be stood on its head, and it will be Labour which gets chucked out with the garbage cans, haemorrhaging low-ranked list members as it goes.

Uncle Helen has been, probably indisputably, our most popular Prime Minister of recent times; but come Christmas, it will be a real struggle finding anyone who can actually remember having voted for her.

Her replacement during Labour's next few years on the Opposition benches will be Phil Goff; and when, in three, or six, or nine years' time, he gets his day in the sun, we will, having tired by then of Bill English (who will replace John Key), happily forget that here is a man who reputedly raised the Viet Cong flag over the Auckland University registry building on the day that Saigon fell, who held hands with Yasser Arafat, and who advocated legalising sex for twelve-year-olds. Is this really someone who we want for Prime Minister in 2017? Probably not, but we won't remember any of this by then.

Why did National get dealt such a beating at the polls in 1999? Anyone remember? Was it dissatisfaction with Jenny Shipley which tipped it? Now be honest – how many of you had completely forgotten about Jenny until I reminded you just then? She was our first woman Prime Minister, you will recall. Did the job for two years No, really. It wasn't Helen Clark. She was second.

How about 2002, and an even worse drubbing? Can we blame Bill English for that, and will we remember what it was he did wrong, come 2011 when we make him the Prime Minister?

And why did the Nats – admittedly only just – lose again in 2005? Was that down to Don Brash? Maybe; but in accepting that, we also have to remember that it was Don Brash who rescued National from near-oblivion. Labour only just squeaked it in '05, winning by a mere two percentage points.

If Dr Brash made one fatal mistake in 2005, it was to intimate, too publicly and too close to the election, his approval for such things as privatisation, and asset sales, and so forth. Really, stunts like walking the plank and clambering awkwardly into speedway cars had nothing to do with it. It might have made him look like a bit of a goose, but we don't crucify politicians for that in this country, which is just as well for the likes of Pete Hodgson with his funky chicken dance, or the Scary Singing Sisters of the last Labour Party "Congress". No, the only people who really get worked up about that sort of thing are the media.

We the People (well OK, not me, but you know what I mean), having become somewhat gun shy where noises about selling off the family silver are concerned, ducked for cover behind the Labour Government; which is odd in itself, because it showed that we had forgotten about it being Labour who actually invented the process in the first place.

That's right; Rogernomics was a Labour initiative. Remember? Roger Douglas? Moustached chap, used to be Minister of Finance. Sold everything out from under us. Good Labour man. Privatised most of the Government, turned whole Departments into dole queues. Got a gong from the Queen for his efforts, and then went off and started the truly Right-wing ACT Party.

Quite why Rodney Hide thinks it's a good idea to bring him back from the dead escapes this writer; perhaps he has forgotten that most of New Zealand is un-amused with the idea of privatisation. I do hope National remembers this, come the end of the year.

ACT itself may well still make a showing this year, thanks to MMP; a system which, despite its faults, is undoubtedly better than the FPP sham it replaced. Voices in our society continue to clamour for the return of the old ways; we have forgotten, no doubt, the bad days when Labour won more votes than National but still didn't become the Government, when Social Credit attracted twenty percent of the electorate but occupied just two percent of the seats in Parliament, when the support of fewer than four of every ten voters was enough to ensure one-Party rule. Why have we forgotten this?

For the same reasons, I suppose, that many people also call for the reduction of the size of Parliament from 120 MPs back to 99. We have forgotten that the original Royal Commission which recommended the adoption of MMP also said quite clearly that the size of the House of Representatives should increase to 120 members whether the voting system was changed or not, simply because electorate and international commitments meant that fewer than 100 available lawmakers were not able to adequately staff Parliament's Select Committees, which do the real work of the House.

People draw comparisons between the size of the New Zealand Parliament and the Sydney City Council, and ask why, when both are administering a similarly-sized population, does one have to be so much bigger than the other; they forget, perhaps, that the

Sydney City Council does not have to concern itself with Health, or Welfare, or Education, or Defence or Foreign Affairs or any of the other matters which are the responsibility of the Government of a Nation State, but not of a local authority.

I know a good many people who will be voting National this year because they are disgusted by what Labour have done to New Zealand's defence forces. I share their sentiment, but I wonder whether they may have forgotten that it was a National Cabinet which scuttled the Navy's third and fourth ANZAC Frigates, and which failed to sign off the F-16 lease deal, making it possible for Clark & Co to cancel it altogether. Max Bradford, indeed, is on record as questioning the need for the Air Forces' strike wing, long before Helen Clark got the knives out for it. Remember Max? He was Defence Minister in the last National Government. He was also the Energy Minister who told us all that chopping the country's electricity generation into bits and selling it off, would mean lower power prices for everyone. Hmm. Well another winter is upon us, and my power bill is twice what it was in 1999, and competition or no, we still don't have enough power stations, and it's going to be a cold winter like '92....but I guess we've forgotten 1992, just like we've forgotten that privatisation aside, the Government (ie us) still owns half the generation capacity and all the national grid, and so why are we paying twice what we were, for our own power, from stations which we had already paid for, when we're not making any new investment in additional generation? And why – if Labour are so much about looking after the people as they claim – have they forgotten to do anything about this over the past nine years?

I think what cracks me up most of all is Winston Peters. No matter what happens, or what he gets up to, we keep forgetting what he's done, and we keep forgiving him. I think it's hilarious. I might even vote for the man myself this year. I mean I haven't done that before, and it's probably his turn.

Winston backed National when everyone expected him to back Labour, and he got away with it; and for good measure, backed Labour when everyone expected him to back National, and got away with that, too.

As I sit and type, and the Siege of Helengrad has already begun, Winston's support is on the rise yet again; people are forgiving him already, and forgetting that this increasingly unpopular Government has only been able to stagger on because of his support for it – but they're forgetting about that even while he's still doing it!

Long-time chameleon Peter Dunne has had so many changes of flag over the years that in fairness, people can be forgiven for forgetting what it is that he actually stands for. I do hope they'll remember, however, that he voted in favour of Sue Bradford's anti-smacking Bill. In fact, all but seven of our elected representatives supported this particularly onerous piece of legislation; something we should all remember come the election, and perhaps more importantly, we should all remind them of afterwards – just in case a few of them decide to forget which side of the fence they were on. Perhaps a good time to do this will be when we get our referendum on the matter – when we give them cause to not forget that it is We, not Them, who are actually in charge.

Investigate, June 2008

Chapter Four

Pinko's, Liberals & Lefties

"I don't like corruption. I don't like bent cops, or bent politicians, or bent judges, or perverted priests or embezzling executives or lying lawyers or dodgy accountants, or civil servants and military officials who sell out to the system in exchange for promotion or profit or power"
— Prosser, Investigate, October 2006

The Good Ol' Boys

I got called a redneck the other day. I don't do the insult thing, so naturally, I took it as a compliment. The accuser was some wowser who'd taken objection to one of my rare, and moderate, opinions. The incident didn't trouble me, though it did, as many of life's encounters are prone to, set me to thinking. What is a redneck?

I receive, amongst the volumes of correspondence which fill my email, regular despatches from a contact in the US; a Vietnam veteran, ex-Special Forces, and now a prolific social and political commentator. Much of what he sends is humorous, and a proportion of this is aimed at poking fun at American Rednecks. I trolled through my inbox files. Surely the New Zealand redneck cannot be the same species as his American counterpart?

In general terms, I've more often thought of myself as a classical liberal than a raging fascist. I mean I'm a winemaker – almost by definition, that paints me as being urbane and sophisticated, one would think.

So I wondered, what are the attitudes which make a redneck in New

Zealand today, and do I, however unwittingly, fit the description?

I like to call a spade a spade. And unlike some metropolitan commentators, I actually know what a spade is. I own several, I know how to use them, and I don't mind getting my hands dirty. Does this make me a redneck?

I also like to call an idiot an idiot, and a hypocrite a hypocrite. I don't like the liberals pinching the term liberal any more than I like queers pinching the term gay. I mean if people want to be weak, stupid, effeminate, erectile dysfunctional, naïve, apologist, namby-pamby, thumb-sucking, lefty pinko fantasy-land morons, let them find their own word for themselves, and leave "liberal" for us genuine freedom-loving, gonad-equipped, libertarian go-getters.

I don't like part-Maori hypocrites demanding compensation for injustices which weren't done to them, from people who wouldn't have been responsible for them if they had been. If people want to identify with their 1/16th Maori ancestry, I say good on them. But when they ignore the other 93.75% of their lineage, and want a free ride from me because of something which happened to their great-great-grandfather, 100 years before my old man got off the boat, I say they can go fish. Here's a question; if I stump up for an inflation-adjusted increase on the muskets and blankets which your great-grand-pappy took in exchange for some property which he probably never lived on, let alone owned individually, will you give back the vote, rugby, Christmas, trial by jury, the right of free passage on the Queen's Highway, metal, the wheel, beer, tobacco, spuds, mutton, the protection of the Crown, and everything else which the evil white man brought with him, along with 15/16[th]s of your genetics? No? Didn't think so. Am I a redneck yet?

I don't have a problem with people being queer if that's their kick. I know some excellent poofters. So long as they don't do it in the street and frighten the horses, what they get up to in the bedroom is their own business, in my libertarian opinion. But I draw the line at gays getting married or adopting children. Why? Because marriage is the preserve of us regular straight folk, and because kids need to be raised by a mum and a dad. It's bad enough that so many of our youngest generation live in fractionated families and separate households, without deliberately making things worse. It happens that some people have children, and then swap teams. That's different. But choosing to be gay from the start, doesn't come with the right to partake in shaping the next generation. Getting married and raising kids is about the kids, not about us. If you want a pet, go and buy a dog.

Those same kids have a right to a balanced real world education, with male teachers as well as female, regular men with kids of their own, ordinary straight blokes who coach sports, and go to scout camps, and cook barbeques on the beach, and drink beer, and who aren't child molesters or rapists or anything else the Sisterhood would have them branded as. The hysterical shriekers who scream satanic abuse, or mass molestation, or ritualised slaughter of the innocents, or whatever other insanity their twisted minds can create, need to be taken out and given a cold hosing down, along with the slack-jawed cardigan-wearers who permit such parasitic drivel to colonise the thought processes of policy making. Reality check, people! 99.999% of men are not paedophiles! Film at eleven!

I don't go to Church. But you know what? I don't object to people who do. I celebrate Christmas. I take Easter off.. If I ever had to serve on a Jury, which I won't because I live in the wops, I'd swear on the Bible, and mean it. I sing God Defend New Zealand, rather well if I say so myself (and while I'm on the subject, I refuse to sing it in anything other than English). I respect the Christian under-pinning of our officially secular society, even if I don't necessarily claim it as my own. If the price for this is to have primary school kids put up with half an hour of Bible instruction on a Wednesday morning, I'm all for it. But do I want the country filled up with Muslims? No. I don't particularly want the influence of Islam here at all, however many fine examples of individual Muslims it may be possible to find. Why not? Because it's just not necessary. We can get all the immigrants we need and more from "traditional source countries", and still leave people in the queue. Diversity is just close enough when it's on TV, thanks very much.

Have I qualified as a redneck yet?

I light my rubbish fires with gasoline. But I don't spray the weeds when the breeze is getting up, because I'm a qualified chemical handler and I care about the environment. Yeah, I drive a 4WD. There are frequently a few dogs in it. But hey, it can snow any month of the year hereabouts, and I have lots of dogs, and they like to go places. And yes, I also frequently carry a rifle – properly secured, of course. One often encounters animal pests on vineyards; rabbits, and possums, and, err, ahem, fallow hinds. You know?

Up the road in the Maniototo there aren't too many vineyards; but the good ol' boys up there are ever vigilant, and there are scant few road signs which don't sport a few bullet holes or a peppering of shot-gun pellets. The hand-wringers may despair at such antics. Personally I'm inclined to cut them a little slack. These young men, and others like them, all over the country, are the muscle, nerve, and sinew of the Heartland, where the nation's wealth is actually earned, before it gets theorised about, and squabbled over, and turned into latte, by the armchair commentators, and the welfare wets, and the rest of society's passengers who are happy to be generous with everybody else's money in support of their own trembling sycophancy. If the boys get a bit loose on Friday night, or after footy practice, does it really matter, and does having such an attitude paint my neck with rouge?

I like the Yanks. I like the Aussies and the Poms and the Canadians too, for that matter. Like the Paddies and the Scandinavians, they're People Like Us. I like and respect the Indians as well, and the Israelis and the Russians and many of the Europeans. But I feel most com-fortable in the company of the peoples who are most like me. Am I a redneck because of this? Yep, I'll bet some of the lefties are frothing at the mouth by now. I like the Yanks because of their attitude. I like their cars, their courage, their camaraderie. I like the fact that thanks to the Yanks, I don't have to speak Japanese. I want us to be friends with America again, and to exercise with them, and benefit from their generosity, and have their ships come visit, like things were in the old days, when the sky didn't fall just because the US Navy was in port. And I don't have a problem with nuclear propulsion, mostly because the factual record shows there hasn't ever been a single problem with it – unlike diesel powered shipping, the disastrous litany of which has wrecked more coastlines than most Greenies have ever seen.

I don't like pacifists. I don't think they're very bright. I struggle to find an idea more monumentally stupid than the notion which says we live in some special bubble of human history, where all wars have now ended, and we will never again need the Air Force which we lost because it didn't fit with some naïve fantasy promulgated by people who have never lived in the real world. Things are not different now. We are simply at a point in time which is in between conflicts. I do think the Chinese are coming, and I do think it blindingly obvious that we need to resurrect and maintain effective combat forces and reliable military alliances – whatever the cost. To repeat a phrase which I coined a few years ago, I think it a mighty coincidence that "Benign Strategic Environment" and "Mad Cow Disease" have the same initials.

I don't like corruption. I don't like bent cops, or bent politicians, or bent judges, or perverted priests or embezzling executives or lying lawyers or dodgy accountants, or civil servants and military officials who sell out to the system in exchange for promotion or profit or power.

I don't like politicians who delve into the gutter and stoop to personal attacks, or lie and duckshove and avoid the real issues, or cheat and steal and attempt retrospective legislation, or commit fraud and bend the rules and blame other people, instead of getting on with the job, and having the balls to admit when they were wrong, or that they made a mistake, or that they're only human and they're sorry and they'll do better next time.

Now I don't think I have too many attitudes which are too far removed from the great majority of ordinary, mainstream, moderate, right-thinking New Zealanders.

But if all the above makes me a redneck, then I'm guilty as charged, and proud of it. I reckon I'm in pretty good company.

Investigate, October 2006

The Wolf who cried, 'Boy!'

Human beings are a curious species. We profess to possess intelligence, worldliness, and a healthy skepticism which, it pleases us to believe, keeps us one step ahead of the odds; a foot in front of the charlatans, the politicians, the dishonest and the predatory. The wolf is kept a good pace from the door by way of our insight and foresight, our shrewdness and cunning, our wise understanding of the darker recesses of the human condition, of the desires and motivations of those who would seek to confound and exploit us to their own ends.

Singularly, we are surely so; in fact, I have yet to meet a fellow individual who was not thus endowed with a fine appreciation of the true character of our rulers and commentators – nor who was reluctant to admit it.

Strange, then, that en masse, we display behaviours which are almost entirely at odds with this understanding. *Homo sapiens*, collectively, often appears to be reactive, gullible, and easily frightened. Indeed, it is this propensity for alarmism, and a tendency to believe that the worst is imminent, which permits the powers that be to impose upon us the very same social manipulation which we so gleefully deny is even possible.

American journalist Henry Louis "H.L" Mencken, whose assessment of US politics was that it involved 'the worship of Jackals by Jackasses', described popular willingness to be led, conned, and saved from fictitious dangers, in appropriate terms;

"The whole aim of practical politics is to keep the populace alarmed, by menacing it with an endless series of hobgoblins, all of them imaginary."

And he is correct, of course, as proven by the history of mankind over the past few centuries. Unsubstantiated and sometimes irrational fears in the minds of the populace, have been transformed into all manner of Governmental edicts and directions, policies, punishments, laws, and even wars.

I mean think about it. Whether you believe the Devil to be real or not, Old Nick never once came striding through the towns and villages of yore, trident in hand and forked tail swishing; but people's desire to believe that he might, was enough to see many a poor soul strung up, run through, or burned at the stake, for the crime of encouraging him.

Likewise, the old lady in the run-down house on the edge of

town was, in all likelihood, no more than a simple widow with a penchant for amateur medical herbalism, rather than a baby-eating fiend possessed of a compulsion (and the ability) to render small boys into flying potion. This reality, however, did not save many a supposed witch from drowning on the ducking stool, in a summary execution demanded by the shrieking hystericals of the day and sanctioned by the appropriate authorities.

And I wonder, I really do, how ostensibly intelligent folk (albeit without the benefit of modern toys and tools), could convince themselves that a person, once bitten by a suitably magically affected dog, could be transformed into a rabid half-wolf, half human, bent on mayhem and thirsting for blood, by the simple and quite natural mechanism of the lunar cycle arriving at its smiley-face stage. Too preposterous for words? Never mind, he's a werewolf, cut his head off anyway.

In more recent times, we have stampeded in fear from such varied threats as communists, satanic ritual abuse, and alien invasion. The American 1938 radio broadcast of HG Wells' *The War of the Worlds* had panic-stricken citizens phoning the authorities, loading shotguns, fleeing their homes, and hollering for the National Guard; no-one, apparently, stopped long enough to ask whether perhaps the radio show wasn't actually a true account of a genuine happening.

From then on, through the 1947 tales of crash-landed space ships in Roswell, New Mexico, to the UFO-cultism of the 1970s, a seemingly sizeable chunk of humanity has been convinced that a takeover by the extra-terrestrials was due to happen any day. In 2008, of course, now that everyone has video cameras on their cellphones, no-one sees flying saucers anymore; but the books, movies, and doomsday cults spawned by this once-great popular culture are testament to something which was made real, and in many cases acted upon, by humanity's need to believe – and by someone shouting "wolf".

The witch-hunts of the McCarthy era, likewise, never meant that the US was over-run with communists both overt and secret, that every second person was spying for the Soviets, that there really were Reds under the bed. What it did mean, however, was that lives and careers were overturned and in many cases ruined, through an all-too-willing population's knee-jerk response to someone yelling "commies!".

Perhaps some of this is understandable, and perhaps not all of it is a bad thing. This reactive behaviour may be connected with the human fight-or-flight response, an essential part of our self-preservation mechanism. Our earliest furry mammalian ancestors, faced with the dangers posed by ravenous dinosaurs, had two choices: stay and be eaten, or run away. We today, all of us, carry the genes of the ones who decided to run away. Perhaps this is why we startle easily, because we are hard-wired with a survival instinct to dash for safety first, and ask questions about the nature of the danger second. Such a response may be commendable; but maintaining a fear that something is dangerous, in the face of evidence that it is not, is probably silly.

Hundreds of innocent parents in Cleveland in the UK did not, in fact, sexually abuse their children in the late 1980s – but the modern-day equivalents of the shrieking hystericals of yesteryear had the authorities up in arms simply by shouting "paedophile", and invoking the panic gene.

Naturally, we are still doing it today. All someone has to do is cry "wolf" about a supposed impending Y2K bug, for example, and we run for the safety of hills made from new computer equipment. Cry wolf in the form of SARS, and we rush to hide behind face masks. Cry "Bird Flu", and the result is the same….and on that subject, can anyone suggest what the nation might do with a rapidly outdating stockpile of Tamiflu tablets?

This is not to say that we shouldn't fear anything at all, nor that there are not real dangers of which we should be cautious. Rather, my point is that we are all too quick to bolt for the trees when danger threatens, but often slow to come down again when it has passed, or worse, reluctant to admit we were wrong when it is proved that the danger never was.

Of course, I'm working my way towards Global Warming. I can't leave it alone, and besides, it fits the theory very nicely.

"The Globe is Warming, and it's all our fault," shriek the hystericals. "The polar bears will die and we'll all be drowned by rising seas. Look, the ice is melting! Flee! Flee!"

"Oh dear, whatever will become of us," reply the rest of us, as we duck for cover behind wind turbines and Emissions Trading Schemes.

After a wee while, from atop our solar-powered battlements, we can see that none of it is actually true; but the hystericals, thrashing wildly at molecules of carbon dioxide with their organic bamboo swords, aren't listening.

They're not concerned that the earth is in fact cooling, and has been for ten years now; that polar bear numbers are on the rise, that total ice mass in both Greenland and the Antarctic is increasing, that much of the Northern Hemisphere has just had its coldest winter in most of a century, or that changes in CO_2 concentrations actually follow shifts in temperature, rather than preceding them. No, they're happy being hysterical, and appear quite incensed that the rest of us are refusing to stay panicked. The initial reactions to suggestions that something was up with the climate are understandable; the continued insistence on worrying that we are faced with dangerous warming, in the face of all the evidence that we are not, is silly at best.

What, then, may be the motivation of the hystericals? Did they slip through the net, perhaps, on a day when the dinosaurs weren't hungry? Or could there be another agenda at work here?

The cynic in me has pondered this question, and wonders if there could be a buck to be made in it, for someone, somewhere. The idea of profiteering from mass panic is not, after all, without precedent.

There is the Peak Oil delusion; the idea that oil is about to run out (in thirty years or so, just like it's supposed to have been running out in, every year for the last thirty years) – unless, of course, the barrel price can be maintained at close to a hundred bucks, in which case, there'll always be plenty of it.

There's the Global Credit Squeeze delusion, a truly brilliant con predicated on the myth that Bank loan money is taken from someone else's savings – rather than being the newly and privately issued credit which it actually is – and which justifies the continued upward march of interest rates.

Just lately, there's the World Protein Shortage delusion, which, despite being without foundation, has rocketed the price of cheese in New Zealand supermarkets to $15 a kilo, or about twice what it was less than a year ago, and yes, I do do the supermarket shopping in our house. I'm quite progressive that way.

All these panics, based on imminent and disastrous shortage, have us scurrying for our wallets without a second thought; our security is at stake, we must stock up or perish, for the survival gene has been tickled.

So where, one may ask, is the money to be made from the Global Warming panic? To this writer's mind, it lies in the control of energy; the power sources which fuel the developed world, which advance technology, learning, medicine, and the progression of the human condition. Under the agenda of the Global Warming alarmists – today's hystericals – such energies will be subject to the edicts of the United Nations, that final bastion of collectivism in a world which has otherwise rejected it. The taxes, the carbon credits, the emissions levies paid by the confounded and frightened peoples of the world, will go to line the coffers of this new evil empire, ably – and perhaps, in some cases, unwittingly – aided by the Green activists, and their naïve, idealistic media lackeys, who come among us as wolves in sheep's clothing.

Perhaps we should all be very wary of those who cry Wolf.

Investigate March 2008

Chapter Five

The Benign Strategic Environment Myth

"Hospitals in the Auckland area alone, annually discharge more radiation into New Zealand waters than has been released in total by the US Navy, globally, since the USS Nautilus first put to sea in 1955"
– Prosser, Investigate, November 2003

The Nucleus of the Issue

If ever you want to know whether or not something is truly important, give it the "so what?" test.

Some examples:

"I'm late for work." So what?

Alternatively;

"I'm late for the airport." So what?

Or ponder these:

"I spilt coffee on the new sofa." So what?

Compared with:

"I spilt petrol on the barbecue." So what?

It becomes apparent that the potential consequences of any given course of action may be more important than the action itself. Here's another one;

"Allowing nuclear-powered ships to visit New Zealand ports will mean the end of our nuclear-free status."

So what?

What, in all reality, is the worst that may happen because of this?

Nuclear propulsion was never intended to be included in the

nuclear-free legislation as it was written. The reference to "propulsion" was a one-line modification of the draft law, bulldozed through the Labour party caucus against the wishes of then Prime Minister David Lange, by a small but powerful cabal of MPs including Helen Clark. It was a deliberate act of anti-Americanism, motivated not by any concern for the environment or for issues of safety, but as a statement of socialist and anti-militarist intent.

Naval nuclear propulsion systems are in a different category to Chernobyl or Three Mile Island; they are differently designed and constructed, better contained, better shielded, and not subject to civilian incompetence. There has not ever been an incident with a nuclear powered vessel of any nation, not even the Soviets. The same cannot be said for diesel powered shipping, which regularly wreaks ecological carnage on harbours, coastlines, and oceans the world over.

Contrary to popular film and television myth, a nuclear reactor is not a bomb waiting to go off, and power stations do not spectacularly explode in an eruption of irrevocable calamity, with regular abandon, the instant something goes wrong.

The most common mishap resulting in radiation discharge from nuclear power stations is the leakage of primary cooling water or gas, into the secondary, or steam-generating circuit. Such potential leaks are monitored for, easily detected, and able to be quickly isolated.

The worst-case scenario is a complete or major loss of primary or secondary coolant, resulting in a full or partial meltdown of the reactor core, with a subsequent fire and release of radiation.

Since naval reactors are cooled ultimately by the ocean, it is difficult to envisage such a meltdown occurring while the sea remains full of water.

And despite the scaremongering of Greens and other socialists, such incidents simply have not occurred throughout the history of naval nuclear propulsion. Hospitals in the Auckland area alone, annually discharge more radiation into New Zealand waters than has been released in total by the US Navy, globally, since the USS Nautilus first put to sea in 1955. Sorry to dampen the rantings of the ill-informed pacifist Left, but this much is fact.

Nor does harbouring nuclear capable vessels make us any more of a target than we already are; Waihopai does that all by itself, and if we think we've annoyed the Yanks and the Brits by going nuclear-free, watch what would happen if we tried to get rid of Echelon.

Perhaps it is time we took the stance that we have 'made our point' on the nuclear issue. Tactical nukes are long gone from the surface. The US publicly declared its surface Navy to be free of nuclear weapons more than ten years ago. And aside from the Aircraft Carriers, propulsion is gone too. The new generation of US warships is conventionally powered, and the next generation of subs will run on hydrogen fuel cells.

Now that the rest of the world has "seen reason", we need to extend the olive branch; reach out and show we can meet them half way, that we are friends, and that we are prepared to compromise and make allowances, as they do, as friends should.

In any event – how much good has being nuke free actually done us? Are European consumers queuing up to buy our "Green" produce at any price we care to name? Have we been made a permanent member of the UN Security Council? Do our exports enjoy unhindered access to markets which shun the products of nations who have not declared that they are banning the US Navy from visiting? Have we cleared our foreign debt and been given the Nobel Prize?

Or does the rest of the developed world not actually give a continental, apart from a few loony vegan hippies who get a disproportionate amount of airtime from overseas TV crews because they're entertaining?

Do thousands of young British and European backpackers avoid Australia on account of it allowing US nuclear ships to visit, and Sydney having a nuclear reactor? No. More of them go there than come here.

A large chunk of Europe, Britain, and North America depend on nuclear power for their electricity, and folk there live long, happy, prosperous lives, without dying of a hundred different cancers – at least, not at any greater rate than we do. Clean, green Canada, Sweden and Switzerland have nuclear power. So do friendly, peaceable Finland and the Netherlands. Australia, Denmark, even Jamaica, and 60 other countries, have "research" reactors. Their economies boom, and the sky doesn't fall, unlike our ranking in the OECD standard of living tables.

Do millions of foreign tourists come here to avoid nuclear power? It would appear not. They come to see the South Island, to ski, fish, play golf, climb mountains, parapunt, bungy jump, take photos, walk in the bush, and because they were going to Australia anyway. Apart from generally agreeing that it's a good idea, the rest of the world doesn't really care about being nuclear free, and if they do they certainly aren't prepared to match that concern with dollars.

As it happens the developed world is moving away from nuclear power as a first choice where it can. Apart from the well-recognised problems associated with disposing of the waste, Uranium is like any other precious metal; its supply is not inexhaustible, and deposits of high-grade, easily accessible, economically extractable ore are becoming increasingly difficult to find. When other, non-nuclear, power generation technologies which have been kept under wraps for some considerable time are brought on stream, it will likely be done away with altogether. But that isn't the point. The point is that we should show our friends that we are still friends in the meantime, despite their not having the hydroelectric advantages that we have had.

Don't get me wrong, I don't want to live next door to a nuclear power station; but then I wouldn't want to live next door to Huntly or Clyde either.

But if my American friends want to bring their perfectly safe power plant with them when they come to visit on their boat, I don't have a problem with that.

Not that it is ever likely to happen, of course. Of the approximately 300 ships and submarines in the US fleet, only around 80 are nuclear powered. Of these eighty vessels, we can scratch 21 off the potential visitor list straight away. They are ballistic missile subs, which are not in the habit of advertising their presence or movements by making social calls to known ports.

Knock off another eleven, these being Aircraft Carriers which quite simply won't fit into our harbours, and the guest list is down to four dozen or so *Los Angeles* class attack submarines, of which only half are based in the Pacific.

And the Americans are not stupid, nor are they motivated by a desire to cause ill will where none is necessary. However, like us, they have a point to make, and they are making it. We have already made ours. They are not about to put their Navy into two categories just to suit New Zealand, when there is no good reason for doing so.

Diplomacy and good faith can easily break the current impasse; these people are our friends, for God's sake.

If we were to simply invite the US Navy to make such port visits as it deemed appropriate, they would not respond by sending an atomic boat just because they could. They'd send a cruiser and its escorts, or a destroyer, or a couple of frigates. The crews would spend their money, and drink our beer, and impress the locals by being the charming, friendly, personable people that they are, just like the way it used to happen in the old days – when the sky didn't fall just because the US Navy was in port. And if we thought the America's Cup was good for business, have a think about how much a visiting Navy can spend.

There is no historical or good scientific reason for excluding nuclear-powered vessels from our waters, and no reason at all for shutting out the conventionally powered US Navy. Neither-Con-firm-Nor-Deny is ancient history. There are no nuclear weapons on board the US surface fleet.

At the nucleus of this matter there is not a concern for the environment or a statement of belligerent independence; there is petty intransigence and an agenda of anti-Americanism, backed up by insupportable propaganda and the misconceptions of a hoodwinked public.

New Zealand can do better than this.

Investigate, November 2003

Aged yet not Infirm

Shortly after taking office in 1999, Prime Minister Helen Clark began making noises about the Air Force's well-used fleet of A-4K Skyhawk attack aircraft. Having already welched on the F-16 lease deal negotiated with the United States by the outgoing National administration (regarded throughout the aviation and military world as the steal of the century), Ms Clark publicly announced that the Skyhawks were "clapped out", and that furthermore, in her "informed" opinion, the Air Combat Force itself was neither affordable nor necessary.

Shortly after Don Brash assumed the leadership of the National Party, Clark again made disparaging comments concerning age; this time, relating to the good Doctor Brash's years of experience in living on earth – many more than her own – insinuating, it could be said, that such greater experience somehow made Don Brash less well qualified to govern the country than any other person who was perhaps more youthful.

All too often, academics who embrace socialism, seeking to impose their own elitist ideals on a population whom they only-semi subconsciously regard as being beneath them, fall victim to a naïve and narcissistic cult of self, wherein all teachings and learning which went before – as well as those of society's elders, who, from their experience, strove to promote such learning – are cast aside, in a vain attempt to remake the real world according to the childish fantasies of those who have never lived in it.

Perhaps Ms Clark has succumbed to this same trap. Certainly she appears to believe that the venerable are not to be venerated.

In terms of the Air Force's now grounded Skyhawks, Clark could easily be described as plain wrong, and demonstrably so, and possibly also of being just a little bit economical with the truth.

Even without taking into account the pictures reputed to exist in the *New Zealand Herald* archives of a young Helen Clark heading up a protest march against the acquisition of the Skyhawks in 1970, her opposition to the retention of the Air Combat Force based on its age, fails to pass inspection. This was, after all, at the beginning of Helen Clark's political career; a career which has been characterised by an anti-American, anti-military, particularly anti-Air Force stance.

Yes, the Skyhawks were getting on a bit. After all, those particular airframes were due for retirement in 2008.

But what does that mean?

Helen Clark is the Prime Minister, head of the SIS, party to the best information that the MoD can provide. She should, realistically, be well versed about the military, its hardware, capabilities, and the application of same.

That she appears not to be is more than a little worrying; perhaps our esteemed "leader" is not being provided with the best in advice and information, or perhaps she has chosen to be disinterested in the most important responsibility of Government, that being the defence of the nation.

Of greater concern is the possibility that Ms Clark has decided to ignore such accurate and good quality intelligence as is provided to her, in favour of her own preconceptions and ideology.

Or perhaps she was simply following a misconception popular amongst certain of the fringe groups who are part of what, until very recently, used to provide a workable degree of support for the minority Labour-led Government, and which also has followers amongst the wider electorate.

Certainly we have something of a predilection for baseless urban myths in this country. Along with the legend which proclaims that Vegemite is made from vegetables and Marmite from meat, and the theory which suggests that leaving a plastic soft-drink bottle half full of water on your lawn will magically repel the neighbour's dog, there exists an equally bizarre belief that the McDonnell Douglas A-4 Skyhawk is somehow a second-rate aeroplane.

"Heinemann's Hot-Rod" (after designer Ed Heinemann) or "The Bantam Bomber" as it is affectionately known in military circles, is anything but second rate. Designed to be capable of carrying and delivering a nuclear weapon, and still used in the front line by Israel – a state with access to whatever it desires in military technology – the Skyhawk holds a number of standing aircraft performance records. Not the least of these is the fastest aileron roll rate capability of any production aircraft in history, which is part of what makes it such a potent anti-shipping strike weapon.

In addition, the Project Kahu upgrade, completed in 1991, made the RNZAF's Skyhawks the electronic equivalent of any F-16 currently in service with any European Air Force. The Prime Minister appears to have completely failed to understand the significance of this fact.

Supporters of Clark's insane (as well as illegal and unconstitutional, according to Section 24 (d) of the Defence Act 1990) decision to axe the RNZAF Strike Wing, happily parrot her cry that the A-4 was an old design, and therefore should be got rid of.

The Skyhawk prototype first flew in 1954, and the aircraft entered production in 1956, making the design about fifty years old; to which this writer's response is "so what?"

Many of the most "advanced" aircraft flying today harken from the same era, and are destined to continue flying for many years to come. The Harrier jump-jet began life in 1960, and the F-16 which was to have replaced the Skyhawk in RNZAF service first flew thirty years ago, in 1974. Just filling existing orders will keep the F-16 in production for at least another five years, and with maintenance and upgrades, the type will still be on active duty in 2035, making it more than sixty years old.

The Boeing CH-47 Chinook, the big, twin-rotor, troop and APC-carrying helicopter made famous by footage from the Vietnam war, began its design life in 1959 and first took flight in 1961. Seen in every US and British action since then, most recently in Afghanistan and Iraq, the latest round of upgrades will take the Chinook's service life past seventy years.

The ubiquitous B-52 heavy bomber, answering a 1949 design call, first rolled down the tarmac in 1952, entered service in 1955, and saw every subsequent action from Vietnam to Kosovo to Iraq. The USAF plans to keep the Buff flying until at least 2037, by which time the design will have passed eighty-eight, and the youngest airframe still dropping bombs will be seventy-five years old. That's right; seventy-five.

Even the good old Boeing 747 Jumbo Jet, still happily rolling off the production line in Seattle, Washington, dates from 1965. It'll be forty next year.

Why are such museum pieces still flying? Perhaps the answer should be, "why not?" With maintenance, service, and upgrades, far in excess of anything the average motorist would ever contemplate, an airframe can carry on working long after the motor vehicles which carried its builders to the aircraft factory have been recycled into baked bean cans. As for the relative age of designs, I wonder if Ms Clark and her cohorts have ever stopped to ponder beyond their own myopic prejudice? The laws of physics and of aerodynamics facing today's aircraft designers are the same as those discovered by Richard Pearse and the Wright Brothers in 1903. Air is still air, a wing is still a wing, and on top of that, the jet engine today is essentially the same as it was when Frank Whittle patented his first turbojet in 1930.

Real advances in aeroplane technology are few and far between. Designing and building a brand-new aircraft of any type is not simply a matter of bolting together a few off-the-shelf bits from "Plane Parts 'R' Us" and selecting this year's fashion colour.

The USAF's next new-generation fighter, the F-22 Raptor, began with a design brief in 1981, first flew in 1990, and won't enter service until late 2005.

Such realities are not limited to aircraft design; next year's Toyota Corolla will have begun life as a sketch on the back of an envelope a decade ago, and it will be powered by an internal combustion petrol engine whose basic design is more than a century old. Even your brand-new dishwasher took six or seven years to travel from the top of someone's drawing board to the underside of your kitchen bench.

This writer's favourite hunting rifle calibre, the .270 Winchester, was developed in 1925, from the 30-06 Springfield which entered production in 1906 and saw the American soldier through WWII.

Against such comparisons, the relatively youthful, 1940-vintage, Dr. Don Brash appears to be in good company. At 64, The Don is far from obsolete, and as the father of a ten-year-old, it would be reasonable to hazard a guess that his ideas for change, and vision for the future of New Zealand, are not the only potent force he still has to offer.

Nor are many of those same ideas themselves new.

Don Brash, new perhaps to parliament, but well-schooled in life, brings some very tried and trusted philosophies with him as part of his fresh approach to the issues facing this country.

Old-fashioned values such as personal responsibility, self-discipline, moderation in all things, a hard work ethic, honesty, straight talking, fair-handedness and prudence, along with the solidly admirable values of tolerance and social justice, are the mark of this son of Presbyterian forebears; a man who espouses an approach which dates from a couple of millennia ago.

Perhaps Helen Clark is right to be worried by the rise of Don Brash; a new man with some time-honoured suggestions, gaining the hearts and minds of a people grown tired of the increasingly unsettling direction of a Government led by an unworldly woman with ever more unworkable ideas.

Is Don Brash, the "old man" of Labour ridicule, the right Doctor to take New Zealand back to the future? The next year-and-a-half will tell; if New Zealanders like Don Brash's prescription, and the polls suggest that they do, then the detractors of age and experience on the Brave New Left could find the next election a bitter pill to swallow.

Investigate, April 2004

Foreseen Circumstances

When Alexandra flooded (yet again) a few years ago, local clinician Laurence O'Connell posted a wry and frustrated sign on the office door of his hastily abandoned practice. O'Connell was one of those forced to evacuate by the floods; the sign read "Closed Due To Foreseen Circumstances".

The town's only optometrist had been at the forefront of efforts to persuade Contact Energy, and Electricorp before it, of the necessity of dredging the Clutha River upstream of the Roxburgh dam, in order to protect the town of Alexandra during times of flood on the Clutha and Manuherikia rivers.

But the electricity giant concerned had other ideas, and relied instead on its own preferred method of lowering the floor of the Clutha River. It is called flushing, and centres on allowing large volumes of water to periodically surge through the floodgates of the Roxburgh dam, lowering the level of the lake behind the dam and, it is hoped, taking quantities of accumulated sediment with it.

All this is good in theory; however, as pointed out by Laurence O'Connell and others, and as evidenced by the flooding of Alexandra, it doesn't actually work.

Yet Contact persists with its policy, even after the floods, even after the payouts, even after the remodelling of a large part of downtown Alexandra and the removal of many historic buildings. In spite of all this the generating company insists that flushing works, and that it is a viable and practical option.

The frustration of the good optometrist and many others with this approach is easy to understand. What is perhaps less easy to understand is why it is that this situation is being allowed to continue. Ultimately one is led to wonder if perhaps it is a lack of knowledge, insight, mental processing capacity and leadership at political level, which can be held to account.

When presented with the facts of the situation, a lay person does not appear to have any difficulty in grasping their apparent truths. You dam a river. Silt borne by the river, which would ordinarily be carried downstream to the sea, is deposited behind the dam, raising the level of the riverbed. This in turn raises the level of the river, reducing the capacity of the river valley to carry increased water flows. In times of flood, which are a natural phenomenon on rivers and do occur (despite the best efforts of engineers), water accumulates in the river valley, builds up, backs up, and causes flooding outwards from any point of the constriction of its flow – in this case, a dam. Common sense indicates that if the level of the riverbed is higher, so the level of the flood will be higher.

That the level of the riverbed must be lowered in order to prevent flooding upstream is not disputed by Contact Energy. The point of contention is over the method employed in order to achieve this aim. The Optometrist and the Frustrated People contend that dredging is the only method which will be effective. The Generating Company and its Engineers insist (in spite of all evidence being to the contrary) that flushing will suffice.

And there rests the basis of a quandary. When educated professionals, entrusted with the responsibility of designing policy on which the lives, livelihoods and wellbeing of the People will depend, insist on following a course of action which produces results that appear to be at variance with that aim, and which appear to fly in the face of common sense, one is forced to consider whether one of two disturbing scenarios may be unfolding.

It is possible that the professionals and officials involved are professionally incompetent, and in the absence of checks and balances of a managerial structure above them, the trusting naiveté of the People concerned allows this incompetence to translate itself into policy and action.

It is possible that the professionals and officials involved are in fact competent but are cynically disinterested, or motivated by concerns outside the stated aim, and that once again, without checks and balances, public apathy or ignorance permits flawed ideology to prevail.

In either event, the end result is the same; the line promoted by the experts was incorrect, and the town was flooded.

There are some eerie parallels between this failure of the system to protect Alexandra from a known hazard, and the current parlous state of New Zealand's external military defences.

Perhaps those promoting flushing are concerned by monetary issues. It is understandable that people accountable for a public budget should seek the most cost-effective option. It is bizarre however that they should select an option which, irrespective of its cost, is not effective at all. It is even more bizarre that those people who are directly affected by this lack of effectiveness should allow such a course of action to be followed.

The eerie parallel to this state of affairs as it relates to the defence of New Zealand, centres around the insistence of the present Government on prioritising the Army as the focus of defence spending, and on its questionable action in dispensing with the Air Force as an effective military entity.

New Zealand's lack of either a written Constitution, or an upper House of Parliament, to act as a bulwark against the excesses of incompetent Government, is disturbingly similar to the planning and management structure whose deficiencies have allowed Alexandra to remain at continued risk of flooding.

In a sense, for a nation to maintain an Air Combat Force can be likened to running dredges on a river. You don't need many of them, they don't require many people to operate, and for the most part, so long as they are doing their job, people are unaware of the consequences of being without them.

And yes, they do cost a little to own and operate, to maintain and run.

By contrast, flushing can be likened to maintaining an overseas focused, peacekeeping-oriented land force. It's spectacular and makes a great deal of noise, and gives people the impression that something big is going on; but unlike the dredging, won't provide those same people with any protection in the event of a flood.

Like the dredges, the flushing will cost money to perform, in terms of time and inconvenience, and reduced generating capacity. Certainly flushing is a cheaper option than dredging; an equation that is far less favourable, however, is the comparison of the costs of maintaining infantry battalions against the relative cheapness of providing for fighter squadrons.

And if cost were to be the only or major consideration, then a little lateral thinking can be called upon. In the Waikato, river dredgings are dried and mixed with clay, becoming a product known as Waikato Pea Metal. This highly sought after material is sold to eager market gardeners, home owners and landscaping suppliers as a mineral enriched soil conditioner. It's worth a mint.

By the same token, excess military training capacity is a valuable, saleable commodity.

Britain has subsidised its military for many decades now by providing training to virtually anyone who can come up with the cash. The cost of training an air combat pilot has been estimated at around $NZ25 million – and Singapore is having its next generation of fighter aces trained in Canada. How many foreign high school students, I wonder, does New Zealand need to attract in order to make up for each one of these opportunities lost? Add to that the sixty-one million dollar maintenance contract with the Royal Malaysian Air Force lost by Pacific Aerospace in Hamilton when the F-16 lease deal was cancelled, and the ongoing business losses which will be suffered by Air New Zealand's maintenance division when it can no longer source internationally respected staff ex of the RNZAF, and the cost to the nation of being without this valuable resource will rise dramatically.

Flushing, incidentally, generates nothing in the way of secondary income. Neither do land based peacekeeping forces.

On the flat, fertile, peaceful delta that is New Zealand, talk of floods – and wars – seems unrealistic, laughable even. These are things which happen to other people, in faraway places. We are happy here, in our pleasant backwater, with our heads in the sand – or perhaps in the silt.

Far upstream however, beyond the halting hills of the Benign Strategic Environment Ranges, in the high catchments of the Middle East, the headwaters of the River of World Affairs, clouds are gathering. A storm is brewing. First in Afghanistan, then Iraq, and soon Syria, it is beginning to rain.

We are no longer dredging our river, and we are no longer prepared for a flood. Indeed, we have laid up our dredges, offered them for sale, and laid off their operators, and are relying instead on two quite incredible assumptions; firstly, that we can always depend on our friends to help us fill sandbags, and secondly, that we firmly believe there will never be another flood.

Alas, our friends, both upriver and down, are sufficiently disenchanted with our irresponsible refusal to maintain our section of the watercourse that we will be left to fill our own sandbags; a proposition which, even if we did have a sufficiently large population to provide for it, would still prove sadly ineffective.

It appears to have escaped our political leaders that the next flood on the River of World Affairs will be a Big One. To survive it we may need to both dredge and sandbag. Dredging we can do ourselves; for sandbagging we will require the assistance of our friends and allies. They however have indicated quite clearly that they are not interested in helping us fill sandbags unless we show a willingness to dredge our section of the river.

There are good reasons for the views held by our neighbours. Dredging is a skilled operation. It requires a fair degree of technical expertise, backed up by a support infrastructure which not every nation possesses to the same degree. Our dredges and their operators were counted amongst the best in the world; indeed, we were respected and appreciated for helping keep the waterways clear well beyond our own boundaries.

Sandbags on the other hand can be filled by any Joe Schmoe with a shovel. But in order for the technique to be effective, a nation requires lots and lots of Joe Schmoes.

New Zealand simply does not have that many Joes. When we were providing dredges beyond our own river limits, our neighbours (who have lots of Joes with shovels) were only too happy to give us the assurance of sandbag-filling assistance. However, now that we have told them that dredging is too expensive to maintain, and that we believe there will be no more floods, their attitude has changed, quite understandably, to one of "Well, fill your own damn sandbags then, and much good may it do you."

And much good it won't, as is patently apparent.

Two situations can be safely predicted at this point; two circumstances easily foreseen. Firstly, that there will shortly be another flood; and secondly, that after it, the accumulated silt of the New Zealand public's apathy will be gone. What a great accomplishment it would be if we could learn from the lessons of history, and clear the apathy by returning to dredging now, rather than waiting for the lesson to hit home by watching all we hold dear being washed away in a flood. After such a flood, of course, without preventative measures in place, it is quite possible that rebuilding will not be available as an option.

When circumstances can be clearly foreseen and their repercussions are beyond acceptable countenance, it becomes the responsibility of those people who will be affected by them to instruct their political leaders to follow a clear course of common sense, rather than an unworkable one guided by flawed and unrealistic ideology.

After all, floods do happen.

And so do wars.

Investigate, December 2003

Your Country needs You

"Ask not what your country can do for you – ask what you can do for your country." So said John F Kennedy in his famous 1961 inaugural address. Kennedy's speech was a call for strength and sacrifice from his fellow Americans, rather than a call to arms; but sometimes, sacrifice requires the strength of arms, and for a country such as New Zealand, it is perhaps only that call which ultimately makes sense.

Compulsory Military Training was last exercised in this country from 1950 until 1958, and again between 1962 and 1972. Under its final incarnation as National Service, young men were required to register for a ballot based around birth dates, the lucky winners being rewarded with the opportunity to train and serve for a period in the Armed Forces. More than 85,000 New Zealanders were conscripted under CMT over the course of its final two decades. It is surprising how many you bump into even today, and quite telling in that not one, of the many I have met over the years, remembers it as being anything other than a positive and beneficial experience.

The enlightened scheme was brought to a premature end by the spineless peaceniks of Norman Kirk's Labour Government, and no administration since has had the foresight or testicular fortitude to reinstate it. For this writer's money, it is time New Zealand did just that.

Militarily, socially, and economically, there are many good solid reasons why our nation and its people would benefit greatly from bringing back the draft. I'm not talking about a ballot, or any other selective form of National Service; rather, the universal enlistment of every capable New Zealand citizen for two years, from the age of eighteen (or at the end of their formal schooling, whichever comes first), followed by a week or two's service a year, every year thereafter, until retirement age. A year's basic training could be followed by a year's service in the Army, Navy, or Air Force; or indeed a year in the Police, the Fire Service, a professional Coast Guard, or even a full-time Civil Defence Corps.

There are pros and cons with every proposal, of course; but your favourite commentator believes that in this case, the potential positives outweigh the negatives. Young people – and their parents – would have the surety of knowing that, after the end of high school, there will be two more years of certainty in life; a guaranteed job, a respectable income, a structured environment which encourages savings. On top of that, the Services promote the continuation of sport and fitness which many find it difficult to maintain when education finishes and real life begins. Along with this is the provision of medical and dental care, and perhaps most importantly, the encouragement of self-discipline to bridge the gap between the relatively cloistered and subservient existence of childhood, and the freedom of the adult world of work or varsity.

Militarily, a return to National Service would help to rescind New Zealand's current laughing stock status, and restore us to the type of credibility enjoyed by the likes of Switzerland, Singapore, and Israel, and those other nations with comparably small populations to our own, whose Armed Forces nonetheless enjoy genuine international respect; Norway, Denmark, Finland, and Sweden.

Given our very small population base, the independent defence of New Zealand's undeniably large land, sea, air, and coastal territory is not realistically possible without large-scale mobilization, which conscription would provide. This is not so much from the manpower made involuntarily available by it, as from an expansion of the professional core of the military – enabled by the increased resourcing of the Armed Forces which conscription would obviously require, coupled with the increase in voluntary enlistment which would naturally result from a greater number of people experiencing a more credible Defence establishment. Singapore, with a population of five million, has a professional military numbering around 35,000, roughly three times the size of New Zealand's, with an equivalent conscripted enlistment of about the same at any given time, and a further 350,000 trained reservists. Any potential aggressor would think twice before considering an attack on Singapore; New Zealand does not offer anything remotely like a similar capacity for resistance.

Socially, the nation would gain by instiling a sense of duty, responsibility, and patriotism in a new and disciplined generation; a respect for law, order, and the older citizenry; the promotion of a work ethic, self-respect, and the realisation that dreams and goals can be attainable through training by those who might never have managed to achieve them before. Young people given a taste of actual success are far less likely to turn to crime and dereliction, than those whose experiences serve to constantly remind them that their place is at the bottom of the heap.

Economically there are benefits too. The Forces may serve as a training establishment not only for skills and practices of warfighting, but for the trades and disciplines which support them. The Armed Services need personnel trained in mechanics, engineering, electrics and electronics, radio and communications, IT, transport logistics, and even plumbing and carpentry; as well as, of course, medicine, science, and a raft of other necessary specialties. Utilising the military for this purpose may be likened to putting an ambulance at the bottom of the cliff; but people, three decades of failed management in education and social policy has left us on the edge of that cliff, and right now, we don't have another ambulance. Young people properly trained in all the skills which the military requires for its own purposes, can take those skills out into the workplace, to the greater benefit of the nation as a whole.

There will be naysayers, of course. There will be the pacifists, the weaklings, the other cowards and bludgers who don't want to fight, and who will conscientiously object. Well, I say let 'em. This isn't the Soviet Union. If people really don't want to serve in the military, they can spend a couple of years picking up rubbish off the beaches and digging out long-drops for DOC instead; though naturally, they will forego any benefits offered to those who do choose to accept their civic duty.

Some will argue that those of a criminal disposition will end up being trained in the use of weapons – yes they will, but so will everybody else, including the decent majority who vastly outnumber them.

There will be those who ask how we are going to pay for all this, to which I say we pay for it out of the savings we will make through creating a better society. We will spend less on Police, Courts, and prisons, because more of our people will eschew crime and violence, instead thriving in an environment which offers a sense of purpose and self-worth. We will spend less on health, because more people will stay fitter and healthier for longer in life, under a regime which requires and encourages it. We will spend less on welfare, because people will learn responsibility, resilience and self-reliance, and the pride and satisfaction which this brings.

The experiment with anarchic liberalism foisted on New Zealand since the 1970s has failed this country dismally, and we now lack any alternative social regimentation with which to replace it. We do not have the class structure and traditions of British society, the Bible and Constitution culture of the Americans, the unionised solidarity of Australia. But we do have the inherent fighting nature of our peoples, and the proof of its efficacy in our recent past. Maori, Saxon, Celt, Viking; we, all of us, once were warriors. I say it is time we took up arms once again, and put our troubles to the sword.

Investigate, May 2011

Chapter Six

Climate Change

*"The 60m blades of the proposed Otago turbines will be
manufactured in Denmark from carbon fibre and carted halfway
around the world in diesel powered cargo ships, then trucked from
the port, over 150km of new roads, to sit atop 100m steel towers –
most likely forged in the smoky foundries of China or Germany –
which are transported the same way. And when they finally get here,
the first thing they will do is push the power prices up"*

– Prosser, Investigate, December 2006

A Burning Question

A millennium dawns, and a power and environmental crisis beckons. Or does it? The globe is warming, oil is running out, and it's all our fault, apparently. Mankind's fondness for fossil fuels spells doom for us all, or so we are told. The earth will warm, the seas will rise, crops will fail, coastal lowlands will be inundated, polar bears will die out, and yada yada yada.

This is partly true. The climate is changing. Temperatures world-wide are increasing. It is happening; it just isn't happening for the reasons that that Greenies tell us it is.

I was raised as an environmentalist. I love the earth. Like most farmers, and most hunters, I'm a true Green, and proud of it.

But unlike the ultra-far-red-leftists of the party which bears the same name, Greenies like me prefer to base our opinions on fact, rather than on dogma, ideology, and bad science.

We are in good company. British botanist, Professor David Bellamy, has published a paper outlining how it is that atmospheric carbon dioxide levels are increasing because of global warming, and not, as the flat-earth zealots of the Kyoto Cult claim, the other way round. His findings are based on thirteen thousand years worth of archaeological data since the last ice age.

Bellamy refers to the Milankovitch cycles, which measure changes in the earth's climate brought about by variations in the tilt of our planet's axis and her orbit around the sun. These changes occur gradually over long periods – up to 100,000 years – and their effects, along with those of the known 300-year and 22-year weather cycles generated by sunspot activity, have been inscribed not only in the fossil record, but also in human history. 1000 years ago, the Vikings grazed cattle on the lush pastures of what are now the frozen wastes of Greenland, and Britain had a wine industry. 750 years later, the climate had cooled to such a degree that people could ice-skate on the River Thames in London.

Bellamy also quotes from the Oregon Institute of Science and Medicine, whose petition against the Kyoto Protocol has been signed by some 18,000 scientists worldwide. Its central claim is simple; "Predictions of harmful climatic effects due to future increases in minor greenhouse gasses like carbon dioxide are in error, and do not conform to experimental knowledge."

Kyoto proponents would do well to acquaint themselves with a little of that experimental knowledge. We are told that melting ice caps will cause sea levels to rise. This is patently untrue, and easily demonstrated. Fill a glass to about three-quarters with water. Drop in a few ice cubes. Mark the water level with a felt-tipped pen.

In an hour or so, when the ice has melted, come back and check the level. You will discover that it hasn't changed.

The science behind this is very, very, third-form simple. Ice is less dense than water, which is why it floats. Because it floats, it displaces water, pushing the water level up. As the ice melts, the displacing ice is replaced by water, of increasing density, at lower volume, meaning that the overall level remains the same. Melting ice caps will have no effect at all on sea levels.

For the record, the Northern ice cap has no land mass under it. It is all floating sea ice. Most of the icebergs released by the Antarctic, are also sea ice, from such reservoirs as the Ross Ice Shelf. Such land-based ice as is released, by retreating glaciers and continental ice masses, is utterly insignificant relative to the volume of the oceans. It doesn't take a rocket scientist to sit down with a map of the world and a pocket calculator to work that one out.

Sea levels will, however, rise with increasing global temperatures. This is because a warming of the oceans causes their waters to expand. Low-lying countries are at risk, unfortunately, and this is a great tragedy of our time; but a greater tragedy still, is the unfettered willingness with which so many otherwise ostensibly intelligent people leap blindly onto a popular bandwagon founded on theory and science which is, plainly and simply, wrong. The burning of fossil fuels by Western nations is not causing the rise in global temperatures, and their cessation in so doing will not halt it, nor will it save those nations which are at risk.

We are also led to believe that methane emissions from New Zealand's three-odd million cows are irrevocably harming the atmosphere, and that we must purchase "carbon credits" from some other country in order to overcome this.

The authors of this particular chapter of the Kyoto fantasy have obviously not thought far enough outside the box to give consideration to the effects which must, by their logic, have been caused by the up-to-75 million bison which roamed North America until the 1830s. One would presume, in keeping with their argument, that the globe should now be in credit from that period.

The fantasists also appear to ignore the fact that the atmospheres of the northern and southern hemispheres mix only at the equator, and even then, by only a minute percentage every year. Even if the "carbon credit" theory were anything other than simplistic misinformation, several centuries would have to pass before the effects of carbon emissions "saved" in one hemisphere, had any measurable effect on those "spent" in the other.

And as an aside, forests are not the "carbon sinks" which the Protocolers claim them to be; living plants emit almost as much

CO_2 as they take in. The only effective way to turn a forest into a carbon sink, is to cut it down for timber, or mill it into paper.

As I write this, on the evening of Wednesday 16th February 2005, the Government of New Zealand is committing the latest in its long litany of ill-informed, incompetent, or deliberate and ideologically-driven blunders. It is ratifying the Kyoto Protocol.

Even as it does, professional activists, from the internationally-franchised business Greenpeace, are occupying the site of this New Zealand Government's single most intelligent and sensible action – the commissioning of the mothballed Marsden-B power station, as a coal-fired electricity generating plant.

They are doing so because they, and the Greens, and any number of other highly-opinionated yet poorly informed protesters, are opposed to the use of coal as a fuel for electricity generation. It is their claim that the burning of coal, or any other fossil fuel for that matter, in spite of a wealth of informed scientific opinion to the contrary, is a contributing factor to the current cycle of natural climate change. I do beg to differ. Mankind, for all his faults, is just not that significant. We are not affecting our planet's climate. It is changing all by itself, without our help, as it has done since time immemorial, not just in the couple of hundred years since modern record-keeping began.

A single volcanic eruption on the scale of Taupo, or Krakatoa, or Mount St Helens, or Pinatubo, releases more particulate and oxidative matter into the atmosphere, than has been created by the whole of mankind since the discovery of fire, modern wars included. Sorry, Kyotoers, but once again, this is verifiable fact.

Ice ages come and go. After them, indeed between them, the climate warms again. Greenhouse fanatics choose to ignore this natural phenomenon, because they have no pseudo-scientific way of explaining it.

Though generally short on alternative solutions, in this case, as an alternative to coal, the protestors make some timid noises in favour of natural gas. This is a curious position. The exhaust products from the burning of natural gas (primarily a mix of propane and butane, with some methane, a little ethane, a smattering of pentane, and a dash of carbon monoxide), are mostly water vapour (the single most effective greenhouse gas, which also sustains life on our planet, and staves off ice-ages), and carbon dioxide.

Strangely enough, the exhaust products from a modern coal-fired thermal power station are also, primarily, water vapour and carbon dioxide.

The reality of black gold today, is a long way from the grim memory of its industrial past. Fly ash is caught by filters. Sulphur dioxide is neutralised with lime, and the resultant calcium sulphate is extracted to be used as a fertiliser. After these processes, there is very little left.

Their other preferred alternatives appear to be the continued destruction and flooding of South Island rivers and wilderlands, and the proliferation of ugly, noise-polluting wind farms – which Europe, incidentally, having had much experience of, is now in the process of dismantling.

Nobody wants pollution. There are very good reasons for mankind to pursue an alternative to oil as a source for transport fuels. But just for the record, oil is never going to run out. Contrary to popular myth, it isn't fermented dinosaur juice. Oil is one of the products which the earth produces all the time, albeit slowly. When we tap into an oil strike, some of the oil comes out under its own pressure, and the next fraction is displaced with water, either sea water or fresh water, depending on whether the find is on land or offshore.

But oil isn't so much pumped, as collected. Oil companies prefer not to spend unnecessary money on extracting this free and plentiful product; when the easy stuff runs out, the well is capped, declared "dry", and the company moves on to the next find. At that stage, the reservoir usually still contains around 80% of its original oil.

Oil is handy and versatile stuff, providing us with plastics, artificial fibres, and a host of other products, from cosmetics, to agrichemicals, to road-building materials.

That said, it isn't the cleanest thing we can put into our fuel tanks; but neither is it, nor coal, the cause of global warming.

Worldwide, a commercially-driven and media supported campaign of mass hysteria over climate change, is using fraudulent science and bogus evidence, to convince foolish Greenies and ignorant politicians to spend vast amounts of money on solving a problem which doesn't exist. It is reminiscent of those other great bogeyman stories, about Y2K, SARS, Nuclear War, werewolves, vampires, and Asian Bird Flu.

I end as I began, by quoting Professor Bellamy;

"The link between the burning of fossil fuels and global warming is a myth. It is time the world's leaders, their scientific advisers and many environmental pressure groups woke up to the fact."

(With acknowledgement to David Bellamy, and special thanks to Allen Cookson for some additional information.)

Investigate, March 2005

When the Wind Blows

Spring is nearly over, and this writer for one will be glad to see the back of it. While it might be nice to see the trees greening up and the snow receding after the bleak privations of winter, for many people who work outdoors, muggins included (at least most of the time), spring can be a frustrating and uncomfortable season. It is alternately hot, cold, wet, dry, chilly, humid, stifling, and windy, and on occasion, most of them at the same time.

This season, for grapegrowers and orchardists, has been a diabolical one in terms of frost, and probably less wet than many others, certainly the farmers, would have liked. But what grates most about spring, is the wind.

In the autumn we have the equinoxial gales, but they don't last for very long, and while they may carry off the odd elderly shed or ailing barn roof, and knock over a few macrocarpas, they also provide some welcome respite from the burning heat of summer.

In the springtime, however, it just blows. It blows every day, from nine in the morning till nine at night, regular as clockwork. It's blowing even as I sit and type. Every year it starts blowing at the beginning of spring, and every year everyone says it'll be over by Christmas, and every year it isn't. Most years it'll blow till the end of January, by which time the wind has turned from cold southerly to hot nor-wester, sapping the will and stretching the patience, and driving grown men into licensed premises in search of a little cool amber relief.

And then it stops; and almost the next day, is forgotten…and come the heat of summer, when it's forty degrees hereabouts and dead calm, and a gentle breeze would actually be quite nice, it's almost forgiven.

That's the thing about the wind, you see; it doesn't blow all the time, at least not always in the same place. Not even in Wellington – just like it isn't, in fact, always raining on the West Coast. Certainly, in this long narrow country of ours, there will almost always be somewhere where it's windy. And the wind is a completely free and ever-renewable resource, which we as a nation could and should be harvesting, because right now, as some of us cranky doomsayers have been grizzling about for years, New Zealand is running out of electricity.

As I write, both Meridian Energy and Trustpower are planning on building large wind farms in the heart of the Central Otago tussock country. They'll be just the ticket, we are told; cheap, clean, green, renewable energy, which will save the lakes and cut the carbon emissions, light the lights, slash the power bills, drive the heat pumps of a new and wood-fire free world, and generally herald a glorious age of eco-friendly, low-footprint humanity.

Nice theory; what a shame it's a load of rubbish. About the only truth in the propaganda is that the wind does blow, and will continue to, for free – some of the time. This is fine if you have a mobile wind farm which can be transported to wherever the gusts are gathering; unfortunately, such technology is probably still a little way off, and we will have to make do with fixed installations for the time being. These fixed installations are a long way from having a low environmental footprint, and their construction is a very long way indeed from being clean or green.

Power companies and the supporters of windfarms have spent inordinate amounts of money on producing splendid brochures and photo-shopped montages of the planned turbines, elegant structures sweeping majestically against a backdrop of empty skies and wide open country, within which they are scarcely visible. And, true enough, from Auckland, or Wellington, or Christchurch, or anywhere else whose back yard they're not in, they won't be visible at all. From the farms and tourist trails of the Otago back country, however, (or the Manawatu, or the Wairarapa, or the Hawke's Bay, or anywhere else earmarked for despoliation, come to that), they'll stick out like the dog's proverbials; garish white pylons nearly twice as high as a rugby field is long, and covering almost as much sky as one and a half times its area, spread out by the hundred across the roof of what little remains of our wilderness country, and with the rotor tips lit up at night to warn aircraft of their presence, beneath the glittering heavens which till now have remained as free from light pollution as ever they were when dinosaurs walked the earth.

So much for the emotional argument. It is true, as a wise man said to me on the subject, that these ugly, noisy, monstrosities don't have to be there forever. Unlike a hydro dam, if and when something else comes along, we can always take them down again (though probably not their 650 cubic metre concrete foundations). Economic reality, however, says that we won't be able to. These windfarm projects will cost billions, and that money must be recouped over the coming years, not only to pay for the development, but to return the owners an acceptable profit. Once upon a time, when we were the owners, that profit went back to the nation, in the form of cheap electricity; now, in our brave new world of privatised power, it goes largely offshore. Hilariously, in the case of the Government's own state-owned generators, the profit from the sale of electricity – the price of which has doubled since the "market reforms" – is delivered directly into the Government's coffers, where it is now called a dividend instead of a tax! (How's that surplus, Dr Cullen?)

Factor into the equation the reality that the turbines will only be producing at capacity for a fraction of the year – between a quarter and a half of it, depending on whose global averages one chooses to believe – and the anything up to 30% transmission loss suffered in delivering the power to market, and it becomes apparent that the precious kilowatts which do actually reach the customer, will need to be very pricy indeed, in order to make the exercise a successful one for our admirably capitalistic generation industry.

On top of that, the National Grid is already stretched, and new infrastructure to carry the increased generation will be neither cheap, nor paid for by anyone other than the consumer. Either way, it is likely that we will be locked into using, and paying for, the power from these windfarms for at least a half century.

No electricity generation is actually clean, and we are foolish to believe that it is. Hydro dams built from concrete by definition require cement works, no turbine or generator in the world can be manufactured without steel refining and heavy engineering, photovoltaic panels use more energy in the refining of their selenium cells than they will produce during their serviceable lifetimes, and even the good old Kiwi DIY rooftop black alkathene solar water heater depends on polyethylene pipe, which is made from oil. This oil doesn't just dig itself up, ready-refined, and transport itself around the world unaided. It needs ships, which need shipyards, and vehicles, and pipelines, and the same goes for the construction machinery needed for building dams and thermal stations and even wind farms.

The 60m blades of the proposed Otago turbines will be manufactured in Denmark from carbon fibre and carted halfway around the world in diesel powered cargo ships, then trucked from the port, over 150km of new roads, to sit atop 100m steel towers – most likely forged in the smoky foundries of China or Germany – which are transported the same way. And when they finally get here, the first thing they will do is push the power prices up.

In spending the aforementioned billions on the wind projects in question, we are ensuring that this money is not available for anything else. We need more electricity, certainly, but at the same time, there are, with a little lateral thinking, some ways in which we could both reduce growing electricity demand, and localise its production.

As I may have mentioned before, about a quarter of New Zealand's electricity generation, and around half the average household power bill, is consumed by domestic hot water heating. The money spent building the Clyde dam, for example, would have paid for almost half a million domestic solar water heaters.

A company in Scotland (see www.renewabledevices.com) manufactures domestic wind turbines, which are almost silent, and produce about 1.5kw of power – when the wind is blowing, of course. Perhaps a large number of small turbines, say on the roof of every house (and owned by the homeowner), in cities and towns where the power is needed, would make more sense than a small number of large turbines out in the backblocks, where it is expensive to produce, wasteful to transport, and detrimental to tourism. Think about it; the structure to get the turbine up in the air is already there – it's called a house. Ditto the access roads, and on top of that, we won't need to upgrade the Grid, because we're making the power where we need it.

Of course, such a solution is not likely to find favour with either the Government or the power companies, because it means a whole lot less money for both of them. But at the end of the day, it's our money they're spending, and our wild open country which they're hell-bent on wrecking in so doing.

If our Governments' lunatic adherence to the crackpot Greenhouse theory hadn't convinced them that CO_2 was evil, we could build thermal power stations, quickly, cheaply, and handy to town, and run them on some of the 2000-years' worth of free coal supply, with which Mother Earth has blessed our fair land, or fit every house and commercial building with a gas-fired co-generation unit (and a dozen energy-saving lightbulbs).

Maybe we could tap the hot air which emanates from the Beehive, or make biogas out of the base material from which the attitudes of Kyoto believers are formed; but until we can find a way of storing the wind, or turning it on and off as demand dictates, the large remote windfarms currently being suggested by the greedy and the powerful (no pun intended), are never going to deliver on the promises of their promoters. It will be an ill wind indeed which blows them our way.

Investigate, December 2006

Profits of Doom

Chicken Little, so the story goes, was out in the woods one day, when an acorn fell on her head. Convinced that the sky was falling, Chicken Little ran off to warn the King. On the way, as we all know, she collected a number of her friends, who, upon hearing the story, became likewise immediately convinced of the imminent collapse of the sky, and who undertook to accompany her on her mission to convey the awful news to the aforementioned monarch.

As history records, Chicken Little and her assembled fowl (Henny Penny, Ducky Lucky, Goosey Loosey, and Turkey Lurky) eventually met up with Foxy Loxy, who, not being a bird brain himself, cottoned on swiftly to the reality that the sky was not, in fact, about to impose its presence upon them; but that if the feathered fools of his new acquaintance believed it was, then there might be a buck to be made, or at least a meal to be had. Offering his services as a guide, Foxy Loxy led Chicken Little and Company not to the King via his promised shortcut, but instead to his own lair, wherein he proceeded to dispatch and consume them at his leisure.

The moral of the story: if you're stupid enough to believe something ridiculous, don't be surprised if somebody else decides to exploit your stupidity for their own gain.

Human history is littered with examples of mass foolishness and subsequent expensive solutions to non-existent problems. Creating an irrational fear in the minds of the proletariat, of some fictitious ailment or impending disaster, and then selling them the remedy, has been a standard marketing ploy for centuries. From snake oil, to water fluoridation, to tinfoil hats and mass inoculations and antibacterial soap, we've been sold them all. Governments, too, have been in on the act, ensuring their ongoing support by continually rescuing grateful voters from imaginary calamities or crises of their own creation. It is apparent that there exists, somewhere in the human psyche, a primal need to believe that the worst is about to happen; and a steadfast desire to hold on to this belief, once attained, in spite of all rational argument and physical evidence to the contrary. Over time, the cynical and the manipulative have learned to take advantage of this trait of the gullible and the educationally challenged, by offering a salvation which, once proffered, will be seized upon and held with the same fervour and conviction as was the original perceived threat.

This might be funny were it not for two disturbing trends. The first is that, in recent years, scientifically ignorant but egotistically self-important individuals and organisations within Governments, who craft and implement responses to perceived situations, and within the media, who disseminate such information, have expanded and accelerated the process of Alarmism to the point where it now dominates human consciousness and activity at a level not seen since the witch-hunts and Devil-fear of the Middle Ages.

The second is that some of the "solutions" currently being touted, to some of the "disasters" supposedly facing the earth and all who sail on her, are actually at risk of creating a very real threat to the safety of mankind and his fellow travellers, in place of the imaginary ones which they are intended to counter.

A few years ago, when concern for the ozone layer was the fashionable *cause du jour*, much ado was made of the need to replace chlorofluorocarbons in aerosols and refrigeration plants, with hydrocarbons or hydro fluorocarbons. It is true that chlorine and bromine act as catalysts in the destruction of ozone; but these elements are dissociated from their source halons and freons by the same solar ultraviolet radiation which both creates and destroys ozone itself, depending on the level of such radiation being emitted by the sun at any given time, which, as with everything to do with the Big Yellow, is far from consistent. CFCs in the miniscule amounts produced by man may, or may not, have had anything to do with ozone depletion – and it is worth remembering that the Antarctic ozone hole was first recorded in 1956, and may have been coming and going cyclically for millennia – but in the meantime, everyone has had to have their car air conditioner re-gassed, at not inconsiderable expense.

Remember Y2K? It was going to be the end of the world; every computer on earth was going to crash simultaneously (depending on one's time zone, of course), the water and sewerage would go out, the traffic lights would fail, nuclear power stations would melt down, global communications and banking would cease to function, and, we were quietly told, computer geeks all around the world were fleeing their workstations for the safety of survivalist bunkers in the desert, leaving the rest of us to face the wrath of everything from home appliances to digital watches which would probably go rabid and turn on us. Then, at the stroke of midnight, December 31st 1999,…um…nothing happened. Of course, by then, the world had already gone out and spent literally billions on new computers, just in case. Fortunately for unbelievers such as Yours Truly, the old stuff kept on working just fine.

Not long afterwards, we were all supposed to die from SARS. That didn't happen either, because the threat was never real, but millions of people spent millions of dollars anyway, on millions of face masks which wouldn't have protected them if it had been. I mean come on – a paper dust mask, which doesn't even seal, let alone filter, to protect you from an airborne virus? It sounds disturbingly similar to the Cold War advice about putting your head into a paper bag in the event of a nuclear attack. Quite what that was supposed to achieve I'm not sure; give the propagandists something to laugh about, I suppose, while they were pocketing the money from selling so many paper bags.

This writer can remember being told that oil was going run out in thirty years, every year for the past thirty years. The latest prediction has Peak Oil occurring in 2038…hmm, that's about thirty years away. Meantime, we must buy while we can – at sixty-odd dollars a barrel. Memory tells me that at the time of the first oil shock in 1973, when oil hit the dizzying high of US$23 per barrel, the actual cost of unearthing that barrel and getting it to the refinery was seven cents.

We have always been like this. I suspect that the concept of Vampires was invented by a garlic merchant. Today we live in fear of Bird Flu, a disease which cannot be transmitted from human to human, and which shows no signs of mutating into a form which can; meanwhile, millions upon millions of dollars are being spent on stockpiling a well-known proprietary drug, which, not being a vaccine, couldn't cure it if it did.

But the most immediately dangerous of the current follies of Man is of course Global Warming. Popular conviction that this entirely natural and totally unavoidable phenomenon is the fault of mankind, via his supposedly unholy relationship with a completely innocuous and absolutely essential trace gas, namely carbon dioxide, has led to the promotion of some bizarrely impractical, and predictably expensive, solutions.

Trading in Carbon Credits has already begun; exactly how one country or company paying another for the right to continue polluting is supposed to save the planet escapes me, but apparently the market is speaking even as I write. Even if there were any validity to the Greenhouse Theory, the supposed offset effect of a CO_2 producer in one hemisphere crediting their production against a sink in the other, is negated by the reality that the atmospheres of the two hemispheres only mix at the equator, and even then, by only 1 to 2% per year. The dangerous aspect to our Government's irrational embracement of this process, and its forced sequestration of the said credits from the private forestry sector, means that no-one is planting trees in New Zealand anymore, because to do so will prove uneconomic. Consequently this country is currently undergoing a net loss of forest cover, for the first time since plantation pine was established in the 1920s.

Carbon hysteria has also resulted in calls for Biofuels to replace mineral oil-based fuels, on the presumption that they are somehow "clean and green" in greenhouse terms. This is bizarre because the primary byproduct from the burning of ethanol, methanol, natural gas, rapeseed oil, palm oil, or, in fact, anything with carbon in it, petrol and diesel included, is – tada – carbon dioxide. (Hint for the Greenies – there's carbon in biofuels. Lots of it. That's why they burn.)

The danger in accepting this insane theory is that serious proposals are now being made for the growing of food crops such as maize, purely for the production of motor fuel – and this in a world which has a growing population, a shrinking availability of land, and where people are already starving.

Furthermore, even at best, efforts towards replacing a significant percentage of our existing motor fuels with bio-alternatives will be nothing better than an exercise in tokenism, and within that, they will tie up large tracts of our agricultural land in producing fuel, which can be easily provided by mineral oil (which isn't running out), instead of food, which can not. The sheer volume of motor fuel required can never be matched by anything we can grow in crop form or harvest from existing wastes. Fonterra, for example, produces whey ethanol at an approximate volume of around **100,000 litres per month** (the bulk of which currently goes to feed the appetites of New Zealand and Australian vodka and RTD drinkers). By comparison, New Zealand consumes petrol and diesel at an approximate volume of around **10 million litres per day**. This does not include marine diesel, aviation petrol, or jet fuel. Do the maths. Biofuels are neither significant nor sensible nor sustainable.

Turning food which is already in short supply, into fuel which isn't, under these circumstances, on the basis of a completely spurious theory, is worse than madness; it is evil.

Carbon neutrality is also a red herring. The total amount of carbon present on Planet Earth was fixed at about the time of the Big Bang. CO_2 released by the burning of coal made from plants which died millions of years ago, will be absorbed by the plants of today; the whole process is cyclical, and neutral by definition.

Beware the prophets of doom who insist that the sky is falling. It isn't. However, they may well be trying to sell you an acorn-proof hat.

Investigate, April 2007

The Iceman Cometh

I was going to sound off about electoral reform this month. I got quite fired up about it; BCIR and why "They" don't want us to have it, unaccountable list MPs with hidden agendas (such as anti-smacking bills), State-sanctioned propaganda campaigns funded by stolen taxpayers' money (oops, I mean State funding of political Parties), the advantages of the Preferential system over MMP, and the like. Then, with the Smacking Debate still raging, I thought a rant about the merits of corporal punishment might be apropos.

However, there is another pressing issue, which simply won't go away. I have gone into it before, including recently.

It's Global Warming, of course; but more to the point, it's that Global Warming actually isn't happening.

It's not only not happening because of any of the various activities of mankind – burning fossil fuels, farming cattle, wanting to have selfish and non-eco-friendly things like electricity and houses and jobs and so forth; it's simply not happening at all.

Now before the Greenies start frothing at the mouth, and I get labelled a "Climate Change Denier" – a title I would actually wear as a badge of honour, rather than reviling it as one would a swastika – climate data from around the world shows very clearly that Global Warming, if indeed any such thing ever existed, finished almost ten years ago. We are now in a period of cooling. NIWA's own figures show that New Zealand's annual average mean temperature peaked in 1998. Every year since then has been successively colder, with the summer gone being the coldest recorded in 14 years.

Are we in fact heading for an Ice Age? Quite possibly, and quite possibly very soon. Russian scientists believe that it could begin as early as 2012 – ironically, the year in which the Kyoto Treaty is due to expire.

Khabibullo Abdusamatov, from the Pulkovo Astronomic Observatory in St Petersburg, suggests that reduced output from the sun will trigger a period of global cooling similar to the so-called "Little Ice Age" of the 17th century, which lasted for more than sixty years. During this period, canals in Holland froze solid, and ice fairs were held on the frozen surface of the River Thames in London. Curiously, weather records from this time regularly, and inexplicably, fail to appear on the graphs and charts produced by Global Warming doomsayers, including the famous (or should that be infamous) "hockey stick" model much beloved of a certain US ex-Vice President. Abdusamatov believes that the effects of cooling could begin to be seen in as little as five to seven years from now, and be at their most extreme between 2055 and 2060, following a major decline in solar output between 2035 and 2045.

Now isn't this a turn-up for the books. Just when we think everything is sorted as regards Global Warming – which appears to have morphed into "Climate Change" as even the most ardent opponents of human civilisation's advancement, realise they may have been sold a pup in terms of the now entirely discredited Greenhouse

Theory – those pesky Russians come along with a bunch of irrefutable facts, which shoot the whole "Inconvenient Truth" campaign down in flames.

So how does Ivan know that the sun is going to have a wee snooze between 2035 and 2045? Well, because it's done it before. Often. Predictably, and regular as clockwork. The Big Yellow, it would seem, is quite a creature of habit.

Ice Core data from Vostok Station in East Antarctica has faithfully recorded the true patterns of the earth's climate, over the past 415,000 years. The graph resulting from it is quite chilling, no pun intended. We do, it would appear, stand poised on the very brink of an Ice Age.

The data records the Milankovitch Cycles, variations in the angle of tilt of the earth and in her orbit around the sun, and in the sun's own output. It doesn't leave out "inconvenient" bits like the Little Ice Age, or the Mediaeval Warm Period, when the Vikings were grazing cattle in Greenland.

There are other inconvenient truths out there as well. The Greenland Ice Sheet is thickening, not thinning. Ditto the East Antarctic Ice Sheet, which covers about 97% of the Antarctic land mass, and accounts for almost nine-tenths of the fresh water on planet earth. Why, I cannot help but wonder, do a small but vocal group of somewhat fringe scientists, and a large number of politicians and broadcast journalists, insist on showing us repeated images of ice thinning on the 3% of Antarctica (mostly on the Antarctic Peninsula, and to a degree on West Antarctica) where it is actually happening, probably because of temperature changes brought about by shifting ocean currents, and demanding that we believe the world is undergoing disastrous warming as a consequence?

And then there's the famous picture of the sad-looking polar bear, hopelessly marooned on a tiny shrinking ice floe, drifting forlornly in the middle of a huge and warming ocean, and staring oblivion down the barrel…as it turns out, the picture was taken several years ago, in the summertime, when the ice always breaks up, by a geology student who never knew it had been hijacked until she saw it on the Internet, let alone gave permission for it to be used or captioned in the way it was. The bear (who, being a polar bear, is a good swimmer anyway) was apparently very close to the shore, and according to the photographer, appeared quite contented. Polar bear numbers, incidentally, are on the increase in Canada – where, as a further aside, this year's annual seal cull has been set back because many of the ships used by the cullers have become trapped in unseasonably heavy pack ice. "The worst in 20 years", was how one veteran described it.

And New Zealand's glaciers are growing! That's right; Fox and Franz Joseph are advancing, not retreating. So are 35 other glaciers in the Southern Alps. OK, this probably isn't an entirely fair observation, because glacial advance actually has more to do with relative precipitation in the mountains than it does with temperature; but this writer finds it intriguing that glaciers are also advancing in Chile, North America, and the Indian Himalayas.

How quickly might the next Ice Age be upon us? Some people think it may impact over as short a timeframe as three years; others, even faster. Author Robert Felix (http://www.iceagenow.com/index.htm) certainly thinks so.

Doomsday scenarios such as the one portrayed in the film *The Day After Tomorrow* may be a little far-fetched; or maybe they're not. Woolly Mammoths frozen in the last Ice Age, 10,000 years ago, have been discovered with green food still in their mouths. Maybe they were just in the habit of chewing their food for a really long time – you know, for several years – or maybe the onset of cold, in some places at least, was rather quick.

We don't know exactly when this next Ice Age will begin. We do know that there will be one, because that is what our planet does, in regular cycles, and we also know that it is, at the very least, if not overdue, then due to happen right about now. In fact if the temperature of the breeze outside is anything to go by, it may have started already.

So why, in the face of physical evidence, current weather recordings, the historical record, fossils, tree rings, ice cores, satellite data, and a majority of scientific opinion – or at least question – are we being fed the complete opposite of what is actually happening?

Has belief in Global Warming become, as Czech President Vaclav

Klaus has asked publicly, a religion in its own right? Ask the Believers, and they will say that any who question the doctrine of Climate Change, must be in the pay of Big Business, the Oil Companies, or other Evil Anti-Ecologists. Personally I think such conspiracy stuff is a bit crank, but then I believe the Yanks did actually go to the Moon, too.

There is plenty of international commentary on the misinformation distributed by the global warming industry. Our media in New Zealand, particularly – and once again, predictably – the State-owned broadcast media, have shown little interest in reporting such commentary. The excellent documentary "The Great Global Warming Swindle" which screened on Britain's Channel Four a month or so back, may be found in its entirety on YouTube, free from editing, censorship, or plain indifference, at http://youtube.com/results?search_query=global+warming+swindle, along with several other serious and sober investigations. I don't imagine TVNZ will be showing it, while the present Government has plans to indoctrinate our schoolchildren with the Al Gore film instead.

I leave the last words to two commentators who have neither vested interest, nor reason to oppose any view of the majority of the scientific community;

"It could not be a worse time to abandon our own traditions of reason and tolerance, and to embrace instead the irrationality and intolerance of ecofundamentalism, where reasoned questioning of its mantras is regarded as a form of blasphemy. There is no greater threat to the people of this planet than the retreat from reason we see all around us today." – Nigel Lawson, former Chancellor of the Exchequer in Britain, address to the Centre for Policy studies, 1 November 2006.

"The climate changes naturally all the time, partly in predictable cycles, and partly in unpredictable shorter rhythms and rapid episodic shifts, some of the causes of which remain unknown. We are fortunate that our modern societies have developed during the last 10,000 years of benignly warm, interglacial climate. But for more than 90% of the last two million years the climate has been colder, and generally much colder, than today.

The reality of the climate record is that a sudden natural cooling is far more to be feared, and will do infinitely more social and economic damage, than the late 20th century phase of gentle warming." Professor Bob Carter, geologist and paleoclimate researcher, James Cook University, Queensland.

Here endeth the lesson.

Investigate, June 2007

Chapter Seven

Welfare Dependency

"People aren't on benefits because they're struggling; they're struggling because they're held down by benefits"

– Prosser, Investigate, August 2004

The Caring Society?

The Budget has been and gone and, predictably in this pre-election year, the Labour-led Government has desperately attempted to shore up its flagging support by way of more and more handouts to those in society regarded as "less well off".

If Ruth Richardson's infamous 1991 carve-up was the Mother of All Budgets, then Michael Cullen's 2004 version could be described as the Nanny of Them All.

Labour is in serious trouble on several fronts, and Dr. Cullen's budget needed to pull something dramatic out of the hat in order to slow the haemorrhaging of its voters.

Thanks to the seabed and foreshore, the turning point of *that* Orewa Speech, and Helen Clark's bungled response to both, Labour's Maori support is now gone regardless. Middle New Zealand (which was turning back towards the Right at the last election anyway) has found new favour with National, and an unlikely hero in the respectable and conservative Don Brash. And as the new Maori Party enters the fray, it is likely that Labour will suffer even further, as the Parties of the Right find their ranks swelled by a political form of "white flight" in the face of it.

So Labour's budget has reached out to what remains of its loyal constituency; those on low incomes, and New Zealand's vast ranks of welfare beneficiaries.

Understandable perhaps; but is it healthy, I wonder, to lengthen even further the apron strings of Nanny State, and to enlarge the nipple for those who suckle at the nation's breast?

Despite the doubtless honourable intentions of the 1930s architects of "welfare from the cradle to the grave", the reality of welfarism is that it traps those who it claims to help, in entrenched poverty, both materially and psychologically. The economic, social, and medical evidence of this is now irrefutable.

The mentality of dependence instiled into the New Zealand psyche by three generations of entrenched social welfare provides fertile ground for the seeds of socialist vote-buying. Its mechanism is simple enough; those who live from the handouts of others remain, (albeit subconsciously) psychologically locked in a developmental stage equivalent to its physical counterpart at the beginning of life. Any threat to the food supply results in anxiety, and the promise of more food engenders contentment and approval.

This reality carries through to electoral support, even when the food supply is being guaranteed at the expense of the very security of the provider.

Welfare is a necessary, even an honourable facet of a civilised society. We look after the young, the old, the sick, and the weak, the victims of misfortune or of the destructive actions of others; those who, for whatever reason, cannot look after themselves. It is this that sets us apart from those societies which do not care; from those who, unlike ourselves, do not strive to achieve a greater humanity. We are morally superior to these nations. However, we do not bask in such self-anointed glory, or even visit it much in thought; we simply do it, because it is the right thing to do, more so than because there but for the grace of God go any of us.

But welfare needs to be a safety net for those who fall victim to life's misfortunes; and not, as it has become in New Zealand, a hammock for generations of those who cannot be bothered.

The psychology of welfare dependency follows a predictable progression, from grudging acceptance, to gratitude, to pleasant satisfaction, to expectation, to demand with the conviction of right; at the same time accompanied by pitiful self-justification, founded on an ever-increasing sense of inadequacy.

To take ever more from those who have vision and purpose, and who desire and strive to better themselves, and to give ever more to those who do not share these ambitions or motivations, is not sustainable.

Taxing the "rich" and the industrious, so that the lazy and the self-pitying are not required to work, is not sustainable.

Part of this situation is society's own fault. We have allowed a myth to perpetuate itself in this country. For many generations we have relentlessly promoted the idea of equality alongside the concept of egalitarianism. These two precepts are not the same thing.

In an egalitarian society such as that which we uphold and take pride in, every man and woman has the same rights, freedoms, and opportunities.

But this does not mean that every person has the right to expect that they will achieve the same level of success.

Disregarding fortune bestowed by inheritance or winning the Lotto – chances both so rare in everyday society as to be statistically irrelevant – success will depend, as it has since the human race began, on a combination of talent and one other factor. This factor is effort.

Call it endeavour, enterprise, or plain good old-fashioned work if you prefer, but the meaning is the same.

In an egalitarian society, everyone has the right to the opportunity to achieve their best. What this best may be, is determined by each person's inherent, inherited abilities, and by the degree to which they make effort to achieve their aims.

Those who will not make the effort cannot expect to achieve equality with those who do. By the same token, those of us not gifted with certain innate abilities should not expect society to provide, by some unexplained right, an equal standard of living to someone else who, for whatever reason, has the good fortune to have been born with rare talent. It is unlikely, for example, that this writer will ever be an All Black, or a concert pianist.

Those political leaders who seek to impose equality on people who will not strive to achieve, by taking the means for this from people who will, all for the sake of their own electoral expediency, are behaving in a manner which is neither sustainable nor responsible. The truth of this is self-evident.

There is another self-evident truth contained here. It is that those who support such politicians, and who are their primary beneficiaries, are themselves ultimately responsible for the consequences they will have to face, because of the reality of the nation created in their name.

There is a degree of discipline required if New Zealand is to free itself from the dependency of the welfare trap. And, unless we can shed the ingrained idea that it is not possible to make ends meet without some form of Governmental subsidy or handout, we will not, as individuals or as a nation, progress – economically or personally.

Discipline means a number of things. In this case it can probably be summed up by the term "delayed gratification".

I do speak from experience here. Growing up, my family was never materially well-off, and I went without many of the niceties of life which others appeared to have in abundance. It didn't kill me. In fact I would venture that I had, and learned, other things, which have stood me in better stead.

During my early twenties, due to what I will now describe as poor choices made by myself under the prevailing economic situation, I had a couple of short bursts on the dole.

That didn't kill me either, but neither did I enjoy it; nor, indeed, did I choose to remain unemployed. There were other things I could do, new skills I could learn. I did so. Nothing stopped me.

I will go so far as to say that there is, very probably, little stopping others from following the same path, save for their own inertia, and the lack of motivation provided by the knowledge that the benefit will always be there.

Pause a moment and imagine a New Zealand where the benefit won't always be there. Say, for example, that the unemployment benefit lasts for a maximum of six months. After six months, there is no more benefit. What are people to do?

The human animal's priorities are determined by the necessities of life. When these are met, there is time for rest and contemplation. Reality is thus: if the individual knows that the rent is paid, there is food in the fridge, and the rugby is on Sky at the pub in two hours, he or she can happily sleep in till ten, walk down to the dole office in bare feet, sign in, and take the rest of the day off.

If however the rent isn't paid, and the fridge is empty, the same individual will instead become motivated to do something to help him or her self. This may involve learning how to do something new, or perhaps actually doing something regarded as menial; it may be poorly paid, or it may involve moving to another area. The footy might have to wait. It might actually involve going without, or, to put it another way, delayed gratification.

The individual required to fend for themselves does, in spite of insistence to the contrary, become a better and more resilient person, with greater self-esteem; less inclined to commit crime, and with a higher regard for the value of effort and for the rewards that such effort can bring.

Without going into the causes of social decline which has lead to such a huge number of solo mothers in this country, there is equally nothing stopping groups of such individuals, particularly in suburban environments, pooling their resources to enable each mother to, for example, work four days a week, and provide child-care for the group on the fifth – nothing, that is, other than a lack of motivation to so do, and the provision of an alternative income by the State.

We are not doing people any favours by allowing them to wallow in indolence and self-pity. We are in fact harming them, and destroying the foundations on which the decent society of the future must be built. The children of the third welfare generation need to be rescued, not spoon-fed and indulged. They will gain far greater learning, understanding, and self-respect, by seeing their role models as contributors, than by being shackled to a world of bitterness and poverty where none may rise above the lowest common denominator of the tag that is "beneficiary".

The whole concept of the Welfare State has been wrong from the start, and the Great Nanny Budget will only make it worse.

People aren't on benefits because they're struggling; they're struggling because they're held down by benefits.

Investigate, August 2004

Team Who?

I'm part of a majority!

This is a rare occurrence indeed, but recently, better than 50% of respondents to a Holmes poll felt that HelenClark Inc. shouldn't waste further precious taxpayer dollars on the "America's" Cup.

And indeed, where is the potential value to the New Zealand taxpayer, in subsidising this pastime of billionaires? There are some jobs for boatbuilders, true; though invariably, foreign challengers will bring their own craft with them from overseas.

We are told that staging events such as the Americas' Cup brings unprecedented publicity to New Zealand, and a level of exposure for our manufacturers and tourist destinations which cannot be matched by other forms of advertising.

This is a myth, and it is time New Zealand woke up and smelled the coffee. 12-metre match racing is the preserve of a very, very tiny minority of the world's very, very tiny rich elite. Most of the earth's population simply are not interested, and will receive little coverage of the event anyway, other than as an occasional item on the late night or back page news.

We were given the same line over the hosting of the APEC summit a couple of years back. It filled the headlines and swamped the news bulletins for weeks; New Zealand was in the spotlight, the eyes of the world were on us, this was going to be an economic El Dorado.

Reality check, people; APEC happens every year, in some city or another. The only reports the world hears about it are the same as those we receive here – a small item on page two, mentioning that an obscure second string Minister has given a speech at the APEC gathering, which this year is in Blahblahville, overseas somewhere. It just isn't news, and it just doesn't rate.

The Americas' Cup, beyond our own introspective and sports-obsessed shores, is about as important. Throwing good money at it, in the vain hope that it will encourage tourists to come flocking here, is plain bad housekeeping.

A challenge in Europe, if mounted seriously, will cost at least NZ$200 million. This expenditure comes with no guarantee of, and indeed little chance of, success.

If we win, we might get $600 million back on this investment, once only, in four years' time. Big deal. Yawn. I can spend $200 million for you establishing vineyards, and guarantee you a minimum gross return of $400 million after year four – and every year thereafter, till the vines die, which, even with phylloxera, won't be for around a century. These are conservative figures, taking account for the bursting of the wine bubble, which hasn't happened yet.

If we lose, we get nothing. And we lose the two hundred million bucks we stake out.

Why do we have such a limited chance of success? Because we don't have the best sailors anymore, and we don't have them because we can't afford them, and we can't afford them because we insist on believing that a first world lifestyle can be paid for out of the returns from a third world economy.

We have a cheap, miserly, outlook in this country. We hold the curious belief that we can offer a professional somewhere between a third and a tenth of what someone else is offering them to do the same job, and expect them to jump at the chance. Why should they? Patriotism? Why is anyone going to pass up between 70% and 90% of their potential income, to support a society with raging tall-poppy syndrome? Even when a fellow Kiwi produces world-beating success, for "us" or for someone else, we persist in trying to knock them down to the level of some national lowest common denominator. One thing is certain, and that is that while we as a people are so frightened of, or so threatened by, success, we are unlikely as a nation to experience it.

How does Switzerland, half the size of the North Island, population just one and a half times that of New Zealand, and few natural resources, throw up a billionaire yachtsman challenger with a personal fortune three times greater than the combined wealth of our country's five richest? Simple, really; Switzerland has industry. They make, and sell to the world, things that the world needs and wants. Forget watches, chocolate, dairying and bank accounts, and the other window dressing for which the Swiss economy is famous.

Switzerland has real industry. Industrial chemicals, pharmaceuticals, fertiliser, steel, heavy engineering. They take raw material and turn it into value-added finished product of high quality and high price.

And they have a clean green image. Maybe this image is fake; but with our 2,4,D, our 2,4,5,T, our 1080 and our landfills, maybe so is ours.

We are told we need to be more like the Swiss, but the only industries we are advised to emulate are the minuscule ones, banking and tourism.

We are told also that Ireland is an example to follow, and the percentage returns from her recent forays into mobile phones, software, and microchips, are lauded. But we are not reminded of the major contributors to the Irish economy – which is twice the size of our own, despite being a similar population occupying the equivalent of the other half of the North Island. Steel, coal, railway irons and rolling stock, glassware, textiles, chemicals, electrical machinery, and of course alcoholic beverages, accompany that nation's EU subsidised agriculture, as the big players, and the big payers.

And Ireland is regarded as being clean and green as well.

It is the billionaires who have made their fortunes in these real industries who can indulge in the luxury of Americas' Cup match racing. For the most part they do this for themselves; there is little emphasis placed on national interests. Main street Switzerland regards the fact that one of their compatriots has brought "home" the Cup as little more than a curiosity. By the same token, if in four years' time it departs again, there will not be a period of national mourning such as we have seen here.

It is puzzling that ordinary New Zealanders should claim such ownership of a syndicate which has so little to do with them, and which offers them so little in the way of access or opportunity. From Korean red socks and Chinese "Loyal" flags, to the family of five sponsors – a Japanese car company (Toyota), an American-owned phone company (Telecom), a Japanese-owned brewery (Steinlager) and a German software firm (SAP), there is very little connecting Team New Zealand to the nation and people for which it is named. In reality the New Zealand content has been our superb sailors and boatbuilders; yet we do not extend the same pride and support towards those who construct and crew equally foreign yachts as we do to those whose boat happens to be black. Perhaps it is somewhat apt that the only real New Zealand sponsor is Lotto – an organisation built on the dreams and wild fantasies of ordinary folk, who will probably never be allowed anywhere near a 12-metre yacht.

So, the Cup is gone, maybe never to return; and to the detriment, in real terms, of probably only those few investors who have speculated on future property values in and around the Viaduct Basin.

Rather than sending good money after bad in the hope of clawing it back, on the basis of a few somewhat dubious claims as to its actual value, New Zealand may be better to invest in some genuine wealth-creating infrastructure.

Boatbuilding is something we do better than almost anyone else, and shipbuilding is something with which we already dabble. $200 million put towards growing this industry could prove an infinitely more sensible and profitable venture in the long term than the vague chance of some increased tourism revenues.

From submarines to superyachts, trawlers to tankers, freighters to frigates, our maritime nation could easily supply the world with the best available boats that all its people need and use everyday, instead of concentrating on one obscure racing sloop which a tiny minority use once every four years.

Then, in the future, when the Cup is raced off the coast of Portugal, Denmark, Brazil or California, the New Zealand industry-made billionaires who challenge for it can be accompanied by the well-off ordinary New Zealanders who work for them, travelling in a luxury cruise liner built right here.

That sounds more like Team New Zealand to me.

Investigate, April 2003

Chapter Eight

Silly Little Girl Syndrome

"New Zealand society, Western society in general, has been hijacked by a conspiracy of Silly Little Girls. They're everywhere; in the schools, in the media, in the public service, in the judiciary, even in Cabinet"

– Prosser, Investigate, May 2006

Boys to Men

Many moons ago, at an impressionable age, I was given a small red book which was to guide, and mesh with, much of my way of thinking during the following few years. It was not Chairman Mao's Little Red Book, and not the Bible, the Koran, or the Kabala, either. It was the Kiwi Joker Book, a slim satirical work, the brainchild of a one Gavin Wainwright.

Gav's tome epitomised the thinking of generations past, on such subjects as sex, dress, etiquette, table manners, drinking habits, suitable occupations, and acceptable names for one's dog. It was a celebration and a reaffirmation of a glorious past era, when real men were real blokes, and sheilas were happy about that.

The Kiwi Joker Book advised that a good job for a real joker involved either killing things which were alive, or tearing down things which were not. A job was not acceptable if one had to sit at a desk, wear a tie, or shave more than once a week. Approved occupations included construction worker, demolition worker, freezing worker, farmer, deer culler, test pilot, and anything to do with concrete.

Attire for the real Joker could include Swanndris, gumboots, or anything nicked from the job. The Real Joker ate red meat (preferably still kicking), drank beer, shot things, and ran over possums in the car. He loved his dogs, his kids, his sheila, and his country, and he drove either a station wagon (for carrying dogs and four-by-twos and keeping them dry) or a ute (for carrying dogs and four-by-twos and not caring if they got wet). He had sex whenever he wanted, which was whenever his sheila wanted it too, and he never paid for it.

My copy of the Kiwi Joker Book accompanied me to Britain and Europe on my OE; such passages as I recall or quote are taken from memory, as it is a very long time since, dog-eared and beer-stained, I passed it on to another young man, a fellow traveller from home. I needed it no longer; its work was done.

That work, however, is not being done in New Zealand anymore. Our society is failing those who come after us. We are breeding an emasculated generation of boys, who are quite seriously in danger of not being able to become the men their forebears were. Why?

Because our society, New Zealand society, Western society in general, has been hijacked by a conspiracy of Silly Little Girls. They're everywhere; in the schools, in the media, in the public service, in the judiciary, even in Cabinet.

Everywhere we turn, the foundations of masculinity, the pillars of male-ness which have underpinned the construction and development of our very civilisation, are being undermined, by Silly Little Girls. And we are putting up with it.

Today's boys, raised evermore in a society of single-parent families, lack the role models which we, as the generation who came before them, had to look up to. Many do not have fathers or father figures in their homes; a dwindling number of grandfathers are unable to stem the tide of poor fathering provided by the procession of inadequate partners and deviant boyfriends served up to so many kids, by an ever-increasing number of single mothers.

There are scant few male teachers in our schools, and their numbers are dropping all the time. Those who remain are hamstrung and muzzled by the priorities of an education establishment which has fallen victim to the shrill dictates of a regime founded and controlled by Silly Little Girls. Even those other stalwarts of commonsense, the caring grandparents and the sensible middle-aged mothers, are fast disappearing from the classroom.

I probably had thirty or more teachers through my school career. I remember about a dozen well and fondly; they were mostly men, strong characters, disciplinarians, strict but fair. Those who taught technical subjects, woodwork, metalwork, tech drawing, had been tradesman before entering the teaching profession. They were real men before they became teachers. We feared and respected them. They coached rugby and wielded the cane. We listened to them, and because of that, they taught us. Where are they now?

Such men are no longer attracted to the once-respected calling of the teacher; the commonsense of ordinary discipline has been replaced by the stupidity of political correctness, promoted, once again, by the pervading cult of the Silly Little Girls. They are unwilling to take the risk of being accused of sexual impropriety with children the same age as their own; we are not all rapists, for God's sake, and the hysterical rantings of unbalanced, frustrated, man-hating socialists doesn't make us so. What does it say about our society that a man can't even sit next to a boy on a plane, in a seat he didn't even choose, without being labelled a paedophile?

Boys of my generation played Cowboys and Indians, Germans and Americans, Bullrush, rugby, and scrag. It made us who we are. Nowadays, a generation of boys is learning Peace Studies and sewing, and they're not even allowed to have water pistols unless they're pink and don't look like the real thing. Why? Because some Silly Little Girl says so?

Back then, if someone was a bully, you ganged up on him and thumped him. Today, boys are suspended for such forthright action, and far from receiving a simple, effective, appropriate, and deserved thumping, the bully will be counselled, mollycoddled, apologised for, and ultimately sent away unmodified and unhelped, to fester into the psychopath of the future.

Only this week as I write, a protective Dad, a real man in my considered estimation, ran foul of the law by administering a clip to the ear of the boy who had been bullying his daughter. Fining him $500, the judge, in tones reminiscent of the Silly Little Girl, proclaimed that "Big people shouldn't pick on little people". No, they shouldn't, lest the remaining real men in our society should stand up and thump them. The judge, seemingly, has failed to realise that the judicial system **is** the Big Person, and what is worse, that in this case, it is also the bully; that the actual bully has learned only one lesson from this, that being that he can do as he likes to others without fear of retribution, and that Silly Little Girls, even if they have become judges, ultimately rely on the strength of body and force of reason provided by real men. How else does she suppose her judgement may be imposed or enforced? By other Silly Little Girls?

The school, as we all know, will do nothing at all as far as any effective response is concerned, in spite of their pontifications to the contrary; and the parents of the bully, who have already failed, and probably deserve a thumping themselves, will do nothing either.

The buck stopped with one real man, and our society and our judicial system, opposed as it is to common sense and to real men, turned him into the villain.

This garbage has to stop. It is ridiculous for masculinity to be promoted as something bad, and grossly irresponsible for society to allow our future men to be reshaped into some gender-neutral shadow of the heroes of old who got us as far as we have come. My old man never put up with it, and still doesn't; why should I? Dad served his military with pride, taught me how to use a rifle, ride a bike, box, study, and think for myself. What are we teaching our boys today? Shoot straight, talk straight, be straight with people, stand up to bullies, and help those in need? No. We're teaching them to whimper and snivel and deny the testosterone in their blood. Boys are made to be men. They need to play war games, and kill animals, and roll in the mud; they need to have rough-and-tumble, to sort out their differences with a few punches and be mates again afterwards, and to play team sports, and weld metal, and hammer stuff, and mess about with cars, and stash girlie mags under the bed where they think no-one will know about them.

And they need to grow up into men who will look after their mothers, and protect their sisters, and respect their old man; and stick up for their mates and help out the little guy and do the right thing, because society needs them to do that, or society won't survive, regardless of what the Silly Little Girls think.

And they need to marry and have kids, and raise the next generation of boys who will become men, and raise their daughters to become women, and love them to bits without the remotest intention of mistreating or abusing them, and 99.999% of us don't, believe it or not, in spite of what the shriekers and the social engineers and the anti-family brigade would have people believe.

I have a day off tomorrow, a rare thing during vintage; so I'm taking Junior down to the mine tailings next to the river, with a couple of rifles, and we're going to shoot a few bottles. He's twelve, and developing quite a good eye; and his dad thinks it's a good thing, too.

As Gavin Wainwright said, in his insightful book twenty-something years ago, "Blessed are the Little Boys, because they are the Keepers of the Clear Vision."

New Zealand has lost the Clear Vision, and we are in danger of losing a generation of boys who may never really become men.

The Kiwi Joker Book was meant as, well, a joke; but there are, as is well known, many a true word spoken in jest.

The end is not quite nigh, but unless we can rediscover the art of turning boys into men, it very soon will be.

And as plain as it is that the world can be broken down into Earth, Fire, Water, and Air, so it is that the Real Man is an amalgam of Concrete, Gelignite, Diesel, and Testosterone; and the sooner we get on and tell the Silly Little Girls with their weak PC drivel to sit down and shut up, and get some real male role models back into the home, the schools, TV, public office, and the Beehive, the better it will be for all of us.

Investigate, May 2006

Spare the rod

And spoil the child, so the old saying goes. In this supposedly enlightened age, many would claim that we now know differently; but do we really?

As the "to smack or not to smack" debate rages on, is it possible that we have simply forgotten what the old adage actually meant – or did we never really know?

Claims and counter-claims are made by those on either side of the argument. People opposed to smacking proclaim that physical discipline constitutes abuse, that it is adult violence towards children and has no place in modern civilised society.

Those in favour hold that in many cases it is not only wholly appropriate, but in fact the only effective method of teaching children a lesson.

It is this perhaps which is the crux of the matter. As parents, we are responsible for teaching those in our charge the ground rules for a life in which they, in time, will become equally responsible adults, and in which they will likewise bear the duty of educating the generation which comes after them.

We, as parents, must to the best of our ability, knowledge, and understanding, teach our charges the best way of navigating a successful path on life's journey; we must show them the difference between right and wrong, correct and incorrect, safe and unsafe, acceptable and unacceptable.

The original quote goes back to Biblical times.

Without suggesting that the "Good Book", as some call it, is somehow to blame for the quandary which modern society is experiencing with regard to corporal punishment, it is entirely possible that the misinterpretation of its message, both deliberately and inadvertently, has contributed to the present debate, by providing a mechanism by which certain of society's sadists can excuse their perversion of choice with some apparent justification.

Certainly, throughout history and across many of the world's cultures and nations, conformity to accepted or desired standards of behaviour has been enforced by physical means, by the weak upon the strong, by the many upon the few, and by adults upon children. It is possible that this enforced conformity has its roots in the interpretation of religious dictate, though it is altogether more likely that such teachings themselves reflect the general way of humanity which existed long before they were written; perhaps even the correct way for humanity.

Whether or not one subscribes to the philosophy outlined in the Bible, or any other Holy Book for that matter, a number of current realities are beyond question.

Firstly, there exists within human society a level of physical violence, which is often directed by those who are capable of wielding power, against those who are incapable of resisting it.

Secondly, there exists within families, family groups, and wider and tribal societies, a tradition of physical discipline, applied by those members who are older, more experienced, and presumably wiser, upon those who are younger and in need of direction and learning.

Thirdly, these first two realities are not the same thing.

Fourthly, these first two realities have lately come to be confused as the same thing, and as a consequence, the smacking/no smacking debate has come to prominence, with legal moves initiated by both sides.

The lack of separation between violence and discipline in the minds of some, is not without understandable cause. The institutionalised brutality inflicted on many of my father's generation by the English boarding school system, was promoted by that system as being a tool for positive character-building, and as a forerunner to the military discipline to which many, if not most, of those subjected to it, would later graduate.

In addition, too many of those charged with parenting the next generation, confuse the responsibility to instil an understanding of right and wrong, with a right to impose their own will and control.

Compounding this is the reality that it is a rare person indeed, who is able to learn solely from the experiences of others. Most of us appear to need some form of experience ourselves. And, until we are able to distinguish between moderately safe experimentation and sheer blind curiosity, we require guidance from others better experienced, in order to preserve our own physical safety.

And in spite of the Shangri-La fantasies promoted by the non-smackers, babies are not little adults, born into this world with a fully developed ability to reason, to communicate with all others, or to observe and assess the realities of the world they inhabit. They are babies.

Little children are not the equals of more mature citizens, in terms of knowledge or understanding. They are little children.

Adolescents are not capable of making informed decisions concerning whiskey, motor cars, or ballot papers. This is why we have rules dictating that they shall not have the right to make such decisions.

Physical "discipline" is not about violence. It is about protection. Simple logic dictates that it is not possible to reason with a child who is so young that they do not understand spoken language. Young children playing with matches, or about to poke their fingers into light sockets, cannot be helped or educated, or protected, by lectures on physics or safety. They simply are not capable of understanding. Children learn by association.

So the child who is about to pull the boiling jug from the bench top gets a smack on the bum, and a growling. The smack is a shock, and it hurts. The shock and the hurt is enough to make the child cry. The child associates the shock, the hurt, and the growling, with the action of pulling on the jug cord. He learns to not do it again, and is protected. Reason can come later, when he is capable of reason and understanding.

The pain and the shock of the smack and the growling, is far less destructive than being scalded by a jugful of boiling water. And as the physical effects of the scalding will last a lifetime, while the fear of boiling water will fade, conversely the physical effects of a smack will be gone in minutes, but the learning will last for the life of the individual.

Later actions such as riding a tricycle out into the road, or running with scissors, or putting firecrackers in the cat's ear, can be dealt with in the same way. By then, the child has not learned everything about right and wrong; but he has learned that his parents love him, and that they will guide him, and that if he fails to listen to instructions regarding correct behaviour and common sense, pain will result.

The child does not necessarily understand about the dangers of traffic, or the wrongness of cruelty to animals. But he understands pain. And a smack is a whole lot less damaging than being run over.

As kids get older, they remain curious, and they find themselves better able to express this curiosity.

Part of curiosity is a desire to find the limits of acceptable behaviour. Children, by nature, will push the envelope. Kids need boundaries, and they will, and do, set about finding them.

When children do not find boundaries, their search becomes intensified, and as such, it becomes more and more destructive, both for the child, and for those around him. Driven by frustration and a lack of definition, young people without behavioural boundaries turn to violence, theft, and antisocial activities; anything, in fact, which will elicit attention and a response.

These older kids – up to about fourteen, in this writer's experience – often know full well that what they are doing is wrong, but they do it anyway, because no-one is stopping them.

In a bygone age, even the threat of corporal punishment was sufficient to modify behaviour. When I was at high school – and I finished the seventh form in 1984 – we knew that the cane existed on the other side of the border between acceptable and unacceptable conduct.

Quick learners discovered early, that it did not pay to push the boundaries beyond where we knew them to be.

In hindsight, many of the most fair-minded and effective Prefects in the sixth and seventh forms, were those individuals who had been caned for misbehaviour in the third and fourth forms.

But this avenue for the learning of discipline is no longer open. It has been replaced by a creeping tide of "Human Rights", of a thinly-veiled agenda to replace the family, and the common sense discipline of loving parents and caring communities, with an institutionalised form of political correctness.

And we are seeing the evolution of the statistically worst-behaved generation of teenagers and young adults in history, because of it.

The cynic in me wonders how many left-leaning teachers have been driven from the profession, by the behaviour of adolescents made uncontrollable through the removal of corporal punishment, which their own naïve and misinformed ideology led them to support.

How many of the supporters of no-smacking, I wonder, have successfully parented children themselves?

Perhaps it is time our society stopped listening to the illogical and sinister preachings of the inexperienced, the intellectually foolish, and the dishonest promoters of some hidden agenda; those who would destroy society and the family, replacing them with some Governmental institution. Perhaps it is time we listened instead to the wisdom and common sense of middle-aged mothers, of loving fathers, of wise and learned grandparents.

We love our kids, and we know we do. We want the best and safest and most productive and enjoyable life for them, and we know we do. And we have common sense and instinctive understanding, and we certainly don't want to hurt our kids, and we damned well will protect them.

And we don't have to justify any of this, to any half-baked sociologists or insidious UN Committees, with their crackpot theories and dubious motivations.

Smacking and violence are different things. Perhaps the day is coming, when we will, by circumstance, be required to stand up, square off, and demonstrate this difference, to those who would seek to destroy our society and our families, and steal our children.

Investigate, October 2004

The Lost Generation

So, Australia is apologising to the people who have come to be known as her "lost generation"; the Aboriginal people who were removed from their families and communities as children, from the late 1800s through to the late 1960s, and forcibly assimilated into white mainstream Australian culture.

Sometime in the not-too-distant future, New Zealand will have a similar apology to make; not to a generation of displaced indigenes, but to an entire generation of young New Zealanders who have been lost to the ravages of the insanity known overseas as "the New Zealand Experiment" – Rogernomics, the Free Market, Pacifism, Feminism, and Political Correctness.

They are the generation who were born after mine; as a child of 1967, I represent the last of this country's children to experience all that which our successors have been denied. We had stability and security, because we had boundaries. We faced challenge. We know how to succeed, because we knew that there was such a thing as failure. Not everyone made the grade. Not everyone was able to be top of the class. We learned of consequence and responsibility, of right and wrong, of duty, humility, and respect. We learned these things because they were drummed into us, because the generation who came before us, like the generations before them, knew it to be of essential importance; and they took it as their primary responsibility to instil in us the same values, the same appreciation of social order, of personal accountability, of self-control.

Perhaps most importantly, and most tragically for those who came after us, we had discipline, where they do not.

We had discipline instiled in us, physically where and when it was necessary, and through that mechanism, we learned to be disciplined in ourselves.

We lived in a New Zealand which still had a sense of community, where the entire village did raise the child, where anyone's mum or dad or auntie was everyone's potential disciplinarian, where a dose of the strap at school for poking someone with a compass in class, or a boot up the backside from the neighbour for nicking apples from the tree in the front lawn, would earn the same rebuke from mum and dad when we got home, rather than, as now, an assault charge against the meter of summary justice, accompanied by a subconscious assurance that we could do whatever we liked without fear of retribution.

Our high schools had prefects and canes, our qualifications and certificates had percentages and pass marks, our universities had required standards of behaviour and academic achievement. We did PE and swimming and ran the cross-country whether we liked it or not, and whether we were fat or spotty (read: image conscious), or culturally sensitive or not, because those in authority, which was everyone who was older than us, knew that it was good for us.

We pushed the boundaries, but y'know, there *were* boundaries, and when we went beyond them, it hurt, so we learned not to. And yes, there were always reprobates, but for the most part, kids didn't go around carrying knives and baseball bats, much less using them on complete strangers.

And then the next generation came along, and the world changed somehow; and somewhere in between, New Zealand went mad. People with curious theories, and potentially questionable motives, took hold of the Government and the economy; they sold off the big Government Department employers and broke up the Civil Service, long a bastion of impartial stability amidst the tumultuous seas of politics. They tipped tens of thousands of gainfully employed New Zealanders out of the likes of the Railways and the Ministry of Works, and dumped them into the dole queues. They occupied the media and the education system, and abandoned the established convention of apolitical conduct within these institutions. They cut the safety nets from under the farmers, while at the same time laying hammocks for uncountable single mothers – and by definition, allowing a generation of single fathers to abrogate their responsibilities. They abolished the apprentice schemes, took corporal punishment out of the schools and replaced it with Peace Studies, turned their backs on our family of Nations, emasculated the military, and opened the doors to a flood of undesirable migrants from second-rate countries with deficient cultures.

In fact, as Rudyard Kipling put it in his chillingly prophetic poem *The City of Brass*, written 99 years ago, they tore up the foundations of a decent and civilised society which had been centuries in the making;

"Swiftly these pulled down the walls that their fathers had made them –
The impregnable ramparts of old, they razed and re-laid them
As playgrounds of pleasure and leisure with limitless entries,
And havens of rest for the wastrels where once walked the sentries;
And because there was need of more pay for the shouters and marchers,
They disbanded in face of their foemen their yeomen and archers."

And we let them; and today, we live with the legacy of that ongoing folly. Children, a lost generation of New Zealand's youth, who grew up in homes that never had fathers, and sat in classrooms which never had discipline, watched over by silly feminist teachers who never had respect for tradition, or personal responsibility, or the rule of law, have grown up into a generation of teenagers without boundaries, or the pride of achievement, or regard for themselves or anyone else. They are becoming a generation of young twenty-somethings who stalk the suburbs with makeshift weapons, living and breathing the gang culture of an animal society from the other side of the world, feeding on hate and resentment, and breeding yet another generation of lost babies, this one born into the squalor of uneducated stupidity and moral devolution.

This thing is broke. It needs fixing, and it is we who must fix it; and we can, but doing so will be neither swift nor pleasant. It requires the testicular fortitude to undo many of the mistakes of the past twenty-five years. Glossing over them will not be sufficient, and neither will the policy initiatives of the major political Parties, announced this week as I write. National's approach has a sensible foundation, but it is weak and not far reaching enough; and as for the Labour Government's policies…well, it's that sort of thing which got us to where we are now, and it stretches credulity to propose that more of the same will get us out of it.

Boot Camp for the undomesticated thugs who roam our streets may be one necessary response, but if we are to require the Army to be the ambulance at the bottom of society's cliff, then we must be prepared to resource it adequately for the job, and not expect it to be ready until it has undone the damage wreaked on its structure, manpower, and *esprit-de-corps* through two decades of downsizing by successive foolish and pacifist Governments.

Rebuilding the education system will be necessary as well, including the return of corporal punishment, however much the idea of tackling the issue makes the hand-wringers squirm. Since the pitiful morons who undid discipline in the schools appear to be completely lacking in the requisite brains or stomach to redo it, I suppose we will have to take on the task for them; along with the re-establishment of the apprentice scheme, for those who simply don't want to be doctors or lawyers or accountants. I mean we do actually need plumbers and welders and bricklayers as well, you know, because the Knowledge Economy is as much of a myth as the Tooth Fairy or the Easter Bunny or Global Warming. Try getting an IT Manager or a Graphic Designer to unblock your drains, or replace the pole fuse, or fix the broken stub axle on the hay baler, and you'll see what I mean.

We need to replace the utterly pointless and destructive NCEA with something meaningful again, and reintroduce kids to the reality that not everyone is going to be a rocket scientist or a concert pianist or the captain of the All Blacks. There is such a thing as missing the grade. And as for keeping young people in school until they're 18 – honestly, Prime Minister, please do give up your day job. I suppose it's our fault for letting you stay in it for so long, but really, what were we thinking? I mean after what cloth-eared, woolly-logic, brain-fog day did we decide that it was a good idea to let child-raising laws and educational policy be decided by someone who's never had kids? Penning up teenagers who don't want to be there, in classrooms for which they have no respect, with teachers who have no way of disciplining them, supposedly to learn about subjects which are of no interest or value to them, is meant to be a good idea….how, precisely?

Perhaps most importantly, we must stem the tide of violence engulfing the lost generation by instiling in them a little immediate respect for the rights and property of others. Tagging is not street art. It's vandalism. Fantasising about being a gangster is neither clever nor funny, and if not the Government, nor the Courts, nor the Police, are prepared to be the answer to the problem, then quite frankly, in this writer's opinion, they abrogate any moral authority to dictate that vigilantism isn't the answer either.

Street gangs, knife murders, graffiti, robberies, beatings, and thuggery from unemployed and uneducated youth, are the legacy of a failed experiment in political correctness, carried out by deluded ideologues and supported by foolish liberals.

This lost generation have to be saved, and quickly, because at the moment they are in no state to raise the next one. We can do this thing. All that is required is a little discipline.

Investigate, February 2008

Chapter Nine

Foreign Ownership

"If we want a prime example of what happens to a people when they start selling off bits of their land to outlanders, we need look no further than the Maoris. I mean do we really, seriously, never learn anything from the lessons of history?"

– Prosser, Investigate, August 2010

Forward To The Past

There is, as everyone knows, no such thing as a Free Lunch. And, as is also patently apparent, there is no such thing as a Free Trade Deal, either. Free Trade Deals, insofar as they are generally offered, rate right up there with the other Great Big Lies – "I gave at the office", "The cheque's in the mail," and "Go on, I promise I won't..." well, you get the idea. The other one.

And, as far as they are generally implemented, supposed Free Trade Deals generally bear more of a likeness to the third (and here unspoken) Great Lie, than they do to anything resembling a level playing field.

However, within this context, there are some Trade Deals which seem more attractive than others. New Zealand has had a trade deal with Australia (Closer Economic Relations) for twenty-odd years, which does not appear to have hurt either partner very much. Today, Australia is about to enter into a much vaunted and long sought-after Free Trade Deal with the United States; a deal granted by the US as thanks and recognition for Australia's unswerving support in the US-led War on Terrorism, and for its commitment of military forces to the Afghan and Iraqi campaigns.

New Zealand, conversely, has been granted no such deal. The official reason for this is that New Zealand failed to offer support to the United States' unilateral military action in the Middle East following the World Trade Centre attacks, where Australia did so enthusiastically. The real reason was, and continues to be, New Zealand's anti-nuclear legislation, which prevents US nuclear armed or powered naval vessels from visiting here.

This is a subject in itself, and one which I have touched on before. For the record, as far as weapons are concerned, neither-confirm-nor-deny is history; there are no nuclear weapons on board the US surface Navy. The Americans publicly stated this, unequivocally, more than ten years ago.

And there are no nuclear-powered surface vessels in the US Navy today either, apart from eleven Aircraft Carriers, which, quite simply, will not physically fit into our harbours. There is absolutely no reason why US naval surface ships should not be visiting New Zealand ports on a regular basis – and no valid reason why nuclear-powered attack submarines should not also be allowed to visit, but that is an argument which I do not intend to revisit at this point.

The point at the moment is that the Australians have been given a Free Trade Deal by the Americans, and we haven't.

We have, however, been offered the chance of a Free Trade Deal by the Chinese – and New Zealand is the first Western country to be afforded such an opportunity by the Great Dragon of the East.

What does all of this mean?

The one thing we can be sure of is that it almost certainly doesn't mean what it may appear to mean on the outside.

Australia's deal with the US may be Free in name, but it is far from free in nature; the powerful US agricultural lobby has ensured that the Australian beef, dairy, and sugar industries will not be afforded the benefits which they may have expected under a trade deal which was truly "free".

Australia's manufacturing, pharmaceutical, and entertainment businesses will, however, be subject to the full force of competition from American companies. The experience of similar firms in Canada and Mexico, suggests that not all will survive.

What can New Zealand firms expect from any proposed "free" trade deal with China? A quick scan through the figures held by the Ministry of Foreign Affairs and Trade gives an insightful view of the products traded by our two countries. China is now New Zealand's fourth largest export market, and our biggest exports to the Great Dragon, by a long chalk, are milk powder, raw wool, and radiata pine logs, followed by animal offal and raw sheep skins. High-tech stuff indeed.

Conversely our largest imports from China include computers, clothing, toys, footwear, and electrical and electronic goods.

Free Trade, in essence, means free access to each other's markets, without tariffs or trade volume controls. This may be good news for New Zealand commodity producers, or it may not; our exporters are selling well in the Chinese market, but in industries which are largely free of artificial prices or controls anyway. A free trade arrangement doesn't mean that the Chinese have to buy New Zealand Made – simply that they can, without suffering any additional costs imposed by their own Government.

At the same time, New Zealand importers of Chinese-manufactured goods may sell their wares in an open marketplace unhindered by the pay rates, safety standards, and quality controls demanded by local producers and authorities.

The much-touted potential goldmine for our primary producers contained in "free access" to the Chinese market may well be smoke and mirrors; and even if it isn't, do we really want to go down this road as a nation – yet again? Think about it; the Chinese aren't currently buying cheese or butter from New Zealand, they're buying milk powder. They're not buying textiles or clothing or even finished yarn – it's raw wool they want. And their imports of unprocessed bulk logs, in 2003, were more than three times the value of all the finished timber bought from New Zealand.

And trade deal or no, China's buyers – like anybody else's buyers – will source raw products from wherever acceptable quality may be had for the best possible price. A Free Trade Deal isn't a loyalty agreement.

Even if it were, Free Trade with China on the basis of raw bulk commodity exports isn't the way to a shining future for New Zealand; it's a clear road back to the past, to the relationship we had with pre-WWII Britain – and this at the very time we are supposedly trying to build a value-added, high-tech, knowledge-based economy.

The restless, fast-growing, Chinese juggernaut has little interest in the humanist concerns of New Zealand or its minute population. Our attraction for the Dragon lies in the quality of the commodities we have available – they have plenty of their own factories, thanks – and in our being both a gateway to, and a guinea-pig for, other markets and similar deals down the track.

China also appears to hold scant regard for copyrights, design registrations, or other accepted conventions of international and trading law. High-tech ideas, particularly software, industrial and clothing design, innovations in engineering and biotechnology, and similar successes in other fields, sold to China under any "special" arrangement, are quite likely to find themselves pirated rapidly onto the world market, with little opportunity for redress, and nothing in the way of royalties, for their New Zealand creators.

Chinese officials have been apprehended in recent years attempting to smuggle New Zealand-developed varietal apple budwood out of this country – in a world where China's annual apple production is now some twenty million tonnes, accounting for more than 30% of the total world crop.

New Zealand's apple exports, by comparison, are around a mere 300,000 tonnes annually. We cannot possibly hope to compete in a free arrangement with such a disparately vast partner, particularly when the potential partner displays an almost open desire to steal our ideas.

At the very least, a Free Trade Agreement with the United States would have provided certain New Zealand producers with an opportunity to compete on a fair basis within some discerning, high-value niche markets, and to have that opportunity protected by some very stout, and proven, legal frameworks and mechanisms. The same cannot be said for any proposed FTA with China.

There is another catch hidden amongst the promises of wealth and All Things Good with which the Chinese FTA is emblazoned.

It is this; other nations, who realise (where we may not) where the Dragon's intentions lie, may not wish to see their ideas and inventions devoured by the relentless and unrewarding expansionism of China. In order to protect themselves and their intellectual property from the clutches of the Dragon, such nations may choose simply to not supply them to New Zealand at all. In this case, we miss out on both counts; and we take yet another step backwards, both in technology and in time, back to the simple agrarian economy which was the structure and the legacy of our colonial past, and which we have struggled so hard these past thirty-odd years to escape.

A deal with Uncle Sam would have been a long way from the answer to all our problems, but there would have been both advantages and safeguards therein which could have made it attractive nonetheless; and in either event, the law and the reasoning which saw us miss out, are so lacking in both logic and foundation, that they need to be swept away regardless.

And when contemplating the possible alternative, New Zealand needs to be very wary of the promises of a smiling Dragon – he smiles only for himself.

Investigate, June 2004

Made into China

Some questions in life fall very easily into the category of "If you have to ask, you'll never know." Why foreigners shouldn't be allowed to buy parts of our country is one of them. They just shouldn't. Why not? Because this is our country, that's why not. If we sell it to foreigners, it stops being our country, and then we don't have a country anymore. Are you with me so far?

As far as this writer is concerned, issues don't get any more basic and simple than this one. This is New Zealand and we are New Zealanders. The land belongs to us and we to it; we are melded, inseparable, one and the same. The nation-state, the people, our identity, national character, personality, values, and worldview, are inextricably intertwined with these islands, the diverse geography and unique ecosystems which have helped to make us who and what we are. If we want a prime example of what happens to a people when they start selling off bits of their land to outlanders, we need look no further than the Maoris. I mean do we really, seriously, never learn anything from the lessons of history?

Recent events surrounding the attempted purchase of the Crafar family's network of dairy farms in the North Island by Chinese interests would make it appear that we do not. It doesn't matter that the China Jin Hui Mining Corporation has recently changed its name to Natural Dairy (NZ) Holdings. It doesn't matter that the company is listed on the Hong Kong Stock Exchange or registered in the Cayman Islands, or that Chinese-born front woman May Wang now has New Zealand citizenship. What matters is that this is Chinese money attempting to procure Chinese ownership of New Zealand farmland, Chinese ownership of New Zealand cows, New Zealand milk production, and the profits from our dairy industry. It wouldn't matter if the intending buyers and their money were American, British, Australian, Greek, Dutch, Portuguese or from the moons of Jupiter; what matters is that they're foreigners, and foreign ownership means foreign control. And foreign control means decisions about what happens in New Zealand being made overseas, by people who do not share our values, and who are not answerable to our laws and conventions, our elected representatives, or our perceptions as to what counts as the national good. It means the rape of our land and the pillage of its profits.

I'll probably be labelled a racist for espousing such views. I really don't care. I've been called worse things than that by better people than my accusers. And in any case I'm not a racist; I couldn't give a wet slap what race, creed, or colour a man is, so long as he doesn't demand special treatment on the basis of any of it, or expect me to adopt his culture in preference to my own. Nor am I a xenophobe; I don't have any fear of foreigners, but neither do I want them coming here and taking over, for which sentiment I feel no need to make any apology. No, in fact your favourite commentator is a Culturist, a term I had coined all for myself before Googling it and happily discovering that someone else had got there long before me and created an –ism with which I can actually identify. Yes folks, you can find out all about it at http://www.culturism.us/ , a site which, for all that it is bound to attract the usual suspect fascists, white supremacists, tinfoil hat-wearers, gun-toting survivalists and other assorted nutters, still has an immense amount of common sense to say about the importance of preserving and protecting our Western culture. Indeed, I say come and live here, by all means, you fine wogs of every hue and visage – in such numbers and with such skills as we determine that we require, of course. But bring only your cookbooks and not your Holy books, adopt our tongue, our dress, and our ways, and give your children the names which we give to ours. Demonstrate that you have accepted our culture, which by definition is better than yours – and if it isn't, what are you doing here – and we will happily accept your place in it.

As usual I am straying perilously close to digression territory. Prime Minister John Key's public support for state-owned Landcorp's bid for the Crafar farms is encouraging, but the cynic in me wonders how much of it is driven by populist political pragmatism, and how much is the product of genuine nationalist sentiment. Public opinion appears to be firmly in favour of the SOE purchasing the farms, in spite of whatever the blogosphere might have to say about the finances of the aforementioned organisation. Personally I think the balance sheets which record what State-Owned Enterprises own, spend, and return to the Government as a profit or a dividend are all smoke and mirrors anyway, and if they're not then they should be. It doesn't matter to me that we paid too much for Air New Zealand or that we bought back the Railways several times over for more than they are worth; what matters is that we own them, and the same goes for the Crafar farms and any other land purchases which Landcorp might make in the future. The best outcome, of course, would be for Allan Crafar himself to refinance and retain ownership of his family farms, but if that isn't possible, then the next best thing in this writer's view is for the State to purchase them and continue to farm them with professional managers, until such time as suitably qualified private buyers can be found.

By suitably qualified I mean, of course, real farmers who are also real New Zealanders. If May Wang wants to put on some gumboots and get up at four in the morning to go milking, I for one will salute her. But stitching up billion-dollar land deals from an office in a Hong Kong skyscraper isn't farming, and I have to confess that I'm not comfortable with the idea of corporate farming at all. Farms should be farmed by farmers. I know I'm a simple country yokel, but some things really don't need to be any more complicated than that. The ability for a young couple to work their way up from being farm workers, to managers, to sharemilkers, to owning a herd, and then buying their own farm and passing it on to the kids, is part of what has made New Zealand and its people what we are today. It sticks in my craw that any foreigner who isn't a New Zealand citizen is allowed to buy freehold title to any land in this country at all, from a house in Auckland to a factory in Wellington to an apartment in Queenstown; but there is something particularly repugnant about the Heartland itself passing into the hands of outlanders. It just simply should not and must not be allowed; this is a truth which I hold to be self-evident. If we allow foreign ownership of our land we not only lose control of our nation, but we put the future out of reach of our children. And if that happens, then as a people and a culture we will cease to exist.

The globalists and internationalists, who are the present-day incarnation of the communists of old, leftist wolves in right-wingers' clothing who masquerade in business suits and bleat about Free Trade and Foreign Investment, will naturally decry such sentiments. Money, power, and control, are the only Gods they serve; they have no loyalty to the nation, its people, or their history.

But the sky will not fall if we deny offshore businesses the right to the freehold title to our land, nor will investment capital flood away from our shores. This is blatant scaremongering from people who have all but sold their souls to the broken ideology of the Free Market in return for the baubles offered by foreign moneylenders. Foreign business people are just that, business people, and realists; and they will take a profit wherever they can, in whatever manner and within whatever constraints the laws of any land may allow. If we as a nation had retained the tariffs which once applied to electronics and motor vehicles, the foreign manufacturers of such would have happily continued to supply us with kits to assemble them from, and today we would still have the factories which used to put them together and the employment and wealth which those factories created. Instead we import cheap nasty rubbish from the same nation which today wants to make us tenants on our own farm land, while New Zealanders languish on the dole, or serve burgers and fries to wealthy visitors from other countries which do still have factories and tariffs. Likewise, Chinese companies are not going to forego the profits from supplying our dairy produce to customers in China just because we refuse to sell them our farms. Get real. They will make do within the boundaries as they are set, just as Fonterra carries on business in China even though it isn't allowed to buy the land on which its factories sit.

The monumental stupidity which is Free Trade doesn't work, and it wouldn't work even if New Zealand wasn't the only country in the world which is actually trying to play it by the rules. America's FTA with Australia is anything but free and fair, and our agreement with China, with its provision for an open door to New Zealand for migrant Chinese labour, will just as surely see our economy crushed, all the more swiftly if we continue to allow foreigners to buy land here.

We could, if we desired, easily create a Crown Leasehold Corporation, which would take ownership of the freehold title to land sold to foreigners and foreign interests, and which would manage their use of both the land itself and any agricultural or industrial production from it; disallowing, of course, such activities as subdivision, land use consent changes, and the export and offshore processing of bulk commodities such as milk, timber, meat, wool, or even oil, coal, and other minerals. Crown Leasehold land sold back to New Zealand citizens would of course include freehold title. Naturally it would require a huge bureaucracy to assess and determine the nature and extent of foreign shareholding, but then we already have a huge and bloated bureaucracy, and it might as well be doing something useful. That is, after all, what Governments are for – isn't it? At the moment we are at risk of being made into a de facto province of China by stealth.

Investigate, August 2010

Sale of the Century

Kenny Rogers, bless his fading star, once told us a story about a gambler. The lead character knew quite a bit about risk taking; he knew when to hold and when to fold, when to walk away and when to run with the cards. Somewhere in the darkness, according to the song, Kenny Rogers' gambler managed to break even. This writer confesses to not harbouring any great deal of faith that John Key will manage the same outcome from his latest gamble.

Calling the election ten months early may be seen as a bold move, an honest and open move, a brave and confident one. Equally, it could be seen as naïve, foolish, and counterproductive. A week is a long time in politics, as I have remarked at least as often as any other observer; and ten months counts as a geological age. Anything could happen in that length of time, and most of it probably will.

Our esteemed Prime Minister – or at least his close advisors – must surely know that, which leaves your favourite commentator slightly perplexed as to why he has done what he has. Promising voters that delivering another term for the National Government will, without any doubt, mean a return to Rogernomics, is perhaps his greatest gamble ever. Maybe John Key genuinely believes that asset sales are the best way forward for New Zealand. Maybe he's taking a punt that his personal popularity will be sufficient to carry his administration through the campaign and back onto the Treasury benches. Or perhaps our best-known currency trader has secretly decided that he's had enough of politics, and is looking for a way to commit political suicide whilst at the same time making his exit look like a terrible accident.

And suicide is what this writer is sure it will be. Too many people were too badly burned by this country's last foray into the stupidity of privatisation, for any agenda which holds a repeat of it as its central tenet to have any realistic chance of winning at the polls. 1984 is still too recent, the memories are still too raw, the pain is still too fresh, for anyone who remembers it to choose to go through it again voluntarily. We remember being lied to. We remember being stolen from. We remember being promised that our debt would disappear and the cost of our daily requirements would shrink, in the face of the power of competition which "The Market" would bring to our basic services and utilities. We remember that none of it was true. We remember that it didn't work. We remember that the trickle down never happened and that power prices doubled. And now Key wants to do it all again. Is he mad?

Asset sales are being packaged differently this time, of course. It's only going to be a "partial privatisation", and the Government will maintain a 51% controlling share. What this means, of course, is that fully half the profits from the services which the SOEs in question provide to New Zealanders will disappear overseas. Naturally, however, as we saw with Air New Zealand, the BNZ, the Railways, and now Telecom, the tab for all new investment will still have to be picked up by the taxpayer. Kiwi Mums and Dads (I have a gene which automatically triggers a "bulls**t" response whenever I hear a politician use the word "Kiwi"), who of course have bucketloads of spare cash sitting around waiting for something to spend it on, will have first rights to buy shares in companies which, as taxpayers, they already own. Am I missing something here, or are we about to be ripped off yet again?

We are told that we have to sell what remains of the family silver because we are drowning in a sea of debt and there is no other way to pay it off. This is an outright lie. Our public debt sits at less than 30% of GDP, 97th on the list of national indebtedness, less than half that of the United States, a third of that of the UK, a quarter of the French and Canadian Governmental liabilities, and barely an eighth of the degree to which Japan is in hock to the global banks. Our total external debt, which includes private borrowings, is half the world average, and only half that of the US and Australia. British debt is nine times greater than ours and Switzerland's more than five times. Selling 49% of our State Assets will have no effect at all on private debt, but will halve the amount of income we currently receive from them. The entire idea of privatisation, partial or not, is absolute rubbish which cannot possibly work, and which, as history and bitter experience has very clearly shown us, does not work.

But John Key, money dealer and master gambler, wants us to

do it again; and furthermore, he believes that enough people will vote for the idea that he will be returned to office come November. That's a big ask, because it relies heavily on more people than voted for National last time voting for them this time. With ACT in freefall and the Maori Party imploding, the Nats are running out of allies, and Key's blunt refusal to work with Winston Peters may turn out to have a sad outcome for one person only, that being John Key himself.

The reason I say that is this; the New Zealand public didn't vote John Key in, they voted Helen Clark out. If Key believes otherwise then it is possible he has fallen victim to the cult of ego, which may be clouding his judgement. Now don't get me wrong, I wanted Helengrad gone as much as anyone, and John Key came across as a nice enough guy. But this supposedly conservative National administration supported the anti-smacking Bill and still does, hasn't given me back my Air Force, won't scrap the ETS, and now it tells me it's going to sell off my electricity supplier to the highest bidder – again. And apart from that, in the past two-and-a-bit years, this Government has done...um...well, nothing, really.

So why should I vote for it again? Truth is, I won't be. This coming election will be about one issue and one issue only, and that will be asset sales. It won't be about global warming, or who wins the rugby world cup, or whether or not Phil Goff dyes his hair. I don't want Rogernomics again at any price, and poorly-spun garbage about partial privatisation won't cut it for this writer. National isn't National anymore, it's morphed itself into ACT, and if I wanted ACT I'd vote for it.

So I am faced with a singular alternative, that being a Labour-led administration, and if a right-winger like me can openly countenance that as being the lesser of two evils, then John Key and the Nats are in serious trouble, because I most certainly won't be alone in my thinking. And if enough conservatives don't want asset sales, but they also don't want a Labour Government which is beholden to the Greens, they will most likely vote for Winston instead, which means that Key will have painted himself into a corner.

If Key is prepared to polarize himself into political oblivion that is one thing, but whether the rest of the National Party wishes to follow him is quite another. Paradoxically, time may prove that National's best hope of retaining power might involve dumping their most popular Leader and Prime Minister ever, and replacing him with someone more driven by political pragmatism than by failed ideology.

If I was a betting man, which I'm not, my pick would be that Key's gamble will fail, and there will be no fire sale of our assets this century.

Investigate, March 2011

Chapter Ten

Nanny State II

"Every time someone comes up with a new product or idea which might be fun, they're the ones jumping up and down shouting about why it mustn't be allowed. They pop out of the woodwork at the first sign of controversy, shamelessly promoted by a sensationalising and probably sycophantic media"

– Prosser, Investigate, September 2007

Enough, Already

There are some people, many of them in fact, who seem almost incapable of minding their own business. Being of a somewhat libertarian bent, this irks me. What motivates them, I wonder? Is it genetic? Are they emotionally stressed? Was something lacking during their childhood?

Certainly, such characters have always been with us; they are the Mother Hen types of old, now morphed into the social engineers of the present. These are the same people, with interests beyond their rightful concern, and opinions beyond the scope of their knowledge. From everyone's interfering aunty, through to a good few members of the present Government, with the media, the pressure groups, and the chattering masses in between, they are the people who steadfastly believe that they can run our lives and make our decisions for us, far better than we poor simpletons could manage the job ourselves.

Well, I'm tired of it. I've had enough of being busybodied. If I want to go for a drive without wearing my seatbelt, or take my old

10-speed for a run without wearing a cycle helmet, whose business is it but mine? I don't ride as much these days as once I did; countless kilometres I clocked in years gone by, to school and back, to work and back, at the weekends just for fun, on country roads and city streets, and never once wore a helmet. I fell off a couple of times, broke a finger, but never banged my head – and if I had, well, it's my head, you know? If I kill myself, or become horribly maimed, is that any concern of the People's Planet Party, or the United Parish of Pigsknuckle Arkansas (Manawatu Branch), or talkback caller, Mrs Outraged of Geraldine?

"But if you hurt yourself you'll be a drain on the nation's medical resources," is the shrill response. Yeah, well, I pay my taxes, and if I want to take my refund via the hospital system, isn't that my free choice in a democratic society? I mean the same connotation could be applied to anyone who eats too much red meat, or not enough red meat; or who drinks un-de-caffeinated coffee, or alcohol, or who doesn't drink enough red wine, or who doesn't go jogging, or indeed who does go jogging, by some estimations – strained knees, ligaments, and tendons, etc. And what if I'm independently wealthy, and have plenty of private medical insurance, would that get me out of paying a fine for not wearing a seatbelt? Or is the "cost of medical treatment" argument just an excuse for the anti-freedom brigade to poke their noses into my personal choices?

If I decide to smack my kids, then that is no concern of other people, particularly those who have never had kids. No, it really isn't. They need to get this idea through their heads, just like it isn't any of my business what they let their kids watch on TV, or what time they send them to bed. Likewise, if I want to fatten them up on tuck shop pies, that's also none of anyone else's business. I'll get fat myself if I want to as well, because my health is my concern, and not any other person's. Maybe I like fat. Maybe I don't care whether I can see my feet or not. Maybe I'll push-play for thirty minutes a day if I decide that's what I want to do, and not because some irritating TV ad tells me I must.

And if the kids want to play violent computer games, I'm not going to stop them. Instead, I'm going make sure they understand the difference between reality and fantasy, and that responsibility is mine, not that of some self-appointed guardian of the public good. The censor-everything mob used to complain about violence in cartoons as well, a generation ago; well, plenty of us grew up with the likes of Roadrunner and Yosemite Sam, with the dynamite and the falling anvils, and we didn't turn into homicidal maniacs.

Some of the busybodies want me to have fluoride in my water supply. Why? Apparently, because it's good for my teeth. Well even if you believe that, and I'm not sure I do, and you don't accept the medical evidence about the poisonous nature of fluoridated water, what on earth is the point in medicating people through their kitchen taps? To have any effect at all the water has to cover the entire surface of the teeth; so the 99.999 (and however many other nines there are) percent of the average household water usage which goes straight back down the drain, via the shower, the bath, the washing machine, the dishwasher, the kitchen sink, the garden hose and the toilet, won't do anything at all; and the minute amount which is actually drunk, without being swilled round the mouth, won't do very much either. If I do want to fluoridate my teeth I can go and buy fluoride toothpaste....but that's not good enough for the busybodies! I have to have my town supply fluoridated! OK, so I'm not on town supply, but you get my point.

I'm having folic acid put in my bread, with the same excuse used as justification. Well what if I don't want to eat folic acid? How do these people come to the conclusion that because they have an opinion on something, it thereby follows that they have a right to impose that opinion on others? This is a basic mentality thing, I'm sure of it. The busybody types are fixated on controlling the lives of other people because for some reason they are unhappy in their own tiny minds. I have a message for them; my life is none of your business!

I like to have a beer or two on a Friday night (tut tut). Sometimes on other nights of the week, too. Heavens above, how irresponsible of me. There should be some kind of mandatory reporting system in place. And you know what, I don't really care if the bloke standing next to me at the bar is having a cigarette. If it bothered me that much, I'd go and be somewhere else. But apparently I'm not allowed to make that choice; no, the busybodies have decreed that none shall light up a smoke in my local pub. Why? I'm damned sure most of them have never been in there.

And that'll be next; some Governmental control freak will want to restrain my imbibing, whether I'm driving or not; bars will be limited as to how much one person can be served in any given session, and the fun police will visit people in their homes to administer random sobriety tests.

I drive a four-wheel-drive. My God! What a selfish waste of the earth's resources! Why am I not riding a bicycle instead? And on top of that, I'm a deadly menace to other road users. Slaughtering them by the dozen, apparently. I should really be driving a Fiat Bambina, preferably one which runs on organic vegetable oil, doesn't go over thirty miles an hour, and has pedestrian-friendly papier-mâché bumpers. Naturally, the said papier-mâché should be made from recycled paper. Heaven forbid that we should ever make anything new.

The busybodies want to ban my truck from the city streets. Everything is like that with them; either ban it, or make it compulsory. This week, they're wanting me to compulsorily learn to speak Maori. Why? What for? So I can communicate with people in other Maori-speaking countries?

And as for what they want me to do for the climate….no, let's not go there. It's been done to death already, they just don't get it, and the error of their thinking will be all too evident, all too soon.. The point is that it's yet another example of busybodies deciding that I need their help in managing my affairs.

It is time we did something about the do-gooders and the social engineers and the control freaks in society. They're easy enough to spot, because every time someone comes up with a new product or idea which might be fun, they're the ones jumping up and down shouting about why it mustn't be allowed. They pop out of the woodwork at the first sign of controversy, shamelessly promoted by a sensationalising and probably sycophantic media.

There's probably some psychological test we can administer to identify these people at a young age, and nip their behaviour in the bud. In fact, we should make the test compulsory. They'd like that. And we should create a lobby group, aimed at de-lobbying the lobbyists. In fact, I propose a website, where busybodies can be identified and decried, a bit like a cyberspace version of the stocks. We can throw virtual tomatoes at them, or better still, virtual beer cans, because after all, our website will be a public place, and they don't like us drinking there.

There would need to be carrot as well as stick, of course, because what we really want to do is cure these poor unfortunates of their interfering ways; so they could have their Nosey Parker rating reduced, every time they DON'T call for number plates on bicycles, or seatbelts for dogs, or pictures of diseased organs on cigarette packets, or muzzles for Chihuahuas or microchips for cats.

Someone else will have to set the website up, because I am but a simple winemaker, and don't know how to do clever stuff like that; but I have sowed the seed of the idea, and together, dear readers, we can make it a reality. Take this message out to the blogosphere, get it on the talkback stations, write letters to editors. A new movement is set to sweep New Zealand. We will Ban the Busybodies, we will Clear Away the Control Freaks, we will reclaim the freedom to live our lives without the interference of ignorant and meddlesome buttinskis.

Make this your rallying call, all you freedom-loving folk who are capable of operating a motor car and a cellphone at the same time, who can choose what colour to paint your houses without help from a council palette, and who have ever spun your tyres in the gravel without signalling the end of civilisation.

We need to take back our society, people. The busybodies have had their day. They are not well; and this writer has had enough of them.

Investigate, September 2007

One More For The Road

I bought a radar detector a couple of months ago. It's the first one I've ever owned. It cost me 400 notes on TradeMe, but it paid for itself inside the first week.

I make no apology for finally deciding to utilise tax-minimisation technology such as my shiny new Whistler® XTR-690 SE. In fact I think it makes me a safer driver, in that I can now drive with both eyes on the road all the time again, instead of having to keep one of them on the speedo, like I have had to do ever since the Police Force became a branch of the Inland Revenue Department.

It's not even as if I drive particularly fast these days. Once upon a time, when I was a testosterone-fuelled young sales rep, I went everywhere at more than 140k. Nowadays, I prefer to pootle along steadily at a more sedate 120 km/h. I'm older, greyer, more at one with the world, and I have less to prove to anyone.

My motivation for purchasing the aforementioned device was the receipt of one too many speeding tickets. I have had six in my driving lifetime; the latest –and last – was, for this writer, the Bridge Too Far.

I have spent a not inconsiderable part of the 27 years since I first got my licence, behind the wheel. As a truck driver, travelling salesman, tourist, and just for fun, I guesstimate I've clocked up around two-and-a half million kilometres, in New Zealand, the UK, and Europe.

In my opinion – about which there is nothing humble – speed and safety are the product of so many, and such varied factors, that simple arbitrary limits are utterly pointless. There are, whether the wowsers believe it or not, parts of this country where one can happily cruise at 180 km/h and faster, without endangering anyone.

Likewise, there are plenty of city streets where 50 km/h is the legal limit, but where, at times, driving at anything over 30 could be rightly classed as homicidal madness.

When it's dark, or raining, or the road is made of gravel, or you're passing a primary school, or a combination of all of the above, of course you shouldn't drive with your foot to the boards.

That much is such a no-brainer that it shouldn't even need a law.

Equally, when it's fine and calm and there is visibility for miles, and the tarmac is dry and so is the driver, then there is no evil inherent in exceeding 100 km/h, and I for one feel no obligation to pay a fine for the privilege of doing so. Silly laws need to be ignored, as do the control freaks and the hystericals who promote them – or, at least, avoided by the judicious use of the appropriate, and thankfully still legal, modern technologies. The Anglo-Saxon in me feels no compunction to obey the law of the land simply because it's there. There has to be good reason for the law to exist first.

Authority is required to justify itself, in my book. Generally, it attempts to do this by identifying a problem, prescribing a remedy for the problem, and enforcing that remedy by imposing various punishments upon those who do not voluntarily adhere to it.

This would be fine were it not for two considerations, these being (1) that deterrence based on punishments dished out to other people doesn't often work, and (2) Government, given the option, usually manages to miss the target completely, by addressing a quite different reality from that which is actually causing the problem.

Speed is an acknowledged causative factor in something like 30% of vehicle accidents. Government responds to this situation by dictating speed limits for motor vehicles for various open and urban roads, and imposing fines upon those drivers who exceed them, generally in such places where the aforementioned drivers are easier to catch.

But speed in itself is never the sole cause of any accident.

It could be said that speed which is excessive for the conditions would fit that description, and if they were serious about reducing the road toll, it is this which the Powers That Be would be addressing. Pardon my cynicism, but perhaps it just isn't as profitable to patrol known accident black spots with marked Police cars, than it is to hide a camera van in the shadow of a motorway overbridge, or an unmarked car in the one dip on a long straight country road. Police cars out patrolling with the red-and-blue flashing lights on, when it's foggy or raining or there's sunstrike, might save a few lives as well. Cameras on poles, hidden in the trees, probably won't. Y'know?

Alcohol is another serious issue when it comes to road safety, and as I write, Government is considering, amongst other things, lowering the legal blood alcohol limit for drivers, from 80mg per 100ml, to 50mg. Nice sentiment. Alcohol causes or greatly contributes to about another 30% of road traffic accidents, and I believe that the

Government genuinely wants to overcome this real and completely avoidable insanity.

But reducing the legal limit from 80mg to 50mg will not achieve this, because it is not the drivers in the 50mg – 80mg range who are causing the problem. Global statistics show that on average, alcohol-affected drivers involved in death and injury accidents return a Blood Alcohol Concentration (BAC) of 160mg, or twice our current legal limit.

One paper from the Journal of Epidemiology, recording actual hospitalisation data from a New Zealand study[2] shows that some two-thirds of impaired drivers returned BACs which were 150mg/100ml or above.

Of the other third, BACs were evenly split between drivers whose BAC was between the proposed new lower limit of 50mg/100ml and 150mg/100ml, and those whose BAC was between 3mg/100ml (almost nothing) and 50mg/100ml.

From this it would seem that if two thirds of the drivers who cause crashes after drinking are already at twice the limit, and the rest pose an equal risk whether they are virtually sober or not, to lower the limit from the present 80mg/100ml to the proposed 50mg/100ml is unlikely to achieve anything at all in terms of lowering the alcohol-attributable road toll, but is very likely to criminalise drivers who are not presently contributing to it.

The world renowned and benchmark-setting Grand Rapids Study on alcohol and driving[3] suggests that in lowering the limit from 100mg/100ml to 80mg/100ml, as we have already done, and as most jurisdictions in North America are either doing or contemplating, we have already taken what is probably the most effective step we can, in terms of disallowing drivers from reaching what appears to be the significant first level of impairment.

Indeed drivers with a BAC of 20mg/100ml (the Swedish limit) would appear to have a lower accident rate than those with a zero concentration, and the increase in risk for levels between 20mg/100ml and 80mg/100ml appears to be negligible. Curiously enough, even in Sweden, the most commonly recorded BAC for drivers involved in alcohol-related accidents is, you guessed it, 160mg.

---

2 http://journals.lww.com/epidem/Abstract/2004/05000/The_Contribution_of_Alcohol_to_Serious_Car_Crash.15.aspx
3 http://www.hsrc.unc.edu/safety_info/alcohol/blood_alcohol_concentration.cfm

Further examination of data from around the world appears to suggest that other factors, and more importantly combinations of them, such as youth, speed, the presence of passengers, other types of intoxication, and weather and road conditions, are far more significant in causing crashes than the differences between simple BAC levels of between 50mg/100ml and 80mg/100ml. As far as enforcement of some of these other factors is concerned, I can report that of the five of my seven step-children who have reached driving age, all have at one time or another been let off with warnings from the Police for breaching age-related driving curfews and passenger restrictions. Perhaps we don't take these things seriously enough as a nation – or at least, the Police and the Courts don't take them seriously enough. Indeed the latest two editions of the North Canterbury News report, respectively, a 37-year-old driver avoiding a jail sentence after being breathalysed at more than four times the legal limit, despite having three previous convictions, and a 19-year-old, finally disqualified after a crash, who had clocked up no fewer than nineteen warnings from Police, for driving unaccompanied on a learner's licence.

Perhaps, as a methodology for reducing alcohol-related motor vehicle accidents and associated deaths and injuries, greater emphasis on the vigorous and visible enforcement of existing regulations, including more road patrols, more checkpoints, random stopping, and booze buses, may be far more effective than the arbitrary lowering of the legal limit, which is unlikely to do very much other than to unfairly target drivers who are not currently responsible for causing the problem.

The same could almost certainly be applied, in conjunction with a return to the discretion of our wise, sensible, and sorely-missed senior Constables of yore, to speed limits.

But even with alcohol and speed removed from the equation, some 40% of motor vehicle accidents require an explanation; and I would suggest that the most likely answer is that, as a nation, New Zealanders are just simply not very good drivers. Given that we have the second highest rate of motor vehicle ownership in the world, this is inexcusable. We are rude, aggressive, poorly schooled on the road rules, discourteous, and technically incompetent behind the wheel. Government's suggested answer is to raise the driving age. Yes, that'll work, won't it; defer the problem for a couple of years, from 15 to 17.

This change is being promoted by people who, like me, learned to drive at fifteen. It has not occurred to them that today's learner drivers will, like us, be no more mature or sensible in two year's time, than they are now. What was different then, was that cars were slower and less accessible. The teenager of 25 years ago couldn't just go out and buy a turbocharged Jap import rocketship for five hundred bucks. If you got to borrow the car at all, it was Mum's Hillman Avenger, which was flat out at 90k, and on top of that, it was worth seven grand, so you'd better look after it, or else.

Why do we not, as a nation, teach kids to drive, and drive properly, in schools? Is this genuinely valuable life skill not more important than some of the worthless PC rubbish which we waste curriculum time on filling their heads with today? Or limit the CC rating and horsepower of the cars they're allowed to drive, by themselves, just like we used to with learner motorbike licences?

Sometimes I despair of our Governments and their ill-advised, headline-driven, knee-jerk approach to policy making. It'd be enough to drive a less responsible man than myself to drink.

Investigate, November 2009

Chapter Eleven

Economic Policy

"Water is a necessity of life and a basic human right, not some discretionary product to be usurped for profit by the grubby little Shylocks of the self-styled "New Right", or any of the other worthless parasites who prey on decent society"

– Prosser, Investigate, April 2010

Depression? Yeah, right

One of the saddest events it is possible to witness, I believe, is the spectacle of a world talking itself into recession. I mean Humanity does some stupid things, it goes without saying; we invent remedies for ailments which don't exist, we run from shadows, we create false Gods to account for entirely natural processes which we term disasters and blame on ourselves (Global Warming, anyone?), we kill one another in the name of various religions, and we fill our bodies with poisonous rubbish and then wonder why we get sick. All of these things are silly and none of them are constructive, and all of them are completely avoidable with the application of a little common sense.

But of all the pointless and unnecessary sufferings we inflict upon ourselves, the self-fulfilling prophecy of the economic recession is probably the most ridiculous. We're having one now, apparently. The Prime Minister says so. The Reserve Bank says so. Other countries say so. And it's on the TV news every night, so it MUST be true. I know I'm a cynic, but I just plain don't believe them. It's a bad one this time, we are told; the worst since the 1920s. In fact we're probably as near to doomed as a civilization can get, without being, you know, actually doomed. And we had plenty of warning, too – the doomsayers were telling us we were going to be doomed for months before the doom started to set in. Yep, those doom forecasts were spot on – looking out my office window, I can see it's dooming outside even as I sit and type. In fact the forecasts were probably the single biggest driving force in creating this 'recession' in the first place. The self-fulfilling nature of the recession prophecy is that when people are told that there is, or is going to be, a recession, they stop spending…and it is a lack of spending, of course, which causes a recession.

I mean think about it. Some things in life are always constant or increasing. Populations are one of them. This big ol' world is just full of people, and it keeps on getting fuller and fullerer all the time. And people eat, and the other end of the digestive cycle happens too, and every day more people are born, and plenty of them are buried, and in between they go to school and drive to work and get married and start businesses and use things up and wear things out, and they make new things and repair stuff and carry out a million and one other activities….and if all these things keep happening because everyone needs for them to happen, then how on earth can we have a recession?

This time of course we are told that it's the fault of the Credit Crunch. Of course. The Credit Crunch is the latest Boogie Monster [what, you mean Michael Jackson is back? Or did you mean 'Bogey'? – Ed.] which the Doomsayers have dragged out of the closet to frighten people with. Ooh, watch out, the big scary Credit Crunch is going to come and eat you in the night. Be afraid. Be very afraid. You won't be able to borrow any money, and then your life will turn to fertilizer, and you'll die, and be unhappy, and other bad things.

So what is a credit crunch? Well, it's when there's a shortage of credit, of course. You know, there isn't so much credit to go round. Why? Well,….um….I guess because it's just one of these natural cycles. Credit must fall from the sky, I suppose, a bit like rain; so obviously, when it's dooming outside, the credit dries up. Makes perfect sense, when you think about it. Hmm.

So why would there be a shortage of credit? What is credit anyway?

Well, it's money borrowed from a Bank or other lending institution, to all intents and purposes. And why would Banks be short of credit to lend out? Well, because they themselves are finding it hard to borrow in order to fund their lending, we are told. So... why would that be? Because people aren't putting their money into Banks anymore? Really? What else are they doing with it then, I wonder? I don't know which is more ludicrous about the reasoning given for the Big Bad Credit Crunch; that anyone in the media or the establishment expected people to believe it, or that so many of them apparently do. Ah, but they're putting it into other things, the Crunchers will argue, like gold, and, um, well, like gold.

OK, I'll bite; say you decide to put your money into gold rather than in the Bank. How do you do that? Well, just like purchasing anything else, you buy some gold off someone and give them money for it...which they then promptly put straight in the Bank. Or are we supposed to think they stuff it under the mattress instead? Easy enough to do with a wad of cash, but a bit more tricky with an electronic bank transfer, I would posit. In fact if anybody can give me a plausible explanation of how anyone transferring their holdings from one investment to another, somehow results in there being an overall reduction in the amount of money held in Bank accounts, I'd love to hear it. And if there there's no less money in the Banking system, the Banks would find it difficult to fund their lending...why, precisely?

It's all rubbish, of course, as the cynics and manipulators of the financial establishment who profit from it understand very well. Fortunately for them, Joe Public mostly doesn't, and they are ably abetted by various cloth-eared academics and other ignorant but egotistical and self-important financial commentators, who mistakenly believe themselves to be informed as to the realities of world economics and money.

The media, bottom-feeders that they are, revel in this sort of garbage. In fact it has become their stock in trade, the sober and objective reporting of facts having long since been discarded in favour of sensationalism, propaganda, and other commercially and politically-driven mischief making.

Banks can only make a profit by lending money, which makes the idea that credit will somehow remain difficult to obtain, completely absurd. So why did it happen in the first place? Simply because a few US Banks got greedy, in this writer's estimation; it is perhaps risky to lend more against an asset than the asset is worth, but foolish in the extreme to lend more than a borrower is capable of repaying. Thus when the value of assets is over-inflated by speculation, which is also driven by greed, and the ability of borrowers to repay loans is dependent on incomes which are in turn backed by over-valued assets, the whole process becomes somewhat tenuous. Like a house of cards, when one bit starts to wobble, the whole thing falls over, requiring it to be shored up by that lender of last resort, the good old Government, by guaranteeing all the aforementioned Bank deposits. We are further invited to believe (and appear to have accepted said invitation) that the Government actually has tens or hundreds of billions of dollars sitting in a piggy bank somewhere, with which to provide for this guarantee, which begs the question, why haven't they dipped into it before now, to clear the hospital waiting lists and lower the teacher-pupil ratio and bring back the Air Force?

The truth is that they don't, of course; the guarantee is backed by nothing other than people's belief that the Government could bail out the Banks if it had to, which because people believe it could, it won't ever have to, because they will continue to have faith in the Banks, because the government is guaranteeing them. See how it works? This is just as well for You The Taxpayer, because imagine if the Government had to pass the hat round to collect money from ordinary citizens before it could pay out on losses from failed Banks? The Deposit Guarantee Scheme is yet another self-fulfilling creation of belief being transformed into economic reality. Once upon a time (not so long ago in fact) money issued by Governments was backed by actual gold which sat in a vault somewhere. People like gold, because it's heavy and yellow and everyone has always accepted that it has value, hence it has always had value (that's that belief-becoming-reality thing again. Gold's just a metal. It's quite a good electrical conductor, and colloids of it in the blood apparently help with arthritis, and having traces of it in the ground helps to grow good apricots, but it doesn't actually have any use or value beyond that, at least not in any real sense. I mean you can't eat the stuff, now can you?) Since the ending of the gold standard, either in 1933 if you want to blame Roosevelt, or 1975 if you want to blame Nixon, the fiat currencies which Governments issue are backed instead by nothing more than people's faith in the strength and stability of that Government, and of the economy of the nation it represents, which is the only reason that a cheque from the US Government is more likely to be accepted anywhere than one from Zimbabwe.

The upshot of the Credit Crunch and its ensuing recession with accompanying mortgagee sales, is that lending institutions the world over, backed by Governments the world over, are now gaining – by default, mostly – a bigger share in the equity of the assets which were originally used as collateral for the loans they advanced, which may well be reason enough for this latest 'crisis' having been manufactured to begin with. Translated, this means the Banks now own more of the world's property, and that You the Taxpayer, along with having your possessions fleeced from under you, are paying them for the privilege of taking it away. Clever, eh.

Personally, I think the whole idea of recessions is silly and unnecessary, and we should simply refuse to go along with it. They talked us into having a property market slump – not a very big one, admittedly, and it appears to be going away again as I write, because no-one really wanted it; they talked us into believing that oil was running out by speculating the price up to $140 a barrel...now that the speculators have lost their shirts, haha, and oil is back down under forty bucks, there appears to be plenty of the black stuff again, ditto the supposed World Protein Shortage.

Let's just not play their silly game, get on with life, go back to spending, and refuse to let them turn a recession into a depression through weasel words and panic mongering. And maybe while we're at it, we could suggest to certain elements of the media that they lay off the fantasy stuff, and get proper haircuts and real jobs.

Investigate, April 2009

Riding the Wave

The 2025 Taskforce on Closing the Gap, and catching up economically with Australia, released its first report before Christmas. Being somewhat preoccupied with a new baby meant that I hadn't read it until last week, and other than third-hand accounts from the media and various other commentators, had very little idea of what was actually in it. Now that I have, I'm not sure whether to laugh, cry, check the date to make sure it isn't April 1st, or simply shake my head and wonder. In essence, the Taskforce's report says little other than "Well, Rogernomics didn't work last time, and in fact it near terminally stuffed the country – let's try it again!"

Seriously. The best brains the Government could recruit, supposedly, have come up with a list of initial recommendations which they apparently genuinely believe will bring this country closer to income parity with our trans-Tasman neighbours. They include lowering taxes for the rich, slashing health spending, cutting welfare, abolishing the Super Fund, privatizing everything which hasn't been already – including local Government assets; charging everyone for water (also privatised), stinging road users even harder for the privilege of driving on the Queen's Highway, corporatising education, getting rid of the last remnants of worker's rights, and giving away our mineral resources to foreign owned mining companies. No, really. That's what the report says. And that's just for starters – it goes on to emphasize the absolute necessity for more time, more studies, more recommendations, more reports, and presumably more fees for the Taskforce's appointees, before any further progress can be made.

Nowhere does the Taskforce offer anything practical. Nowhere does it even suggest, let alone state, that it has examined the better-performing economies around the world and attempted to discover the secrets of their success. Nowhere does it give any indication that it has the first clue about how wealth is actually created.

Now I can't say I'm any great fan of unions, especially when, as they have done in the past, they step outside their brief, and start meddling in politics and other things which don't concern them, like Springbok tours and the enviro-fascist movement. But the average working New Zealander certainly needs some protection against the more rapacious and unprincipled of employers, especially those whose philosophy is and has been represented by some of the Taskforce's own members. And I have long been an advocate of turning welfare back into a safety net, instead of the increasingly feathered multi-generational hammock which it has become in recent years.

But privatization doesn't work, as we have already long since learned in the most painful of ways, and it cannot possibly work, as anyone who isn't a complete moron can easily understand. This is really, really simple. If you own a freehold business or asset, paid for by and inherited from generations of taxpayers past, and you sell that asset to a private buyer from whom you will then lease or buy back its services, and the private buyer intends to profit from this exercise, then the only way in which the private buyer can make a profit is by buying the business for less than it is worth, or selling the services for more than they should cost, or both. Either way, the previous owner, that's you the taxpayer, can only lose out. Anyone who claims otherwise is either thick or a liar, and since the esteemed members of the Taskforce, on the basis of their records, are almost certainly not the former, it could very well be argued that they may instead be the latter.

As for turning water into a chargeable, tradeable commodity, I have to say the idea turns my stomach. There are some limits. Water is a necessity of life and a basic human right, not some discretionary product to be usurped for profit by the grubby little Shylocks of the self-styled "New Right", or any of the other worthless parasites who prey on decent society. These people are not Right-Wingers, whatever they may claim; they're soulless thieves, bereft of decency, morals, or a work ethic, globalists and internationalists by nature, and an internationalist by any other name is still a communist.

Before I digress too far, I should say that I fully support lowering taxes as well, but before a person or a company can pay tax at all they have to actually earn money or make a profit, and focusing on methods of cutting Government spending, and reducing the sovereignty of the Nation State, has nothing to do with encouraging businesses in New Zealand to do better. The Taskforce seems to be suffering from some form of cognitive disconnect with regards to these two issues. Maybe it's because almost none of them have ever had a real job.

Back in the bad old days of Rogernomics, the fools who were running the asylum made bad policy out of poor choices based on incorrect and incomplete information. Then, they presumed that New Zealand could be transformed into the "Switzerland of the South Pacific" by becoming a tax haven, concentrating on banking, currency trading, company registrations, and other non-industries which didn't involve anyone doing any actual work, and we were all going to sit back and do nothing and become very rich. Then, they simply did not understand, and would not be told, that the financial sector was only a very small part of the Swiss economy, which was and is underpinned by real industry – engineering, steel, pharmaceuticals, industrial chemicals and the like.

Today, the Taskforce – the heirs of the Rogernomics doctrine, it would seem, and in at least one case a surviving member of it – presume that Australia's success rests solely on her mining sector, and that we can become likewise rich by digging up our National Parks and giving our minerals to the lowest bidder in return for a peppercorn Royalty. They just don't get it that Australia has real industry as well, manufacturing and processing, with real factories which employ ordinary people, making goods out of raw materials, adding value and passing some of that value on to their workers in the form of higher wages, which the workers then spend into the economy, to everyone's benefit. Australia manufactures motor vehicles, ships, locomotives, plastics, textiles, rubber goods, glassware, industrial machinery, automotive and aerospace products, mining equipment, furnishings and electrical cables; the list goes on, but you get my point.

Personally I'm all in favour of unlocking our mineral riches, as I have said before; but it has to be the New Zealand nation and New Zealand companies and workers who profit from it, not foreign multinationals. Obviously not everyone can go and work in the coal mines of the West Coast, but people do have to get out of bed in the morning and do something productive.

The essential bottom line here is that if South Auckland is to be weaned off the dole, then there have to be real jobs for them to go to instead, and not everyone can be a graphic designer or an IT consultant. If we cannot compete with the Asian economies in terms of producing bulk goods with cheap labour, then we shouldn't try – but that doesn't mean we can't still have manufacturing. New Zealand needs to concentrate on doing things which the Asians can't do, making quality which they can't produce, filling the high end of the market with the luxury goods and premium brands which the discerning buyer in the niche market simply doesn't want to buy from China.

Wealthy car buyers in Japan and America do not seek out marques such as Volvo or Mercedes because they're an economical option, because they're not. They seek them out because they have a reputation for quality and prestige. Engineers in Europe and the United States do not specify roller bearings from Sweden because they're cheap, because they're not cheap. Rather, they specify them because they're known to be of superb quality. Wine connoisseurs in Britain and New England don't buy New Zealand Pinot Noir because it comes in a three-litre cardboard box for $9.95, because it doesn't. Instead, they happily pay $US100 a bottle for it because it is known to be the best Burgundy-style red in the world. So must it be for the rest of New Zealand's production, and thereby for the rest of our economy.

If we can't make footwear or clothing as cheaply as the Fijians or the Vietnamese, then we shouldn't make cheap footwear or clothing; but that doesn't mean that we can't establish a reputation for making the world's finest outdoor and work wear, designer fashions, and specialist safety clothing. If we can't mass-produce low quality pocket calculators and transistor radios in competition with the sweatshops of India or China, then that is not the market for us; but there is no reason why New Zealand cannot make a deliberate effort to become the source nation of choice for the very best of electronic products, audio and military equipment, laboratory instruments and medical technology. Fisher and Paykel, having established a market and a reputation in the US on the back of being perceived as a quality whiteware brand from New Zealand, may yet find that moving their manufacturing base to the third world has been a very silly mistake indeed, regardless of what the moneylenders and the beancounters have to say on the matter.

The inventor and manufacturer of the Martin Jetpack, unable to secure venture capital in New Zealand, is leaving Christchurch for an unspecified foreign destination, even as the Government wrings its hands in despair at not being able to find the way forward for our economy. He is the latest in a long line of New Zealand innovators who have been driven from our shores by the inability of anyone in Government to see the wood for the trees where economic growth and direction is concerned.

All we need is a little Governmental foresight, a progressive tax regime, and a modicum of seed capital; perhaps a Government-backed venture finance Bank, and an understanding and desire to follow the likes of Singapore, Israel, Sweden and Switzerland. Now here's an idea; instead of scrapping the Kiwisaver scheme and using the proceeds to pay off debt, as the Taskforce suggests (how *do* they propose we should fund retirement and pensions, or don't they?) maybe we should just scrap the Taskforce, and use that money to fund some value-adding industries instead? If these idiots get their way, the only gap we will close will be the one between New Zealand and Somalia.

Investigate, April 2010

What Lies Beneath

Glass Earth, a Canadian joint-venture mining and exploration company, has spent the past couple of years using some of the latest and most cunning of technologies to "see" into the earth's crust, a hundred meters and more, in a survey covering several large areas of New Zealand. Their search is primarily for gold, but the sensors used in their geophysical survey – magnetic, electromagnetic, gravitational anomaly, and ground resistance – allow them to detect and identify many more minerals than the yellow metal alone.

Otago, the Central Volcanic Plateau, and bits of the Coromandel and Hauraki regions have been amongst the company's areas of interest. They flew over my house a while back, in a helicopter dangling a probe which looked a lot like a cruise missile; housed within were the aforementioned cunning gizmos, which could see clear through the *Chez Moi,* and into the alluvial gold deposits below (we know that they're there, because some of it came up with the silt when we had the bore blown out, when replacing the pump a couple of years back). Presumably their gravitational sensors also picked up the localised anomaly directly beneath my bathroom scales, the one which makes everything heavier. Expensive gizmos, too; they dropped one not long afterwards, which was apparently a more-than-a-million-dollar oops.

But I digress. This column isn't meant to be a plug for a mining company (though that's not to say that unsolicited donations wouldn't be happily received).

What's important is that someone is doing this sort of research, and that what it's telling us, is that there are plenty of riches beneath the surface of these fair isles.

Glass Earth was first proposed to the CSIRO in Australia, with the intention of mapping the entire kilometre-deep top layer of the Australian continent, to identify the location and quality of all existing and future ore deposits. I presume New Zealand has been chosen as the guinea pig for testing the new technology, and this writer, for one, is glad about that.

There is wealth down there; oodles of it, and it's ours for the taking. Gold, silver, copper, iron, lead, and zinc; as well as tin, bauxite, titanium, and a host of others, including precious stones and rare earth elements; plus lithium, gallium, beryllium, molybdenum, zirconium, tungsten, magnesium, manganese, mercury, nickel, antimony, and chromium. The menu of New Zealand's economically extractable minerals reads like a veritable periodic table.

And there is uranium. Not much, but it's there; or apparently quite a bit, depending on who you ask. Either way, we are unlikely to know in the near future. Prospecting for uranium is now banned, under the regulation of the 1996 Minerals Programme for Minerals Other Than Petroleum and Coal. The reason given in the legislation, for this bizarre policy of self-denial, is that:

2.13 The policy of not allowing prospecting, exploration or mining of the primary uranium and thorium minerals is in accordance with the Government's environmental policy of New Zealand being a Nuclear Free Zone and the New Zealand Nuclear Free Zone, Disarmament and Arms Control Act 1987. Foreclosing the opportunity for permits to be obtained to prospect, explore or mine for the primary uranium and thorium minerals will prevent the Crown from obtaining a financial return from these minerals. The principle of New Zealand being a Nuclear Free Zone and the position the Government has taken to promote international nuclear weapons disarmament are considered to outweigh this factor.

(http://www.crownminerals.govt.nz/cms/pdf-library/minerals/min-prog-for-min.pdf)

All of which strikes me as being a little odd, given that the nuclear free legislation only bans weapons, ships, and the dumping of radioactive waste, and has nothing at all to say about nuclear power or uranium mining. What is the real reason, I wonder, which lies beneath this ban, made all the more strange because it was enacted under a National Government, rather than a Labour one?

And then there's coal. Masses of it. About thirteen billion tonnes, by present estimates, and that doesn't include anything that the coming transparency of the Glass Earth may yet reveal, which we don't already know about.

New Zealand's coal reserve would last us around 2,000 years at present rates of consumption, were we to utilise it as our primary energy source; but we're not allowed to do that either, thanks to the present Government and its ban on the building of any new thermal power stations for the next ten years. Will National overturn this ban, I wonder; or do they share Labour's sub-surface agenda?

Failing that, we could turn it into synthetic petrol and diesel; Southland's lignite alone, converted via the good old Fischer-Tropsch recipe, could provide for New Zealand's motor fuel needs for better than four hundred years, by which time, I have every faith, our descendents should have the hydrogen answer well and truly sorted.

Australia, as we know, has no similar qualms about exploiting her vast mineral resources. While we in New Zealand wail, and wring our hands, and espouse the virtues of windfarms, and relocate precious snails (so we can dig up our valuable coal, and sell it to India, where they're allowed to burn it to make electricity, but we're not…??), and fret about falling lake levels, the Aussies just get on with digging theirs up, and feeding it into the fuel hopper. No power crisis over there this winter, eh.

We worry, of course – or at least the Government, the Greenies, and the other mentally challenged sectors of society, worry – that the burning of coal will somehow magically and tragically affect the climate, and so we must avoid it at all costs.

That every argument and "scientific" theory in support of the Anthropogenic Carbon-Dioxide Global Warming fallacy, has long since been completely disproven and overturned, is now without doubt; what, I wonder, lies beneath the continued adherence to this doomed cult, by its most committed acolytes and their media sycophants? Are they trying desperately to save face, in the face of a deception which is now desperately unable to be saved?

Your favourite commentator is a somewhat cynical cove by nature, and suspects that Government policy with regard to fossil fuels may be driven by a possible desire on the part of the incumbent Prime Minister, to snare herself a Big Important Job with the UN at the imminent end of her tenure; and that to that end, this country must be seen as being supporting of the unjustifiable claims and demonstrably incorrect theories of Kyoto and the IPCC.

Fair enough; Helen Clark, I will admit, is bright enough to realise truth over fantasy when faced with the reality of actual experience over the theory of University idealism; but she's a politician, and we don't expect them to admit that truth, where the future of their careers may be compromised. Certainly we should expect that; but we don't, which is as much a reflection on us as it is on them. This writer recalls being informed of HC's response, when questioned, by a former member of 14 Sqn on an RNZAF Boeing flight, about the wisdom, in hindsight, of disbanding the ACF; the reply, shall we say, would not be out of keeping with the above.

So that explains the Prime Minister's position; but it doesn't excuse the hilarious spectacle of overpaid auto-cue readers, masquerading as journalists on the nightly news, earnestly parroting about greenhouse emissions and carbon footprints, as if the fantastic theory in question were not only true, but that they themselves had the earthliest idea of the reality or science behind it. I have hint for you guys and girls; this stuff is like WWF Wrestling. People talk about it like it was real – but y'know, it's all made up. You did know that, didn't you?

The Aussies don't mind digging up other things either, and as a result their economy is booming. They load iron ore for China as fast as the ships can be turned around, and build railways, and new towns, and pay dump truck drivers $100,000 a year. We, on the other hand, fixate about obscure ferns, and miniscule beetles, and how to make cows give milk without making poo, and wonder why thousands of our finest flee these shores in search of something better than the prospect of $12 an hour flipping burgers for Korean tourists.

There's a connection here, people, I promise you there is. Could it be that there's money to be made from mining and (gasp) industry? I mean real, manufacturing industry? Blasphemy to the Greenies, I know, but we're none of us going to get rich by turning the entire country into a National Park.

What lies beneath our deep green oceans? I'm not referring to submarines, we've talked about that; no, this time I mean oil. Black Gold. The Great South Basin, in particular, though there are others, off Canterbury, Taranaki, the West Coast, and Otago. But the GSB is the El Dorado; maybe twenty billion recoverable barrels of light sweet crude, the finest and most expensive dinosaur juice ever fermented. What is really, I wonder, beneath the lies about why the Government has slashed the Royalty – our Royalty – payable on our oil, to 1%, when the Saudis are charging 50% and the Norwegians 76%?

We could run forever on our undersea oil, and make an everlasting fortune along the way, if only we had the gumption to create a State-owned Petroleum Corporation to dig the stuff up and sell it, like three-quarters of the world's oil producing nations do. Oh well.

Instead we appear lost in a hopeless infatuation with biofuels; what deep dark motivation, I find myself pondering, lurks below the dark deep Greens, and their continued pursuit of this unworkable folly? Turning food into fuel, and driving millions of people into starvation in the process, hardly strikes me as being the most constructive way of proving yourself wrong about climate theory.

And yet there is hope. John Key has at least expressed enthusiasm about the lignite-to-fuel idea; which is almost certainly the best way of using the resource, since liquid fuels burn more efficiently than solid, and there isn't the same resulting slag to deal with. Perhaps, and here's a wild idea, we could bring ourselves to run a few power stations on that same synthetic diesel.

Enough untruths have been perpetuated concerning the hoarded wealth upon which we dwell. It's time to inter the falsehoods which have kept us poor, and dig up the buried treasure of these sceptred islands' store. The lies of the past cannot build our better future; the way ahead lies beneath us.

Investigate, August 2008

Good Bastards One and All

My great-grandfather was a Welsh coal miner. My grandfather followed him down the pit briefly, before thinking better of it and turning to drain laying instead. This was frowned upon in a way by his family and community at the time, because coal mining was, and to an extent continues as, a way of life in Wales, but at least laying drains still involved digging holes and getting dirty, so in the end it was decided that that was sort of alright.

Coal and mining are a way of life on the West Coast as well, and, as we have been so tragically reminded by the Pike River disaster, at times a way of death. The West Coast and New Zealand lost twenty-nine of our finest when the Pike River mine exploded, twenty-nine men taken too soon from twenty-nine families whose pain in some degree belongs to us all. Many of them were native-born West Coasters, some from other parts of New Zealand, some adopted into our nation from the far-flung reaches of the world; all, now, as they lie in the bosom of this fair land, they are all our sons, and they are sons of us all.

Everyone knows that mining can be a dangerous business, underground mining especially so. The risks presented by heavy machinery, explosives, and falling rock in open cast mines, are compounded by the threat of cave-ins, poisonous and explosive gases, fire, and flooding, when the search for minerals moves underground. We who are not involved in mining know these things, but we do not understand them in the same way as do those who live them on a daily basis. Cosseted in our towns and cities, our farms and our factories and our workshops and office blocks, we all rely on the products of the mining industries, but we do not risk life and limb in the pursuit of them. I have enormous respect for those who do.

On the Coast they know it all too well. If you live on the West Coast of the South Island and you're not a miner, then it's a safe bet that you're married to one, or you're a parent of one, or you went to school with one or more. And your business, or the business you work for, will be dependent, directly or indirectly, on the mines for all or part of its viability. Mining and the Coast are suffused with each other, intertwined, inseparable. Coasters dig and quarry the earth which provides the benefits of its riches to the rest of us; gold, silver, and copper for wealth and industry, coal for heat, electricity, and steel; limestone for cement and fertiliser; aggregates for road building and construction. And there are others – titanium, tin, and other minerals used in the production of paints, plastics, paper, textiles, rubber, and PVC. And there is the potential for more; uranium, rare earth elements, antimony, lead, iron, and even bauxite. Mining touches our daily lives because the things we use and depend on every day for our modern lifestyles are made from its products, and the people of the West Coast touch our daily lives because it is they who make that production possible. They delve into the earth to extract her bounty, they put themselves on the line, body and soul; they toil, they sweat, they bleed for us all; and sometimes, they die.

The danger is ever present. The reality of it hits home with tragedies like Pike River, the name of which will pass into infamy along with Strongman, Brunner, Kaitangata, Ralphs, Glen Afton, Denniston, and Dobson – a somber catalogue of New Zealand's too long a history of fatal mining accidents, and a sobering reminder that just as the earth can give up its riches, it can also take away that which is most precious of all.

But West Coasters are resilient people. In spite of the risks and in the face of adversity they remain united and staunch. They're hardy folk on the Coast; they work hard, play hard, drink hard, live hard, in an environment which is as harsh and unforgiving as it is beautiful and bountiful. And despite the ever-present possibility of death and disaster they stay cheerful and optimistic. I never met a Coaster I didn't like, and I have met more than a few. They will survive the agony of Pike River. The Coast will carry on and the mining will carry on, as it should and as it must.

There will be enquiries, as there also should. There will be a Royal Commission. Twenty-nine good men will not go to their graves without us finding out what happened and why, they will not die without lessons being learned so that others may work the mines in greater safety. There will be accusations and perhaps recriminations in the fullness of time, there will be suggestions that things could and perhaps should have been done differently, and that the approach to mining the Brunner coal seam may not have been the same had priorities been set in another manner. But here and now is not the time for that; now is the time for the nation to stand behind the Coast, to let them grieve, to help them recover and rebuild.

Coasters have a proud tradition of self-determination. The West Coast retains a great measure of the pioneering spirit which has all but faded from most of the rest of the country. The Coast was the cradle of the Union movement and the birthplace of the Labour Party, back in time in a more genuine age, when both those organizations were born of necessity amongst men who worked with their bodies to extract the resources needed by a young and hungry colony. It is a different place, honest and forthright, where the values and perceptions of the New Zealand of old have remained pure these past fifty years, while the rest of us have grown jaded and materialistic. It is a place where Rugby League has established itself as a creditable rival to Rugby Union, like almost nowhere else in the country. And when Dominion Breweries, the new Corporate owners of the time-honoured local brewery Monteith's, decided to shift their brewing operation to Auckland, the Coast responded by creating its own brand new, indigenous, and locally produced ale as a mark of defiance. In true West Coast fashion, they called the brew Good Bastards beer. Realising they were beaten, DB agreed to a compromise, and the Greymouth brewery remained open. I for one say good on the Coast. They are an example to us all.

And long may that example continue. We, the rest of New Zealand, owe an enormous and un-repayable debt to the West Coast. They are the Keepers of the Clear Vision, the people who remind us of who we are and what we were, and of how much of our past we have lost, squandered, or become ashamed of. The forestry, the Railways, the fishing boats, the farmland hacked and wrestled and won from the bush with blood and perspiration, with slashers and chainsaws and bulldozers, and of course the mines; this is a raw land where real people still do real work, and these are a gritty folk who embrace that role, and who risk their very lives so that we may all share in the prosperity they create. Once upon a time, all of New Zealand was as the West Coast is now. Today, we do not face death for them as they do for us, and that, I believe, is worthy of remembering and respecting.

Our way of life could not exist without the technologies we have created out of the treasures we extirpate from our planet. Twenty-nine Good Bastards lie under that mountain, and we dishonour them if we allow ourselves to forget that fact. Yes, maybe the mine could have been constructed differently, but it wasn't. They knew that and went in anyway. Yes, the money is good, but the hazards are real as well, and they knew that and still went in anyway. They did so for many reasons, not the least of them being that they possessed a courage which we do not, and that we must never forget. We do not dishonour these men if we continue to mine for coal. We dishonour them if we fail to learn from this tragedy; we dishonour them if we fail to do things differently and better next time, in whatever ways may prove to be necessary; we dishonour them if we give up and walk away.

There is talk of heroes in these early days when memories are most painful and emotions are still visceral. There are the leaders who planned in vain for a rescue, the rescuers who waited so eagerly for a chance to rush to their comrades' aid. All true enough, I would posit; but unsung as heroes are the men who had the guts and determination to walk into the pit every day; those who still do, and the twenty-nine who never came out again.

We will build monuments to these fallen, that much is certain, so that no-one will ever forget their sacrifice; but the greatest mark of respect we can show them is to carry on their good work and to allow West Coasters to continue with their way of life.

We will not give up and walk away, of course, and neither will the Coast. They will soldier on – and we, the rest of us, who have ridden their backs for so long and with so little acknowledgment, must now walk alongside them as they do.

I salute the miners of Pike River, those who perished and those who have lived to dig another day. I salute your grit, your passion, your determination, your bravery; your solidarity, your humour, your tenacity and your humanity. I am humbled by your example and pained by your loss. I say God Bless the wild West Coast. It is this country's last frontier and the final bastion of the real New Zealand, and I and all New Zealanders owe you a debt of honour.

And God Bless you wild West Coasters, good bastards one and all.

Investigate, January 2011

Chapter Twelve

Pinko's, Liberals & Lefties II

"A small and close-knit clique of narcissistic left-wing ideologues and egomaniacs...occupy the broadcast media and exercise a disproportionate degree of influence over it. They are aided and abetted by a similarly miniscule number of loud-mouthed control freaks sprinkled throughout the Parties of the political Left, the environmental movement, and the Trade Unions"

– Prosser, Investigate, March 2010

Quiet in the Cheap Seats

One of the best things about being a conservative, no-nonsense, right wing nationalist social and political commentator, is never having to say you're sorry. It doesn't matter if you upset anyone, because the only people who are likely to be offended by your unabashed dissertations of truth and common sense, are pinkos and liberals and other whingeing minorities whose opinions don't count anyway. And get offended they certainly do!

Veteran hate campaigner John Minto has been at it again these past few weeks. He gets around, does Johnny Boy; one week he's in Auckland hurling abuse at an Israeli tennis player, the next he's at Waihopai in Marlborough, protesting the fact that the Americans continue to cover New Zealand's posterior despite the abuse and disrespect we shower them with.

What motivates people like Minto, I wonder, and why does the media give them coverage in such a massively disproportionate measure relative to the support and sympathy which their opinions actually carry within the wider population?

I first saw John Minto during some protest or another in Auckland in the mid-eighties when I was about 18. He was hiding in a car being driven slowly up Queen St, expounding anti-rugby, anti-white South African, anti-New Zealand Government views, through a loudhailer mounted on the roof. Following him were several hundred scruffy, unwashed, long-haired retards from Rent-a-Mob, carrying what were, even back then, very professionally made and expensive looking signs, and wearing T-shirts with professionally printed slogans.

I was with a few mates from down home on the Hauraki Plains, and our section of the crowd included a number of Australian league supporters who were in town at the same time. Being country boys, charged with patriotic fervour (and the libations of the Queen City's hospitality) we felt it our duty to offer the protesters the benefit of our wisdom; I believe I advised Minto to go back to Moscow, whereupon a particularly ill-nourished, trench-coat wearing, Bohemian albino popped out from the mob, to inform me that John was "from Hastings, actually", as if I cared.

The point about this is that despite the nationwide TV coverage which the protest attracted, and the credence afforded it by the broadcast media, those few hundred ragged marchers were alone in their outrage about the South Africans, their rugby, and New Zealand's association with both. No-one in the crowd was cheering them. Most, had it not been for the not inconsiderable Police presence, would have been throwing bottles along with their derisory comments.

So why do we put up with them? Surely one of the fundamentals of democracy is that the will of the majority shall prevail – with regard to the rights of the minority – but this itself presupposes and demands that the minority must accept the will of the majority. The right to protest does not and cannot include the right to be given your own way, when your views do not represent the prevailing mood or feelings of most of the nation.

As things turned out, Minto and Co. did get their own way, apartheid crumbled – along with, predictably, the economic and social stability of the Republic, and the South Africa we have today is the result. Black South Africans no longer struggle under the yoke of the white oppressor; instead, they struggle under the yoke of a black oppressor, where tribalism and nepotism have replaced racism as the dominant force. Even Minto himself, I am told, now accepts that Joe Average Black Man in South Africa is worse off today than he was under the old regime. We, the majority of New Zealand, can only watch in despair as the South Africa which we knew fades inexorably into the twilight of civilisation. The best we can offer is a new home to her refugees, the people who were and are our familial and colonial kin, and our nearest relatives. South Africans and Rhodesians were always New Zealand's closest cousins, nearer to us in thinking even than our trans-Tasman neighbours; this is a truth which the silent mass of us have always known.

I say the anti-apartheid mob should stop speaking and go away quickly, because they've done enough damage already. No-one who was taken in by their lies twenty-five years ago, still believes them today.

That hasn't stopped Minto, however, from continuing to attempt to destroy other bastions of the light of Western Civilisation as they stand against the forces of Darkness, nor has it detracted from the passion with which the media ply the man with front-page slots and prime-time sound bites.

Minto and a motley collection of leftists and anti-Semites calling themselves "Global Peace and Justice" (why is it that Communists, bent on world domination and the oppression of freedom, always put 'peace' and 'justice' in their titles?) descended on the New Zealand Tennis Open in Auckland a couple of weeks back, having apparently decided that the way to solve the problems of the Middle East was to harangue a tennis player by megaphone. Yeah, that'll do it, won't it. They were protesting about Israel's continued, and in their view unreasonable, insistence on defending itself against terrorist attacks from the Palestinian territories. They'd quite like Israel to just shrivel up and die, and hand over the only productive bit of that entire wretched region, to people who would take no time at all to turn it back into a desert, like it was before the Yids made it bloom, with running water and agriculture and electricity and a phone system, and sealed roads and drains and sewerage and hospitals and a functioning democracy, like what the rest of the Arab Middle East doesn't have.

Why does this irritating little man keep making ridiculous protests like this, and why, I ask seriously, does the media keep feeding the troll?

Frankly I couldn't give a wet slap about the Palestinians, and neither can anybody else I've spoken to. If they could be bothered to get off their backsides and actually do something to help themselves, they might engender a little more respect from the likes of Yours Truly; but no, the Palestinian approach is to blame everyone else, deny responsibility, re-write history, whinge, sulk, and bite the hand that feeds them. (Boy, do we know about people like *that* in New Zealand.) So some of them live in refugee camps; yeah, well, for the record, that's their own fault. When Israel was created, its leaders offered every Arab living within the newly demarcated borders the chance of a new life as an Israeli citizen, with a clean slate and no strings attached. Some took the opportunity, but others didn't. They headed for Jordan, or Transjordan as it was called back then. The Palestinians are, after all, a Jordanian people. The Government of Transjordan, however, didn't want a bar of them, because the Palestinians, even then, had a long-established reputation in the Arab world for being trouble makers. It was the Jordanian Government, not the Israelis, who built the refugee camps, and therein the Palestinians have resided ever since.

My advice to the pro-Palestinian lobby? You're a small upstart minority and no-one cares what you think, so stop trying to influence policy.

Minto's dalliances with the idiot fringe this past month included a day out with that other vehemently anti-American activist of dubious New Zealand allegiance, Keith Locke, decrying New Zealand's contribution to world peace and security in the form of the Waihopai listening station near Blenheim. Unbearably for these people and their ilk, despite their best efforts, Uncle Sam is still managing to keep the wolves of war from the door of the world, and New Zealand still has the temerity to keep helping him!

But I'm not about sounding off at John Minto. He's a sad, angry, and ultimately irrelevant little man. Quite why anyone has a problem with Waihopai escapes this writer. Why anyone has a problem with ECHELON, the UKUSA agreement, or the Western Alliance generally, also has me puzzled. In fact I don't believe the great majority of New Zealanders have any issue with it at all, just as most of the population never had a problem with ANZUS, or nuclear ship visits, or the fact that we once had an Air Force and weren't afraid to use it.

The problem, such as it is, is 'had' almost solely by a small and close-knit clique of narcissistic left-wing ideologues and egomaniacs, who occupy the broadcast media and exercise a disproportionate degree of influence over it. They are aided and abetted by a similarly miniscule number of loud-mouthed control freaks sprinkled throughout the Parties of the political Left, the environmental movement, and the Trade Unions.

These people make a great deal more noise than their numbers actually warrant, and demand a great deal more say in the nation's direction and policy than the popularity of their opinions can justify.

I say they should sit down and shut up.

The Greens are a perfect example; the Green Party (putting the 'mental' back into 'Environmental' since 1990) are positively peremptory in their insistence that we acquiesce to their proclamations and dictates, seemingly oblivious to the reality that 19 out of every 20 citizens regularly don't vote for them.

The Republicans and the Flag-changers are another. I confess a degree of sympathy for both causes, and I will support them in the future when they are done properly and for the right reasons. But now is not the time for either, and the small minorities making the most noise in favour of each are most decidedly the very worst people to be making decisions about them for the rest of us. The great majority of New Zealanders are proud of our British heritage and traditions, proud of our history, and proud of our flag. When we're ready to change, it will be the silver fern on black which we run up the flagpole, not any of the other God-awful abominations put forward by idiots, trendy-lefties, Maori activists or the *New Zealand Herald*.

Likewise, when we decide that the Monarchy has run its course, we will institute a genuine Republic where all citizens are equal, where no-one has privilege just because some of their ancestors arrived by canoe, and where democracy means rule by the will of the majority, not by the bullying of a few malcontent leftist control freaks.

Till then, if the whiners in the cheap seats could hold the cacophony, that would be great, thanks very much. The squeaky wheel may get the oil for a while, but there comes a point when it risks being lopped off with a gas axe, and replaced by something that does its job – quietly – and nothing else.

Investigate, March 2010

When in Rome

I've said this before and I'll probably say it again; Vive la France. I like the French. I mean the Froggies can be an irritating clan at times, they're somewhat prone to self-interest and indifference, they eat all manner of curious things and they're not terribly adept at fighting wars, but they build a jolly good aeroplane, and in recent decades – at least since they got The Bomb – when push comes to shove, they're often the first to stand up and put their money where their mouths are. Since President Jacques Chirac threatened to include nuclear weapons in the range of responses available to France in the event of a terrorist attack on the Gallic nation or its interests back in 2006, the mullahs have gone conspicuously quiet on the sabre-rattling front where the French are concerned.

And by banning the burqa two months ago, France has made a stand on behalf of the rights and freedoms of the West which no other nation has yet shown the intestinal fortitude to match. I say good on them. Their example is one which we should be both swift and proud to follow.

The French law doesn't ban the burqa *per se*, of course, nor any other specifically named head covering. That would be too PC even for them, and probably contravene any number of prissy, touchy-feely, apologist laws and regulations imposed by the EU, the UN, and other equally useless and counterproductive institutions. Rather, it prohibits the covering of a person's face in public by any means; crash helmets, hoodies, hats, scarves, ski masks, balaclavas, and all flavours of crackpot religious garments included.

Naturally, the usual suspects are up in arms about it, and for this writer's money, their outrage is a delight to behold. Muslims, leftists, commies, pinkos, the entire anti-white western civilisation brigade, along with their media toadies, have been right on cue, jumping up and down about human rights and religious freedoms and tolerance and multiculturalism, and all the other garbage which excites such people.

As far as your favourite commentator is concerned, tolerance and understanding have gone too far in New Zealand and the other nations of the developed world, when it comes to the demands of our more recent arrivals with regards to their religious and cultural sensitivities. For too long we have allowed ourselves to be criticized and berated by an ungrateful breed of interlopers who want nothing from us other than the right to use our own freedoms against us, and who offer nothing in return except their demands for our recognition of their retarded and defective culture.

I say enough. The matter of the mask is not about race, and it isn't even about religion. The burqa, the niqab, whatever it happens to be called by any of the various tribes and sects which make up Islam today, isn't mentioned in the Koran, and wasn't ever part of the teachings of that Mohammed fellow who they like to call The Prophet. I don't do religion, as regular readers will know, but neither do I have any time for the preferred faith of the Middle East's majority of residents; that aside, the essence of this issue is culture, and more to the point New Zealand's culture.

I'm tired of being told that we have to put up with being denigrated in our own country, that our unique set of values and perceptions is somehow of lesser worth or value than anyone else's, or even, as it is suggested from time to time, that middle New Zealand doesn't actually have a culture. Absolute rubbish. That's like saying vanilla isn't a flavour. A people don't have to be "exotic" in order to possess customs and traditions which identify and distinguish them.

Meat and two veg with salt and pepper are every bit as deserving of the title "ethnic food" as are popadoms, or chilli con goat, or deep-fried camel's eyeballs. People coming to New Zealand from the far-flung reaches of the earth need to understand that, and to appreciate and respect the things which matter to the prevailing majority culture here.

And they need to understand that as part of that, we don't accept the covering of a person's face in public. Do whatever you like in the privacy of your own home, by all means; if an immigrant wants to parade about their lounge dressed in a tent, I say more power to them. But when you come out in the street, take off your mask, because that is the way we do things here. This isn't about your rights, it's about our rights; our right to see the other person's face as we look them in the eye, our right to not have our sensibilities offended.

We welcome migrants to this fair land from all over our diverse and multi-hued world, and we celebrate the differences they bring with them, the colours and flavours they add to our melting pot, and the experiences they open us to – up to a point. We draw the line at certain things. There are some customs which are contrary to our way of life, some accepted norms of other societies which we reject here, some preferences and behaviours which cause offence and which we deem as unacceptable. Freedom and choice are only paramount up to the point where they begin to impinge on the rights of others.

We embrace new New Zealanders from South and East Asia, but we do not permit them to include dog on their restaurant menus. Likewise we don't allow the smoking of hashish, the stoning of adulterers, or the genital mutilation of young girls, regardless of how integral a part such practices may be of the culture of other peoples and other places. Women are equal here, not chattels or second-class citizens. Rape is illegal. So is wife-beating, and on that subject, you're only allowed one of them. We don't sell our daughters, or choose wives for our sons, or cut the hands off thieves (however much the latter may seem like a tempting response at times); and neither do we accept wearing masks in public. I don't care how sacred it is to any foreign person from a foreign culture in a foreign country; it isn't acceptable to me, and this is my culture and my country, not yours. Get some respect, and conform. I don't care that some women, from nations which I would regard as having a culture from the Stone Age, claim to enjoy being subjugated. I do care that such women and their husbands show enough respect for my nation's social mores, to not flaunt their subjugation in public. I'm not about to cruise down the main street of Riyadh drinking whiskey from the bottle while my missus drives, because I know those things are disallowed by Saudi law and custom. I may think it strange, inexplicable, or pointless, but I respect it nonetheless; and I expect the same degree of respect in return. It is simple politeness at the very least for a guest to offer deference and regard to the wishes and sensitivities of their host.

At the end of the day it is about freedom and choice. You do have a choice, and you do have the freedom to make it, and your options are pretty straightforward and clear cut. You choose to come here from somewhere else for the better life which this country and this culture offers, and you know what is expected and acceptable here before you make that choice. When in Rome, do as the Romans do. And when in New Zealand, do as the New Zealanders do – or go back to wherever you came from, and stay there.

Investigate, August 2011

Apologies Accepted

John Key went down half a notch in my estimation last month. He apologised to the Jews. Quite frankly, I've had enough of people apologising to the Jews. Why is this, you may ask? Is Prosser some sort of anti-Semite, along with his other right-wing attitudes?

Not so. In fact, this writer, just like Mr Key, happens to be part Jewish. My father's mother was from a family of Spanish Jews who fled to Holland at the time of the Inquisition, migrating from there to Britain during the 18th century. That makes me somewhere between a quarter and one sixteenth Yid, depending on whose assessment you choose to believe, and more than entitled to an opinion,

I would venture. If it doesn't, I shall have some very hard questions for certain others, later on.

Mr Key was apparently forced to apologise to the Jewish community after MP Maurice Williamson commented "If some people can't lose weight no matter what, how come there were no fat people in the Nazi concentration camps?"

Perhaps the next Prime Minister felt compelled to express his displeasure at the statements made by his Transport spokesman because of his own lineage; perhaps because of a desire to be seen as politically correct. Either way, it is an Apology Too Far. The war is over. We won. Nazi Germany was defeated and destroyed, her leaders dying either by their own hands, or at the end of the hangman's rope. And Israel today is a proud strong nation, a nuclear power with friends in high places. It is time to let it go. By continually apologising for the wrongs of the past we remain trapped within it, a past not of our making, and one which denies us the opportunity to build the future we desire.

I am well aware of the atrocities of the Holocaust. I have been to Dachau, I have seen the gas chambers and the ovens, I have met with several of my great-uncles who were active in the resistance in Denmark, smuggling Danish Jews to safety in neutral Sweden. They were great men; sadly, now, all but departed, along with most of their rescued compatriots, and indeed, almost all of those who persecuted them. An era is coming to an end. We must never forget the past, nor the wisdom of its lessons; but there comes a time when we must forgive the descendents of those who did wrong, accept the realities of the present, and move on. Only through failing to prevent a repeat of those evil times will we dishonour the memory of those who suffered through them – not by learning to live without suspicion of those who were not responsible.

Just this week as I write, the Simon Wiesenthal Centre has awarded New Zealand – along with Australia, Austria, Scotland and Estonia – with a 'D' grade for "lack of effort" in hunting down any old Nazis who might still be hiding in our midst. Yeah, well, big deal. Personally I think that says more about the Wiesenthal Centre than it does about us. Did we get an 'A' for effort for sending a generation of our finest to fight them in the first place, I wonder?

Myriad other groupings and peoples were persecuted and slaughtered at the hands – or the behest – of the Third Reich. Gypsies, homosexuals, intellectuals, communists, Catholics, the handicapped and the mentally ill, Freemasons, Jehovah's Witnesses, and trade unionists, not to mention millions of ordinary Poles, Russians, and countless others. No-one demands continuous apology on their behalf, nor offers it at the drop of a hat; and nor should they, for what good would it do? That aside, I don't criticise the singling out of one particular race, religion, or people for special sympathy or remembrance; rather, it is the over-reaching and absurd concept of ongoing apologism in itself, which gets up this writer's nose. I mean who is apologising to whom, and why, and what do they expect or suppose will be achieved by it?

I confess I don't really know what it means for me to be "part Jewish". Is it a religious thing, or an ethnic thing? I don't do religion, so that can't be me, and as for ethnicity, well, I'm from good mongrel stock anyway, so what's one more flavour? Did my grandmother's family stop being Spanish when they escaped the Papacy, and when did they become Dutch? How long had they been English before being subsumed by the Welsh? What was my great uncle James Rueben Goulden, when he died at Arnhem? Jewish, or something else? I mean he was as much a Williams as he was a Goulden, and as much an Evans and a Davies as either of the aforementioned. Frankly, I'd always thought he was British. He was, after all, an officer in the British Army, and wearing a British Army uniform, and I couldn't care less what his religion was, assuming he had one. I've never asked.

And should someone apologise to me for his death? Should I expend my life in a festering rage, trying to track down a descendent of some hapless enlisted German soldier, so that he or she can apologise to me for something which happened decades before either of us was born? And for which of his or her *GroBvater's* sins should they be apologising – doing his job? Being a good shot (or even a lucky one)? Losing the War?

This is playground stuff. "He started it!" "No, she started it!"...

and the blood feuds and the ethnic distrust and the *utu* which follows such thinking down through the ages and the generations and the centuries, is every bit as childish and just as ridiculous. We are individuals, born with a clean slate and blessed with the ability for free thought. That we should choose to exercise this free thought by filling the minds of innocent children with hatred of peoples never met, and grievance of wrongs never suffered, is insane.

In the United States, the Reverend Jesse Jackson wants "white America" to apologise to Black America (can we still call them that? Or are they African America?), for the wrongs visited upon their ancestors who came to the new continent as slaves. Reality check, Reverend – your name is Jackson. Which bit of you is going to apologise to which other bit?

It's the apologising which keeps us stuck in the past – all of us, the apologists and the apologees both. The apologists are trapped by guilt, and the apologees are trapped by self-pity, and the whole horrible sorry mess is perpetuated by political correctness. Can't we all just bloody well get over it and move on? People who never did anything wrong, apologising to people who never suffered any ill, for things which happened decades or generations or centuries or even millennia ago, is just silly. I mean England invaded and annexed Wales in 1076…or was it 1078? I forget – understandably, perhaps, because I wasn't born until almost nine centuries later, and on the other side of the world. Should I still be demanding an apology from the English? And the English – should they be seeking apologies from the Normans?

Naturally, I've had enough of Pakeha apologising to Maori, as well. So have a good many Maori. It is mostly only the professional grievance industry who keep this bitterness alive in New Zealand, because they'd be out of a job if we all decided to just shake hands, have a beer, and get on with life – much like the way things were, in fact, before we had a Race Relations Commissioner. Hmm.

The sooner the whole Waitangi business can be put to bed, the better. Yes, bad things happened 150 years ago, to Maori who have been dead for 100 years, and visited upon them by white people who have also been dead for 100 years. Whose fault is it? Ours? It certainly isn't mine – I'm the first generation of my family to be born in New Zealand, and my mother's family, who were the first of my lot to arrive, didn't get here till more than a century after the Treaty was signed. Do I get lumped in with what is supposed to be General Pakeha Guilt, just because I'm a white boy? What kind of racist garbage is that?

And who am I supposed to be compensating? My mate who happens to have a parcel of land on Stewart Island, courtesy of his great-grandmother, but is paler than me? How far must we dilute the bloodline before the right to feel aggrieved is relinquished? What kind of loser actually wants to feel aggrieved anyway? Or perhaps it doesn't work like that; some will try to tell us that it's all down to affiliation, not blood. Well, that brings me back to just how Jewish this writer might be; a sixteenth if you figure it on blood alone (I haven't worked out precisely how Spanish or Dutch I might be just yet, or who might need to apologise to me for that), but as much as a quarter if you take it on affiliation. Either way, it's silly. People who never lost anything, demanding compensation from people who never took it, makes about as much sense as the rest of the grievance and apology industry – ie, not much at all.

Ironically, the comment from Maurice Williamson which kicked the whole thing off, highlights yet another form of apologism. No, there weren't any fat people in the concentration camps – yet still, we apologise today for those who claim that they just "can't" lose weight, despite the fact that they lack nothing but willpower and discipline. As Billy Connolly said; "You want to lose weight? Eat less, move more. Simple."

Quitting smoking many years ago, I complained to a mate that the process was too hard. "I can't," I said.

His face darkened. "Wimp," he replied.

That one-word slap in the face was more effective than any amount of hypnosis or nicotine gum, and I haven't lit up in sixteen years.

Enough of the apologies for all those who choose to be offended; the fat people, the smokers, the weak-willed, the historically aggrieved, and on behalf of the Jewish quarter, or this writer's Jewish quarter at least, for the Second World War as well. Your apologies have long since been accepted. Can we all just climb over it and get on with life now, please?

Investigate, October 2007

The Genie and the Bottle

Aladdin. I dream of Jeannie. We all know the story; a genie, imprisoned for aeons in a bottle, lamp, or similar suitable container, is released by the actions of a curious passer-by. The Genie, immensely grateful at being freed from captivity, grants his rescuer three wishes. The rescuer predictably chooses wealth, love, and something nice for the weekend, and everyone lives happily ever after. The extended version of the story generally involves much hilarity, as the genie, well versed in the ways of 1970s America, bumbles his – or her – way through an on-going series of jolly japes, or in cartoon form, complete with a rather camp British-butler voice, sprinkles various wrongdoers with showers of magic dust and falling anvils.

All well and good; but unfortunately the story as we are told it in the West is incomplete. The traditional Arabian tale is a far darker affair. The genie, or d'jinn, is in the bottle for a very good reason; it's been placed there, supposedly for all eternity, on account of it being a particularly nasty and evil wee beastie, who, left unchecked, would wreak mayhem and ruin on all those it encounters.

Furthermore, the original genie has its own particular slant on the relative fairness of exchanging favours. The rescuer, having freed the genie, is entitled to his or her three wishes; once the wishes are granted, however, the slate is wiped, and the hapless rescuer immediately becomes fair game for the genie. Several millennia cooped up in a bottle has left the genie hungry, vengeful, and, to put it gently, somewhat frustrated by lack of companionship – and the rescuer inevitably becomes the first victim of his various appetites.

The moral of the story, that being its purpose in the Arabian tradition, is to illustrate that there are some things which are best left alone, lest they should come back and bite one in the posterior.

And genies, as we all know, once out of their respective bottles, are notoriously difficult to put back.

This is, or should be, a matter of some concern to those who seek to govern our fair land, because in recent years, altogether too many dangerous genies have been released from their bottles, by the actions of passing Governments and their various leaders. Some of these may be due to curiosity, naïveté, foolishness, or plain lack of grey matter; some, it might be argued, are possibly the result of deliberate social engineering, or perhaps even an agenda other than that placed before the public scrutiny. It is of concern to wanna-be political leaders because in the very near future, in order to prevent this country and what we like to call its society from slipping into a mess of our own making, some hard decisions are going to have to be made. A few genies are going to have to go back in their bottles.

In some quarters, some of this rebottling will trigger much wailing and discontent; but it will need to be done nonetheless.

Top of the list is corporal punishment. Our schools, the education system, the integrity of the next generation itself, is under threat because of the lack of effective discipline in the classroom. Kids cannot be expected to be reasoned with as one might do with an adult; they're kids. They lack knowledge, understanding, and perspective. That's why they're at school. They need boundaries, and the imposition of discipline to preserve those boundaries until such time as they have developed discipline themselves. When they get out of line, they need a whack. As their self-discipline develops, the mere threat of a whack is often sufficient. This is not about brutality, or assault, or the diminution of human rights. It's about common sense.

The age for purchasing alcohol should never have come down, and it needs to go back up. With due apologies to the purists, it isn't good enough that because a person can vote and serve their country at eighteen, that we assume they also have the ability to responsibly regulate their drinking. Rules have always been more like guidelines in New Zealand. Just as everyone accepts that the 100km/h speed limit *really* means 110, or 120 if you can get away with it, so the old drinking age of 20 really meant 18, and naturally, 18 really means 16. And 16 is really too young. Going into a pub with Mum and Dad, or having a few supervised beers at home, is not the same as being able to waltz into a bottle store and stock up on vodka for your 15- and 16-year-old mates.

Sometimes we catch the politicians in the act, and manage to prevent them from pulling the bung from yet another genie bottle; when Phil Goff wanted to legalise sex for twelve-year-olds because they were doing it anyway, the public rightly told him where he could put his corkscrew. I got news for ya, Phil; rape, and murder, and manufacturing P don't need to be legalised either, just because people are doing it anyway.

Growing up in New Zealand, in my generation at least, one tended to assume that the people running the country more or less knew what they were doing. Most kids had a Dad as well as a Mum, and they were married and lived in the same house. When the TV shut down for the night at eleven-thirty everyone went to bed, because they had work in the morning; kids who played up got a smack on the backside, or in the worst cases, the jug cord round the legs, and if we needed any further reassurance that all was well with the world, we could rush out of our classrooms and look up to the sky every time the jets flew over, which was reasonably often. The All Blacks won more often than not, and we were given regular reminders of the many reasons we had for being proud of our military history, involvement, and capabilities.

Somewhere in the last twenty-five years, however, a great deal of that has changed. The Social Breakdown Genie is out of his bottle, facilitated by a burgeoning DPB and the PC-driven removal of physical discipline from daily life. The Profit-before-People Genie got out when the nation's silverware was sold off because owning it didn't fit with some mindless theoretical ideology, and once free, it helped the Social Breakdown Genie to eat the country's work ethic. Indeed, having granted the three wishes of the Cradle to the Grave via the Unemployment Benefit, the Social Welfare Genie has been rapaciously devouring the moral fibre of New Zealand for three generations now.

The Pacifism Genie got loose on a promise of peace and safety in a pink fluffy world, and promptly set about destroying our sense of nationhood. Now, he's emasculating a generation of young men, and next on his agenda is a plan to completely destroy New Zealand's ability to protect itself.

Worse still, the slide towards pacifism, and the measures which have had to be put into place to support it, has seen the politicisation of not only the military, but the Police as well. We know, without having to do an internet search, where this particular road leads; it can happen, that a country of educated people with an abundance of natural resources can slide into a self-made destructive hell. It happened not very long ago, and not very far away – it's called Argentina.

Perhaps worst of all is the Political Correctness Genie. This nasty insidious gremlin is responsible for a multitude of sins, from the electricity crisis because we're not allowed to build power stations, to the destruction of the family because we're not allowed to teach girls to cook, or tell gays that they can't adopt children, to just this week, where we can't tell a South Auckland family who murdered two of their babies that they're a bunch of evil criminal losers, because they happen to be Maori and we can't be being accused of racism.

I say enough of this rubbish. There comes a time when it begins to dawn on a person that the people who run the country are not blessed with any greater wisdom, understanding, or humanity than the average Joe in the street; they're the same people you were at primary school with, and while they've grown older, they haven't necessarily got wiser.

I say that this situation needs to be of concern to our intending leaders because in the cold light of day, there are going to have to be some tough decisions taken in the next few years.

Every one of Those Who Would Be King needs to look themselves very squarely in the eye and ask if they have the intestinal fortitude to lead, rather than to merely govern; it is not enough just to look for ways around the worst effects of the mistakes of the past. Some of them are going to need to be undone. This new millennium requires leadership with courage and vision.

The mentality of welfarism needs to go. The NCEA needs to go. External exams have to be resurrected. Education without effort, success, or failure, will give us nothing but a genderless generation of losers. The RMA has to go as well – this land is our home, and we have to be allowed to live here, to develop it, to profit from it. DOC needs to be disbanded, the High Country Tenure Review Process needs to be abandoned, and having Maori as an official language is a pointless waste of time and money. Our military needs to be rebuilt, by people who can ignore the hysterical wailings of peaceniks, beancounters, and other assorted idiots. The nuclear ships ban is childish folly, particularly given that there is nothing at all in New Zealand law preventing us from constructing nuclear power stations. Corporal punishment must return, as must CMT. I could go on, but I won't. You get the idea.

It is time for New Zealand to look for real leadership, because the going, from here on in, is about to get rough. Anyone can hold the tiller when the sea is calm. Personally I don't trust the socialists or the feminists to hold it when the swell starts to get up, and I'm not at all sure about most of the opposition, either.

We need to trim the masts, batten the hatches, and get a few genies back in their bottles. It won't be easy, but that doesn't mean it isn't necessary. World War Two wasn't easy; perhaps the naysayers and the apologists believe we shouldn't have fought back? This writer doesn't agree.

Investigate, July 2006

10 Ways To Tell If You're An Idiot

Henry Louis Mencken, American journalist, social commentator, and philosopher, once remarked "The most common of all follies is to believe passionately in the palpably not true. It is the chief occupation of mankind."

He was right, of course; human beings, strange creatures that we are, appear unshakeably inclined towards grasping the wrong end of the stick, as firmly, as self-destructively, and as often as possible.

I had a circular email arrive in my inbox the other day. An oldie, but a goodie, entitled "10 Ways to tell if you're Gay." It's funny, particularly if, like me, you're an insensitive non-PC redneck who doesn't consider very much to be sacred, and if you don't care that most of it isn't actually true. I mean a bloke can like cats, and be into interior decorating, without being a bender, but that doesn't detract from the humour of the thing. Stereotypes are funny. I wish the liberals and the other fun Nazis could get that through their heads. It doesn't even matter that it's been round the block more than a few times; some things stay funny, or at least interesting, no matter how many times they get rehashed, like Fawlty Towers and Monty Python. This is just as well for TVNZ's Christmas programming, and indeed the Internet itself, which seems to consist more and more of the same old material doing the rounds over and over. Imagine, perhaps humanity's greatest and most powerful of creations, the networking of hundreds of millions of computers and billions of independent minds, and most of it dedicated to nothing more constructive than the endless recirculation of the same old jokes and the same tired porn images.

But I digress. The email did get me to thinking. Perhaps who-ever crafted it was onto something. Maybe there really are people out there who could benefit from a checklist against which they could measure their foolishness, in the same way that it pleases the aforementioned rednecks among us to imagine that some folk may appreciate having their sexuality questioned.

In keeping with this line of thought, and as something of a social service for the benefit of those members of Government and the media whose personal challenges might be relevant to it, your favourite commentator has drafted just such a list. In no particular order, here are the top ten beliefs by which the uncertain may determine their relative stupidity, or lack of it.

1. Smacking

This is not the same thing as assault. Actually this is a good one to start with, because it's so really very simple. Discipline and correction are one thing, assault is another. Different things, different intentions, different effects, different outcomes. Little children are not knowledgeable adults who can be reasoned with and who can rationalise the consequences of various courses of action. They are little children. They require guidance. Loving guidance sometimes requires instantaneous correction (light sockets and busy roads spring to mind). Boundaries around safety and socially acceptable behaviour need to be learned long before, and indeed in order to facilitate, the development of rational thinking. Pain first, explanation second, learning follows. The pain lasts but a few fleeting moments, the learning lasts a lifetime. Not necessary in every instance, but very necessary on occasion. Smacking is not the same thing as violence. If you can't work this one out, you're an idiot. Please don't make things worse by becoming a parent. Or a teacher. Or a politician.

2. Fluoride

There is plenty enough fluoride to guarantee dental health available from ordinary dietary sources, and plenty more in toothpaste for those who want it. 99.999% of your household water supply goes straight back down the drain, through the bath, the shower, the washing machine, the kitchen sink, the garden hose, and flushing the toilet. There's a great deal to be said for teaching kids to brush properly, and not basing their diets on sugary junk food and soft drinks as well. Too much fluoride in your drinking water, however, can be a cause of brain damage – evidence enough for this writer that the proponents of it have already had their overdose.

3. Biofuels

These wouldn't save the planet even if it needed saving, which remains contentious. They produce the same exhaust gases as mineral fuels (namely, mostly, carbon dioxide, carbon monoxide, water vapour, and soot), in the same quantities per unit energy delivered, because they all work by burning carbon, and there are no free lunches in carbon-oxygen chemistry. On top of this they cause people to starve by turning food into fuel. If you're a believer in biofuels, you're truly certifiable.

4. Flying Pig Flu

Swine Flu, Bird Flu, SARS, AIDS, yada yada yada. SARS came to nothing. AIDS – Newsflash – is still almost nothing, even amongst the "high-risk" communities. Bird Flu…..whatever happened to Bird Flu? Aren't we all supposed to have died from it already? Swine Flu isn't even Swine Flu, for God's sake. It's North American H1N1 influenza virus, and it's only connection with pigs is that some pigs in Mexico caught it from humans. These are beat-ups, people. Nothing more, nothing less. They are the product of an irresponsible, sensationalist, commercially-motivated media and the natural tendency of the human animal towards panic. The end is not nigh. Count the number of times you have been convinced that it is, and it hasn't turned out to be at all. If you still believe it, you're a simpleton.

5. The Credit Crunch

Oh, please. Why would there be, how could there possibly be, a shortage of money available for lending? If, as we are told, bank loan money comes from other people's savings, and those other people still have their money in a Bank somewhere, and the bank is paying them interest on it, then where could the said Bank possibly be getting the interest with which to pay them, other than by making loans? You think the Banks are paying interest to their depositors out of their own pockets? And if those other people don't have their money in a bank, then where is it? If some of them have "transferred" their investments into gold or real estate, what did the people who sold them the gold and the real estate do with the money, other than to put it into a Bank? This is just an excuse to keep the interest rates up higher than they should be. If you believe otherwise, you're a moron.

6. The Centre Line

This is not some magical boundary between the realms of the living and the dead, and crossing it will not automatically result in your tragic and instantaneous death. In fact on many parts of New Zealand's poorly constructed third-world roading system, chopping the inside off a badly designed corner, through which you can see perfectly well, may be your best way of guaranteeing your safety. Likewise, your vehicle will not explode, or hurl itself into the verges – or the oncoming traffic – the instant it reaches 101 kilometres per hour, even when there isn't a passing lane. This won't even happen if your cellphone happens to ring at the same time. If you believe that any of the above is true, you're an idiot. If you're a traffic cop and you believe it, you're a double idiot.

7. Nuclear Powered Ships

These are not bombs waiting to explode. They aren't built the same way, and they can't do that, plain and simple. Likewise, they are not at imminent risk of melting down. Maritime nuclear reactors are cooled by the ocean, so as long as the sea has water in it, this isn't going to happen. Nor do they make us a target for attack, any more or less than we were ever going to be anyway, and they don't make the fishes grow three eyes or the coral reefs glow in the dark, any more than there are monsters in your closet. Understand the science of this technology, and learn the truth of its safe history, before you fly into a blind panic about it. If you're still worried about radiation from nuclear powered ships, you'd best stop using your microwave oven too, because you're an idiot.

8. Peak Oil

The Black Stuff is not running out, and it isn't ever going to. There's more there than we will ever use. The Stone Age didn't end because of a shortage of stone, and so will it be with the Oil Age. See also #5 above....it's a beat-up to keep the prices high, and you're swallowing it. Oil has been running out in thirty years, every year for the last 35 years, and it's still due to run out in 30 years. Believe it and keep paying the money, morons.

9. The Benign Strategic Environment

This only ever existed in the minds of Pacifists and the similarly retarded. We live in a lull in the fighting, that's all, a brief period of relative peace in between continuing bouts of war, which is the natural state of the human condition. But go on, beat your sword into a ploughshare – it'll make it easier for me to come along and subjugate you with my weapons. Oh and by the way, the Chinese have started sending warships out with their fishing fleets, to protect them as they poach in other nations' fishing grounds. Does this suggest anything to the numbskulls among us?

And last but by no means least:

10. Global Warming

Ah yes, but it isn't, is it. No indeedy, it's cooling, and has been for the better part of a decade now. It's the sun which drives global temperature, not humans and their gases, and if the Russians are right, and the sunspot activity stays low, we are headed for the beginning of a mini ice-age, possibly as soon as 2012.

Switching the name of this non-existent phenomenon to "Climate Change" doesn't make it any more believable, because it doesn't make it any more real. The icecaps are not melting, the polar bears are not dying out, the earth is not flat, and we are not affecting its climate – and none of these things will become true no matter how hard you believe in them.

Will they still be telling us to stop burning firewood when there are icebergs in Cook Strait and glaciers rolling over the Port Hills?

If you're a Global Warming Believer, you are a complete and utter fool, and the more letters you have after your name, the dumber you are with it.

Perhaps this topic might be worthy of a sequel sometime. There is, as you know, plenty of material to work with.

Investigate, August 2009

Chapter Thirteen

Law & Order

"A shop owner in Auckland, faced by a gang of thugs armed with knives, defends his life and property, and gets stabbed for his trouble, only to be arrested by the Police for using "excessive force". What kind of madness is this?"

– Prosser, Investigate, November 2008

Natural Justice: a quest for the impossible?

Peter Ellis. David Bain. Scott Watson. Did they or didn't they? New Zealand's legal history is littered with examples of people, mostly men, accused, tried and convicted of heinous crimes; men who serve part or all of their sentences, never letting go of their claims of innocence, and emerging at the end of years of imprisonment to the welcome of friends, family, and supporters who have never lost faith, nor doubted the integrity of those claims.

Why is this so? Why, in our supposedly enlightened Western democracy, do we continue to lock people away, when from the very degree and spread of protest over such convictions, nationwide, through the media, and across all strata of society, there must, by definition, still exist a reasonable doubt as to their guilt or innocence? Are juries, by their participation in the courtroom, somehow party to crucial information or evidence which is denied to the general public, to the media, and to expert observers, despite the full reporting of the detail of evidence and submissions given in Court? Are jurors able to be mesmerised by the compelling arguments of practiced counsel, or overwhelmed by the undeniable weight of scientific and professional opinion? Is the jury system itself at fault? Or could the problem lie elsewhere?

Could it be that the very structure of our legal process is fundamentally and irrevocably flawed, and that it is incapable of determining guilt or innocence beyond a reasonable doubt – in matters of complex nature or contentious issue – because it does not, by design or intention, concern itself with determining the actual truth of any particular case?

This revelation may come as a shock to many, and raise eyebrows of disbelief amongst those who have never had dealings with the criminal justice system, but it is true nonetheless. It is here where I believe the judicial process as it is used in New Zealand is most at fault, and where it demonstrates most clearly that it is inherently incapable of dispensing genuine natural justice.

The Adversarial System of Justice, the system employed in New Zealand, and in Britain, Australia, Canada, the Commonwealth, and the United States, does not ask juries to determine guilt or innocence based on the truth of any situation. Rather, it *requires* juries to determine guilt or innocence *on the basis of the case as it is put* – and on the evidence and arguments held up to support that case, and those put to oppose it. In other words, jurors are required to find a man innocent or guilty according to the nature and detail of one argument accusing him, and another denying it, even though neither of those arguments may have any connection with the actual truth of the matter.

In this writer's opinion, such a system is not merely silly, pointless, and archaically naïve, it is obscene, and to call it a system of "justice" constitutes an abomination in the face of all we have sacrificed to build a world where truth and fair play are supposed to be paramount. A system it may be, but just, it most certainly is not.

Conversely, the Inquisitorial System, founded in ancient Rome, and used today across most of Continental Europe, Japan, and a number of other countries, focuses on discovering the Truth as it pertains to any particular case or inquiry.

Under the Adversarial system, the Judge is an impartial referee and arbiter of the Law. He or she does not intervene in the combat between the defence and the prosecution, other than to ensure that both sides remain within the boundaries of their own arguments, and do not breach either the Law, or its rules as they apply in the Court. Under the Inquisitorial system, the Judge is the seeker of truth, and he or she may call for new evidence, or inquiries, beyond the limits of the arguments presented by the prosecution and the defence. In an Adversarial criminal trial, if the defendant pleads guilty, the prosecution rests, the trial ends, and sentence is passed. Under the Inquisitorial system, a guilty plea from the defendant is entered as simply one more piece of evidence, and the trial continues onwards in its search for the truth. False admissions of guilt, made for who knows what reason, are not considered the end of the matter under inquisitorial judicial regimes.

Why is any of this important to New Zealand? Because, in my opinion, contested verdicts, delivered under the adversarial system, leave too many unanswered questions. Chief amongst these, I would contend, is the question of Whodunnit? If David Bain didn't murder his family, then who did? If Scott Watson didn't murder Ben Smart and Olivia Hope, who did? In Peter Ellis' case, the question is even more complex; if he didn't do it, did it happen at all? Some of the children in the Christchurch Civic Crèche case reported, amongst other things, being taken aboard spaceships, and seeing their friends butchered. Our judicial system apparently found this to be convincing testimony.

Nobody wants to see murderers and child molesters walk free. Personally I'd prefer to see them strung up; but that in itself poses questions, and not least amongst these concerns the degree to which we can have faith in both the judicial process, and the scientific establishment which supports it.

Every time I feel a rant in favour of the return of the death penalty coming on, my conscience throws three little words at me. Those words are, of course, Arthur Allan Thomas. What if we'd hanged Arthur Thomas, and then found him to be innocent later on? A pardon doesn't bring back a dead man. And the whole matter remains as contentious today as it was then. Was the evidence cooked? Did the Police lie? If so, why?[4] Is it really so important to obtain a conviction, to lock somebody, anybody, away, regardless of the fact that a killer may still be roaming free, while an innocent man languishes behind bars?

In a previous life I worked as a process technician for a large photographic company in a major New Zealand city. One of my colleagues, who had previously been employed by a small photographic firm in that same city, once retold to me a story passed on to him by his then employer; a story about two Police officers who, at the time of the Crewe murder inquiry, had brought in a .22 bullet cartridge case for photographing. The officers subsequently collected their photos, but left the cartridge case behind. To the best of my former colleague's knowledge, it was probably still there – and who knows, may be to this day. Could that have been the infamous missing cartridge case from the Crewe inquiry? Maybe, maybe not; the point is that while the Judge in our Adversarial court system would not have been allowed to regard the disappearance of such a piece of evidence as important, an Inquisitorial judge would be compelled to consider it as a crucial marker on the road to the truth. And at the end of the day, after all that has happened, after Arthur Thomas has served ten years behind bars for something he didn't do, been pardoned, compensated, and allowed to get on with his shattered life, our flawed and faulty justice system still hasn't answered the most important question – who did kill Jeannette and Harvey Crewe? The Inquisitorial System would have regarded the discovery of that truth as its most important mission; our Adversarial System simply doesn't care, because that question never applied to the case as it was put.

David Bain may well have killed his family. The Crown contended that he did. A jury of his peers concluded that he did. A good friend of mine, who met David Bain whilst in jail, is of the opinion that he's as guilty as sin. But I don't know. There is doubt in the minds of many; his most famous advocate, Joe Karam, and a host of friends and supporters. There is doubt cast on the integrity of evidence as it was collected and recorded by the Police, and on some of the findings of forensic experts.[5]

But the nub of the matter, as it relates to the Law in New Zealand,

---

4   See *Arthur Allan Thomas: The Inside Story* by Ian Wishart, Howling At The Moon Publishing

5   David Bain was, four years after this commentary was first published, given a retrial and found not guilty by the jury

is not about who killed David Bain's family. The media, and the public, continue to speculate on whether the murderer could have been David's father, Robin, or perhaps someone else entirely. This question, in the minds of the public, and reflected via the news media, is Inquisitorial in nature, and to my mind, it is an approach far more likely to determine the ultimate truth than the process set before the jury, which was simply required to decide between guilt and innocence on the basis of the charges as they were laid. The jury did not have the option of saying "we don't know", or "we think it was someone else". Hung juries come about because of a democratic impasse between the black-or-white opinions which individual jurors are required to form, not because of the grey opinions which their natural sense of justice may give them.

Scott Watson might have murdered Ben and Olivia. Or he might not. Maybe they died later, much later, somewhere else entirely, a long way away, on a mystery ketch which a whole lot of people only imagined seeing. Maybe they're not even dead.

Maybe we put a petty criminal behind bars for seventeen years for something he didn't do, and maybe even something which didn't happen. Maybe Scott Watson – who wasn't an angel – was simply the wrong man, in the wrong place, at the wrong time, who ran foul of a police force, a public, and a judicial system all barking up the wrong tree, and hell-bent on knee-jerk revenge for what they all presumed was a heinous crime.

Maybe there's a real killer still out there.[6]

We will probably never know. Our Adversarial Justice System does not require us to know. It doesn't care. All it asks is that we determine guilt or innocence on the basis of an argument and its counter, irrespective of whether either of these have any connection with the actual truth of the matter.

And the truth is that this ancient, traditional, revered, flawed, stupid, illogical, infantile methodology, may be called many things, but it may not be called natural justice. New Zealanders, and the concepts and traditions of fairness and the human right, deserve better than this.

Investigate, June 2005

---

6   See *Ben & Olivia: What Really Happened?* by Ian Wishart & Jayson Rhodes, Howling At The Moon Publishing

The Thin Blue Line

It's full moon as I write. People go a little crazy at the full moon. I get a bit strange myself; my beard grows faster, my teeth feel pointier, and I have a hankering for my steak even more on the rare side than usual.

I don't stalk the streets with a baseball bat, or congregate in car-parks to inhale adhesives, or scale the local monument with sherry flagon in hand to proclaim a new earth. But some folks do, and full moon is when they appear to do it most often. If popular conjecture is to be believed, on the night of a full moon, the phone in many urban police stations will be off the hook. The Police have limited resources, they can't deal with every call, and when the wolves are howling, it's a fairly safe bet that the cranks will be lighting up the switchboard.

One could understand, and be more forgiving of such a stance, were it not for the irksome reality that these days, the phone also appears to be off the hook for many other incidents, unless of course they involve motor vehicles, and the possibility of a little revenue collecting.

Something has gone rotten with the policing of New Zealand over the last few years. It's difficult to say exactly when or why the rot first set in; but this writer would hazard a guess that it was about the same time that the Ministry of Transport's patrol officers were merged into the New Zealand Police Force. I think we can blame John Banks for that; his promise of "another 900 frontline police" was never going to be fulfilled from any other avenue, despite pro-testations to the contrary.

The merger still rankles amongst those who wore the Police uni-form before it; many of the MOTs officers came on board in a combined force carrying the rank they had held under their old employer, often that of sergeant – a rank few could have hoped to attain within the singular New Zealand Police, given that, in many cases, they had originally failed to meet its recruitment standards.

This is not to say that the MOT was a dumping ground for those not good enough to become real cops….well, OK, maybe it was.

There were some good traffic cops, however. I can vouch for two of them. One was the man who taught me to drive, a family friend who became an MOT officer after 20-odd years in the Army, teaching people how to drive tanks, and spending a stint in Vietnam as a door gunner on a Huey.

A few weeks after I got my licence, he caught me speeding. This was the bad old days of the 80 km/h limit; I think I was doing 90.

Approaching my trembling self with measured sternness, he said, very quietly, "I didn't teach you to drive like that. Turn around."

I did so, and got a size ten boot in the rear end.

"Now drive home the way you know you should."

He got back in his black-and white patrol car and followed me home at about 70.

Was that effective policing? I didn't get my first speeding ticket until some fifteen years later, in 1997. You judge.

The other is a local senior constable who was previously a city council traffic officer in a regional capital not far from here. A finer example of a good police officer you couldn't hope to meet.

I think these are the exceptions which prove the rule.

Unfortunately, nowadays, they are exceptions which appear to be beginning to prove the rule as far as the entire Police Force is concerned.

The focus which the Police used to have, seems to be fading. Time was, the local cop was someone people looked up to. Now, he is becoming someone you watch out for. I grew up in a very small town in the dairy country of the north Waikato. The local sheriff was a rather dour, somewhat blunt, very pragmatic, and extremely well-informed individual. He was, as sole-charge country cops were required to be in that more enlightened age, quite often judge, jury, and executioner, as well as counsellor, dog ranger, rugby coach, and arbiter of law and order. He looked after us, as underage drinkers; he turned a discretionary eye away from our frequenting of the local hotel, but at the same time, made quietly sure that the said establishment only served us in the lounge bar, so as not to provoke the locals, and that they never served us anything stronger than beer. It was illegal, yes; but he knew where we were, and we knew where we stood, and no-one got into any trouble.

I recall an occasion when his remedy to a late evening altercation between two alcohol-fuelled and testosterone-laden 20-somethings (in the public bar), was to bundle them into his patrol car and drive them five kilometres out of town. There, at the side of one of the many main drains which criss-cross the Hauraki Plains, he made them strip to the waist, and jump in. Ten feet wide, nearly as deep, and half filled with freezing cold muddy water, the drain was the place our sheriff had decreed that these two should sort out their differences. Then he made them walk back to town.

Nowadays, he'd be sacked from the force, and most likely hauled before the courts himself, for such a brazen display of effective pro-active Policing, and for the violation of human rights, and blah blah blah.

But also, nowadays, you'd be hard-pressed to find any but the most dedicated of remote country cops performing such a social service at all, with almost no chance of his city colleague doing the same.

No, instead, they'll be out on patrol, filling their quota of traffic tickets. It's safe, it's easy, it's low-risk, and I'd hazard a guess that a good few of them can't be bothered with core policing anymore. The Force has become as corrupted an institution as any other Government department over the last couple of decades, and probably for the same reasons – the increasing politicisation of its direction and focus, and the subsequent misdirection of limited resources into areas removed from those essential to the key elements of frontline policing.

In very recent years, this situation has been exacerbated by the actions of a Minister who was quite plainly being asked to perform at a level well beyond his capability, and a Commissioner who may very well have had a separate agenda.

The public are losing respect for the Police. All too often, these days, Joe Public perceives his local constabulary with a derision which would have been unthinkable even a generation ago. Too often, also, this is because the Police (and the courts, which is a subject in itself) appear to be siding with the criminals, and leaving the innocent to fend for themselves – or worse, to take the brunt of the law, while the perpetrators of crime walk free.

I cast my mind back to my very first column in this esteemed publication. It concerned the treatment, by our Police, of Northland farmer Paul McIntyre, who defended his home and property, and was dragged through the courts for his trouble. Three years later, acquitted by a judge, he still faces the prospect of losing his farm to pay his legal bills.

Only this week (even after the full moon has passed, one could be forgiven for thinking its madness remains), another bold New Zealander has suffered at the hands of a Police Force and a judicial system which appears hell-bent on promoting the rights of wrong-doers, and alienating a once supportive public in the process.

Paul Espiner, ordinary Taranaki bloke, went to the aid of his neighbour, driving away the thugs who were attacking her, and smashing the window of their car with a machete, whilst promising ongoing protection for the otherwise defenceless solo mother.

Espiner, who should have been awarded a medal, instead got a conviction for possession of an offensive weapon, while the house-wrecking, car-smashing, home invader who threatened to kill her, got away with diversion and name suppression.

I mean what is wrong with the cops who prosecuted this man? Are they afraid of the criminals? Are they in someone's pocket? Or are they simply frustrated by their own individual and institutional impotence, and taking out their anger on the nearest available soft target?

In between these two examples have been countless more. A Bay of Plenty farm couple, subjected to a home invasion, wait for help for more than an hour, while the Police, who are doing nothing, tie up their phone line, preventing them from calling the local neighbourhood watch – who are close, available, and armed. The next such couple probably won't bother calling the Police at all.

New Year revellers near Wanaka set fire to a car, and pelt the Police with bottles when they show up to restore order. In Tauranga, a female officer is hospitalised after being assaulted with a wheel rim while attempting to shut down a noisy party. These things don't happen simply because people are drunk and obnoxious. They happen because a respect for the Police, built up over nigh on a century, has been squandered in a few short years, through politicised leadership, Governmental incompetence, and the complicity of a morally and physically weakened constabulary, which is quick to condemn the law-and-order-promoting citizen, slow to prosecute the real offenders, and eagerly embracing of a new and nauseating regime of revenue collecting, in place of the true and essential preservation of justice.

We will have to arm the Police in response, of course, and very soon, at that; but the horse has already bolted. Policing in New Zealand is rotting, from the top down, and from some repugnant bottom line, upwards. Every time the Police warn against vigilantism, or punish someone braver than themselves for "taking the law into their own hands", they lose the respect of yet another formerly supportive member of the public – someone who can see quite clearly through the hypocrisy of a Force which denies the public the right to protect itself, while refusing to carry out that sworn duty itself.

Perhaps there is hope yet. Maybe the Police can turn themselves around, and become, once again, the respected presence which once they were, in the face of institutionalised corruption bred from the ethical anarchy of our Government-driven social malaise.

But I fear it may be too late, and that those of us who hope against hope, for the return of wise, just, discretionary policing, may simply be howling at the moon.

Investigate, February 2006

God Defend New Zealanders

I'm angry this month. Actually I'm disgusted and angry, and I'm disgusted and angry with the New Zealand Police. I've had enough of the increasing ineffectiveness of the Police Force, their changing priorities, the lies about what those priorities are, the creeping politicisation of the command structure and the senior ranks, and the fact that good cops in the street are being tarred with a brush which should, by rights, only serve to smear the few who are responsible for the aforementioned lies and politics.

But mostly I'm angry and disgusted by the tired and predictable bleating about citizens taking the law into their own hands, every time some innocent victim of crime is forced to defend themselves because the Police either can't, or won't, come to their assistance. Too often we are told not to approach escaped prisoners or wanted felons. Too often we are advised to listen meekly to the demands of thugs and robbers, to lie down and be walked over, to give up the money and allow our rights and property to be violated. Walk away, we are told. Scurry off to a safe distance and hide under a rock. Never mind that it's three in the morning, and you're half asleep and/or frightened and in shock. Behave calmly, rationally, and as if you had the benefits of hindsight and safe distance. Call the Police, who will attend promptly, either within 24 hours, or when they have finished writing traffic tickets, whichever comes first. If you're hurt, you can wait for the ambulance too – they'll let it in through the cordon just as soon as they are sure that Everything Is Safe. Just don't bleed to death in the meantime.

Well I say enough of this namby-pamby rubbish. If I want to risk a beating by taking on some criminal, what business is that of the Police Commissioner? How does he know whether I'm a Black Belt or not? Come to that, how does the criminal know?

Perhaps this is indicative of institutional cowardice on the part of the Police. Perhaps they don't want their individual and collective impotence highlighted. Maybe they're actually on the side of the criminals, in some perverse way. Yes, I'm grasping at straws here; but that's because I'm struggling to understand what went wrong with the New Zealand Police, and when, and why. Are we not the nation with the Fighting Quality, birthplace of the All Blacks, inventor of the SAS, home of the Good Keen Man?

How and why, I wonder, did PC stop meaning Police Constable, and start meaning Politically Correct? Whatever became of the Red Squad?

You wouldn't have caught the Good Cops from the Old Days telling people to act like pussies. By the Old Days I mean twenty and thirty years ago, and by Good Cops I mean the ones who were part of their communities, who played rugby and drank at the local pub, who administered summary justice and employed discretion, wisely and as it was needed.

They were the men who would quietly advise you that if you were going to shoot an intruder, shoot him through the head, and then fire a warning shot into the ceiling. That way, it was your word against his, and the neighbours had heard two shots, the first of which was (obviously) your warning, and he was dead, which meant both a just outcome, and whole lot less paperwork for them, and everyone was happy.

They were the men who would chew your ear and then tell you to get home quick, rather than drag the breathalyser out, when they knew you only lived ten minutes away, and a telling off (with optional boot in the rear end, depending on your age) for speeding – at least the first time. They were also the men who would remember your helping hand when they were frogmarching some reprobate out of the pub, and give you a wink and wave through, the next week at the checkpoint. They were the men who would turn a blind eye, when a bunch of cockies decided to lie in wait in a darkened haybarn, armed with pick handles and lengths of alkathene pipe, for the scum who had been stealing fuel and machinery from local farms.

I don't know where those men have gone, and this week I am outraged by their replacements. It's bad enough that a farmer in Northland gets dragged through the Courts for shooting at the scum who were stealing his farm bike. It's bad enough that a good bloke in Taranaki gets charged for taking to the scum who were attacking his solo mother neighbour, dealing to their car with a machete. It's beyond ridiculous that when a decent law-abiding citizen shoots the tires out from under the scum who have been burgling homes in his small coastal town, the cops decide that he's the bad guy, when they themselves were three-quarters of an hour away and were powerless to do anything at all. It's incomprehensible that when some idiot scum tries to rob a gun shop with a machete, and gets shot for his trouble, that the gun shop owner is the one who finds himself in the gun.

The list goes on. A farm couple in the Bay of Plenty are beaten and robbed because not only will the Police not do anything about it themselves, but they tie up the couple's phone line so that the neighbours, who are close by and armed, can't even be made aware of what is happening.

But this week it has gone from ridiculous to insane. A shop owner in Auckland, faced by a gang of thugs armed with knives, defends his life and property, and gets stabbed for his trouble, only to be arrested by the Police for using "excessive force". What kind of madness is this? Only weeks beforehand, another store owner is murdered in his own shop, once again during an armed robbery; and the very next day, yet another is fighting for his life after being stabbed.

Under these circumstances, how excessive can the use of force be? For God's sake, is any use of force in self-defence now considered excessive by our Police if the victim is still alive afterwards, or if the perpetrator has been harmed in any way?

Now it would be easy, I know, to paint the Police as pawns in some greater game here; subject to the whims of Government, shackled by legislation, caught between the proverbial rock and hard place. But that, I think, tasteless pun intended, would be a cop-out. In all the cases mentioned above, it has been the Police who have, at their discretion – which remains considerable – chosen to prosecute. And in all cases where such has been applicable, juries have thrown those prosecutions out again. The same Police, however, regularly fail to bring charges against corrupt and fraudulent members of Government, ostensibly because they cannot see the public good being served by such action. Well, maybe they need to look a little more closely.

In Texas, a man shoots two robbers who are burgling his neighbour's house. He shoots them dead, in the back, with a shotgun, all the while speaking by phone to a Police dispatcher, who is pleading with him to withdraw and wait. But the Police cannot compel the man to cease his vigilante action, because Texas law specifically allows the use of deadly force to protect oneself, and similarly extends those allowances to one's neighbour, down to and including one's neighbour's property. We do not have such laws here, of course, though it is this writer's firm opinion that we should; but we do have a similar sentiment, established and growing, and fertilised to no small degree by the public's changing and ever more cynical perception of the Police, as a result of their actions and decisions in our own cases of this type.

Whilst the public suffer under the ever heavier yoke of criminal activity, our own Police are all too often unable to intervene or respond in anything like a timely or useful fashion, because their resources are otherwise committed; to the important busywork of issuing traffic infringements, for such heinous crimes as driving at 111 km/h on an empty road in good weather, or crossing the centerline of a badly shaped corner, on that same empty road, with visibility halfway to forever. Protesting that they are not, in fact, the roadside branch of the Inland Revenue Department, the Police regularly bore us with the tired old line that no, they don't have ticket quotas for Highway Patrol officers; rather, they have enforcement guidelines.

There is, I believe, an even older line, which goes something like "don't piss on my leg and tell me it's raining."

The thing is, y'see, we know that they're lying when they come out with stuff like that, and it annoys us to the point of losing respect, that they don't have the balls to admit it. And then the next time they say something like "don't take the law into your own hands", well, we think to ourselves, it's our law, and we'll jolly well do what we like with it, thank you very much, especially if you're not going to do it for us.

And it is the fault of the ordinary cops on the front line, because they're the ones who are not standing up to their superiors and telling them all this. They're not facing up to the Senior Officers, and the District Commanders, and the Commissioner, and the Minister, and saying "no, Sir, you will hear me out."

And this is important, because if there's very much more of it, the placid people of this peaceful country will come to regard the Police as being irrelevant.

Policing in a country such as New Zealand is carried out by a very small force (the entire sworn NZ police force could be squeezed into the hall of one of our larger suburban high schools), on behalf of, and only with the willing complicity of, a people by whom they are impossibly outnumbered and hopelessly outgunned.

And it's important because, regardless of any law, on any statute book, in any country, people do have a God-given right to defend themselves; and if – Government and the Courts having already failed us – the Police in New Zealand will not exercise their discretion and their common sense with regard to that right, then there will come a point where ordinary people, their patience expired, will simply stand up and take it by force, and if the Police get in their way, they will be run over.

And if that happens, then God help us all.

Investigate, November 2008

Camp Faraway

The Police four-wheel-drive crests a rise, and I gain my first glimpse of the place I am coming to see. From the road, a tourist or casual observer might think this was a military base; but it's a moot point, because you can't see this place from the road. There's one way in, and one way out – a 21 kilometre gravel track over private land, with a guardhouse at either end.

The first thing to really strike me is the layout. A razor-wire encircled tent city, and beyond it, what looks like a chessboard of fenced sections, a tiny box inside each square. In the distance, inside yet another fence, I can make out a number of long rectangular buildings. We are deep in the Mackenzie Country, west of Twizel, and this is a Corrections Department facility known euphemistically as Camp Faraway.

Not many journalists have ever been allowed to visit here. My host for the day is the Warden, Butch McLovechild. Butch is 48, a former SAS Warrant Officer, the eldest of seven brothers and sisters born to a Glaswegian father and a Ngati Toa mother. His dad was an alcoholic, and his mum…well, today they'd call it bipolar, and maybe even give her some help. Butch was 15 and in his third year of borstal when the last of the wee kids was taken from her. When they let him out, at seventeen, he joined the Army, after the Chaplain at the Boys' Home, who was ex-Welsh Guards, pulled a few strings to get him an interview with the recruiting officer.

"The chopper will be here for you at four," says my Police escort as I step out of the ute. "I'm not driving up here again today!"

"Welcome to Club Med," says Butch with a grin, as we watch the 4WD depart. He's a short, nuggety man, chiseled and clean shaven. He ushers me into the waiting vehicle. As we drive towards the facility headquarters, I get the distinct impression that he could have been a tour guide, had that been what he wanted.

"This is the restricted section," he says, pointing out the tent city. "It's kind of a punishment area." At each corner of the razor wire encirclement, there are watchtowers, with what looks, I have to say, like gun barrels protruding from them.

"These are the Basic cells," my host informs me, as we pass the chessboard. Small areas of grass, maybe 15 metres square, each with a concrete block cube in the centre, heavy wire mesh fences about 5 metres high, topped with razor wire, and separated from the next enclosure by a six-metre gap.

We arrive at the headquarters. "This is where we have induction, the medical wing, the advanced facility, and most of the amenities," Butch tells me. "New prisoners get body-cavity searched, and spend their first week here on detox."

"What about those who don't have drug problems?" I ask.

He smiles. "Everyone does detox," he says. "There's no chemicals here. No tobacco, no coffee, no food colouring, no soft drinks, no preservatives, no sugar."

"What do they drink?" I ask.

"Water, and black tea," says Butch. "And no drugs or alcohol. Goes without saying. Their urine is tested daily. Any slip-ups, and their personal officer will be here behind bars with them."

"What about visitors?" I enquire. "Surely there's a risk they could bring something in?"

"No visitors," Butch answers. "No letters, no phone calls, in or out. Not for the first year. And no illicit cellphones, either. Transmissions are monitored and jammed."

"Isn't that illegal?" I ask him. "I mean, what about their human rights, and so forth?"

"They're not here for a bloody holiday," snaps Butch. "Or even punishment, really," he adds, perhaps a little more gently. "This is a corrections facility. They're faulty. They're here to be corrected. They're entitled to a non-contact visit from a lawyer once a month, and they can pass verbal messages to their families through them. That's all."

"It must be difficult for the addicts," I remark.

"Yeah, Cold Turkey's hard, but no-one ever died from it," says Butch. "The worst ones are the smokers. But here is all about cleaning out and clearing out, making new people out of past mistakes."

"How do you manage that?"

"Hard work, clean living, discipline." Butch is blunt and to the point. "We break down their past conditioning and impose a new regime on them. That's partly why there's no contact with people on the outside. When they arrive they get given a number, added to their surname. They can have their name back when they leave. We cut their hair and put them in overalls. They wash and shave every day. The ones who don't know how, we teach them. And we take everything off them."

"Everything?" I ask.

"No jewellery, no bone carvings, no tiki, not even wedding rings," Butch replies. "And we remove their tattoos as well. The past that made them bad is outside the gate. In here, we remake them."

We walk back out to the basic area, and inside an enclosure, Butch pushes open a cell door. The cell is an eight-foot concrete cube, with a raised slab along one wall, and a steel toilet in the corner. The slab is three feet wide and supports a thin rubber mattress. On the spare foot of concrete at the end of the mattress is a stack of three blankets. The cistern pipe above the toilet has a drinking fountain protruding from it. In the ceiling is a sprinkler, a security camera, and a 60-watt light inside a cage. I'm surprised to see a TV screen behind a sheet of Perspex, built in to the wall.

"They can have National Geographic or the Discovery Channel," says Butch. "And Concert FM or the National Programme. Or nothing."

"What's the daily routine?" I ask.

"They get woken at 0500, get dressed, and march to the parade ground," replies Butch. "Morning drill, then showers and breakfast, and ready for work by seven."

"What do they work at?"

Butch points to an area beyond the admin block. "The quarry, to begin with," he says. "They break rock for road building. By hand. Later they move into scrubcutting," he says, indicating the hill country to the west. "They walk up into the DOC country and slash broom and gorse. Their ankles are short-chained, and the guards are armed with tasers and shotguns."

"And they're paid the minimum wage, naturally," I suggest wryly.

"Yeah, right," says Butch. "It helps pay their keep though. Everything they need, we provide, and anything we don't provide, they're not allowed."

Outside the cell, I survey the grass square. "They're allowed an hour in the pen each day, between work and lockup," Butch says. "When they move into the advanced section, they have neighbours and a bit of association, but for the first year they're pretty much alone other than for work and mealtimes. It breaks the gang affiliations and stops a hierarchy from developing."

We pass the restricted section on the way back to the admin block. "The cells are a constant fifteen degrees all year round," says my guide. "If they get busted down to the tents, for misbehavior or insubordination, they get enough ankle chain to reach the long-drop, and whatever the weather throws at them. It can be forty degrees here in the summer, and minus twenty in the winter."

The cells in the advanced section are the same as the basics, except for the addition of a small barred window, and the fact that they are in a large block with adjoining cells. These cell blocks encircle a common ground recreation area.

"These guys have better jobs," says Butch. "They work in the kitchens and the laundry, and the gardens and greenhouse when they've earned enough privileges. Most of what's eaten here is grown here."

He turns on a TV. "They get extra entertainment, too; BBC World, and yesterday's talkback with the ads edited out," he adds with a grin.

"Sounds like quite the high life," I muse. "How do you deal with fights and so on, once they can get at each other?"

"They've mostly settled down once they get this far," Butch explains, contemplating the recreation ground. "And they know what the restricted section is like. But we fit them with a bracelet and an anklet just in case; we can zap a current between them with a remote trigger, if needs be."

"What about rehabilitation for the outside?" I ask. "Are there courses, or training of any sort?"

"The guys on basic work six days a week, and have life skills instruction on Sundays," replies Butch. "The ones who can't read or write, which is quite a few, we teach them, and they learn about hygiene, nutrition, social skills, manners, budgeting, stuff like that. These are guys with no self-discipline, who don't know how to operate in society. They're everyone from taggers and fines defaulters and boy racers, to drug dealers and drink-drivers and rapists and home invaders. They come in angry, and arrogant, and smart-arsed. They've got no respect, for themselves or anyone else, and they think the system can't touch them. They learn it different in here."

He opens a classroom door. "On advanced, they work five days, have workplace skills-based instruction on Saturday, and get Sunday off. They're allowed a book from the library on a Sunday."

"How long are prisoners here for?" I ask, reaching for my camera.

"No photos, please," says Butch. "Two years, plus whatever they rack up under canvas, and then they're either out, or back into the prison system, depending on their original sentence. If they ever come back, they do a full year on restricted, digging out long drop toilets."

In the afternoon, following a tour of the quarry, and after listening to some of the wailing emanating from the detox wing, I hear the sound of my helicopter approaching. It's a Rescue chopper, returning from a training exercise in the mountains. How appropriate, I think to myself, as I climb gratefully aboard.

"What's your re-offending rate like?" I ask Butch, almost as an afterthought.

He smiles, and pauses before closing the chopper door. "You tell me, once you've got this place built in real life," he says. "Personally I don't think it'd be very high at all."

As we take off, and Camp Faraway recedes into the distance, I can't help thinking he'd probably be right.

Investigate, August 2006

Chapter Fourteen

Heartland

"Ponder this: Greater London covers approximately the same land area as does Greater Auckland. However during rush hour on a working day in London, there are as many people riding the Underground as there are people in New Zealand; and on that same working day, there will have been more people in London than there are in Australia"

– Prosser, Investigate, September 2004

A Driven People

New Zealanders, as a nation, have an abiding passion for the motor vehicle. We love our cars. New Zealand has the second highest rate of private motor vehicle ownership in the world, eclipsed only by the United States.

There are a number of reasons behind our national affair with the automobile. We are a relatively small population, spread across a relatively large land mass. In the early days of the New Zealand nation, towns and cities were few and far between. The railway, as it was installed, was late to reach many localities, and, being narrow gauge, of limited use when it did.

Roads, on the other hand, were the first mark of the explorers and the settlers. The British Army were first to cut tracks through the otherwise impassable forest which was New Zealand, and the settlers who followed widened and improved them, pushing them further, in pursuit of commerce, agriculture, and exploration.

The pioneers of this country, farmers, engineers, loggers, fishers, miners, surveyors, and a host of others, relied on the roads to take them to the far-flung reaches of the new country. Early New Zealanders, both by choice and by necessity, were an innovative lot. They tinkered and experimented, and then, like now, were quick to adopt new technology. When the Horseless Carriage made its appearance, Kiwis were amongst the first to claim it as their own.

Today, we hold fast to that early infatuation, and not without good reason. We are still a thinly-spread people, and the lifestyle and traditions which have grown up here are largely based around the freedom and independence which is the motor car.

We live on one side of big cities and work on the other, or work in the towns and conurbations while making our homes on lifestyle blocks a half-hour's drive from the city sprawl.

On Saturdays, the kids all play different sports, and all in different places; rugby, soccer, hockey, netball and cricket, all played each weekend at different school venues, all miles from home, and never close together.

The walk to the shops enjoyed by the denizens of great cities overseas, is less favoured by free spirited New Zealanders; we prefer to drive in pursuit of the specials offered by competing supermarket chains, however far apart they may be, so long as they offer big car parks, handy to motorway exits.

And on long weekends, Kiwis leave home; we hook up the boat and head for the beach, throw the rifle in the ute (dogs on the back) and go bush, or tie the skis to the roofrack and race for the mountains.

Surfboards, kayaks, rolled-up hang-gliders and mountain bikes similarly adorn our automobiles, and it is a rare New Zealander indeed who has never had cause to tow a caravan, a jetski, a pair of dirt bikes; or a trailer full of firewood, green waste, potting mix, or cement and corrugated iron.

Yep, we love the motor car, and it's an affection we're not about to give up. The more, the flasher, the faster, the more chunky and gizmo-laden, the better.

But cars need roads, and roads, it would seem, are anathema to some in society who appear to not want us to have any freedom of movement at all. Despite the inescapable fact that we are a small population in a big country, there are those who desperately want to get us out of our cars, and into Public Transport instead.

I'm the first to admit to being a tree-hugger, but the attitude of some self-professed Greenies unsettles me.

The public transport model created for London, or Sydney, or New York or Hong Kong, so beloved of many of these sandal-wearing, bicycle-riding Luddites, cannot simply be superimposed on New Zealand. We are not the same kind of country. Yes, we share a language, culture, much history, and many common values; but there the similarity ends.

The reality of New Zealand is that there are just not enough people here to make large-scale public transport viable.

Ponder this: Greater London covers approximately the same land area as does Greater Auckland. However during rush hour on a working day in London, there are as many people riding the Underground as there are people in New Zealand; and on that same working day, there will have been more people in London than there are in Australia.

Does anyone with their mental faculties intact, seriously believe that we can recreate the London Underground, effectively or economically, even for Auckland, let alone for the rest of this vast and empty country?

Do we even want to?

I would guess not. New Zealanders in general show little enthusiasm for more trains and buses than we already have. Consider the options; on the one hand, the safety and independence of your own car, unrestricted by routes or timetables. On the other, an eternity of waiting – probably in the rain – on sparsely patronised platforms, smothered in graffiti and populated by glue-sniffing street kids, for buses which will be infrequent and trains which will be late, operating on timetables which will be inconvenient and to destinations which will be unhelpful.

The Greenies, and the politicians who pander to them, need to get the message; New Zealanders don't want more public transport, and we're becoming tired of having the unworkable idea of it rammed down our throats, as being somehow more morally pure than the way we travel now.

We're happy with our cars, and we want more roads on which to drive them. That is what the politicians must deliver. Make them wider, make them longer, double stack the motorways if that is what is necessary – but give us more roads.

By all means, make our cars more environmentally friendly. We don't mind. Give us petrol-electric hybrids, hydrogen and corn-oil powered cars, solar scooters if need be – but keep your buses and your monorails and your cycle lanes. We're not interested.

Try bringing a supermarket trolley full of groceries home on the bus, or hooking your boat up behind a train, and tell me you still think it's a good idea. And I'm really sure that InterCity would be only too happy for me to stow a dead deer in the luggage rack, while I ride back from the Haast with my .270 on my lap. Yeah, right.

I defy anyone to organise a weekend of soccer, ballet, karate, and the Senior Formal, without a car, and still vote monorail at the end of it.

Roads. We need more roads. Yes, we'll have to bulldoze a few houses. You have to do that for railway tracks as well. Yes, the Eastern Corridor and Transmission Gully will mean losing a few flax bushes and a pukeko or two.

That's sad, but we'll get over it.

And yes, we can afford it. If folk are silly enough to want to pay for toll roads, so be it; but they are completely unnecessary. Even without getting into the arguments of foreign borrowing versus Reserve Bank credit, the $750 + million which the Government steals from motorists each year to flush down the Consolidated Toilet, would, if it were all allocated to roading, provide us with the best infrastructure in the world, all on its own.

And another thing; I, for one, am not about to give up my 4WD just because some cardigan-clad whiner feels like bleating about trucks like mine taking up too much space, or wasting the Earth's precious resources, or being a danger to other cardigan-wearers as they ride their bicycles on the roads – which my road taxes have paid for, by the way.

OK, maybe I have a few more "excuses" than some city folk for choosing a big truck over a little sedan; I have gravel roads and muddy vineyards to contend with, I struggle to squeeze my 6'1" frame into little Japanese cars, every time I think about going back to two-wheel-drive it snows again, and I drove real trucks for long enough to be better at controlling a 4WD, than most of the bleaters and whingers are behind the wheels of their prissy little town cars.

But even if that wasn't the case, I'd probably still choose to drive a 4WD truck, just because I can. I don't poke my nose into the private business of the cardigan-wearers, and I struggle to understand how it is that they feel they have the right to tell me how to live my life.

My decision on what I drive has no more impact on anyone else, than does their decision to smoke, or drink, or eat particular foods, or inoculate their children, or not inoculate their children, or what colour they choose to paint their kitchen.

Middle New Zealand has a message for the Greenies, the Luddites, the Politicians and the Busybodies, and it is this: Keep your buses. We don't want them. Give us more roads. We need them. Pay for them out of the fuel taxes which you're already fleecing us for. And while you're at it, butt out of what we choose to drive on them.

New Zealanders are a driven people, and we've had enough of listening to the nagging from the back seat. We'll take the wheel from here. Those who don't like it are more than welcome to get out and walk. They're mostly hitchhikers anyway.

Investigate, September 2004

Power to the People

Another winter has come – and not yet gone – bringing with it very little rain, low lake levels, and for yet another year, the threat of power cuts.

How can this be?

How is it that New Zealand, ostensibly part of the developed world, can mismanage its affairs so badly that people are faced with having to do without one of the most basic of the accepted and expected utilities of modern life – electricity?

What are our exporters supposed to tell their overseas distributors when goods don't arrive; what are the moteliers supposed to say to foreign tourists when the shower is cold? Are either of these disappointed customers going to offer repeat business? What will they tell their friends about New Zealand?

Every year we have a winter. It gets cold. People use more power to stay warm. This is not a difficult concept to follow.

Every year we have more people. New New Zealanders are born, new immigrants arrive, expats come home. Every year the population of New Zealand grows by around 50,000. Every year that goes by, the number of foreign tourists increases. So there are more people using electricity. This is not a difficult concept to follow either.

Every year we have more industry, more shops, more offices, more factories. They use electricity. Every year, with the relentless march of technology, we have more devices available to us to make living easier, faster, more comfortable. They use electricity.

Every year there are more of us, using more power, on more power-consuming things. And every winter it gets cold.

And every year that goes by, without fail, we don't build more power stations. Hmm.

So we arrive at a point where we have too much demand on our electricity resource, and not enough generating capacity to supply it. What to do? Oh me oh my, let's put it to the committee.

The Labour Government's approach is to pray for rain.

Seriously.

Helen Clark's administration, devoid of creativity or leadership ability, has no other strategy, plan, or even the glimmerings of an idea, for tackling the current and immediately projected shortfall in electricity generating capacity in New Zealand.

The cynic in me could perhaps be forgiven for believing that Labour is well aware that the critical mass in power shortfall will occur in about three years, by which time it won't be their problem. Their approach appears to be to do nothing now, so that they can crow from the opposition benches at whoever inherits the mess they leave.

How very intelligent and responsible – not.

Criticism of the inaction of inept Governments, regardless of how well deserved it may be, does not however solve the problem.

There are several immediate options available to the nation for increasing generating capacity. Most of them involve the further exploitation of South Island rivers.

The rape of the Waitaki, one of the last great wild braided rivers, is one such option, and it looks increasingly likely that the proposed scheme will go ahead. A dam at Tuapeka Mouth on the lower Clutha, flooding the town of Beaumont, is another. Such proposals are not without complications themselves however.

The Waitaki scheme will provide only a stopgap increase in electricity supply sufficient for about four years. It is likely that the scheme will take longer than that to build. Beaumont has been the focus of a heated and ongoing fight by locals who would, understandably, prefer their town to remain above water, rather than being inundated to provide electricity to meet the growing demands of what is perceived as an ungrateful big city "overseas in the North Island".

And it is that 'big city' where most of the projected increase in demand is centred. There are very practical reasons for not building more hydro stations in the South Island to supply electricity to Auckland. Transmission losses, over the national grid, and through the Cook Strait cables, mean that only a fraction of the power generated ever makes it that far. Big power consumers need to be supplied from close by.

There are other alternatives which could, should, and will be explored; wind farms and solar power are both capable of making a serious contribution to the nation's energy needs, as are micro-hydro schemes, wave power, and biomass conversion. Wind turbine and solar panel technologies have made great strides in recent years, but both have a way to go before reaching peak efficiency; and while a Government decree could see a photovoltaic panel, a direct solar water heater, and a windmill on the roof of every house within a few short years, it is likely that the lack of either imagination, or an appreciation of urgency, on the part of the Government, coupled with the steady growth of population and industry, will mean that critical mass arrives before any such sustainable solution is ready to meet it.

The unavoidable conclusion we must face up to is that more thermal stations are needed. These must be built, and commissioned, in the next two to three years, near to the big centres of growing demand; Auckland, and to a lesser extent, Christchurch.

Supplying the rapid growth of Christchurch is a less urgent problem because ample hydro-electric generating capacity exists nearby, and it makes more sense to use it locally than it does to ship it north and lose most of it on the way.

Auckland is a more pressing problem. The solution is simple enough, but it poses a difficult choice for the residents of that city, and for self-proclaimed environmentalists throughout the entire country.

Thermal power stations are quick, cheap, and easy to build, and they make a lot of electricity.

However, they require fuel to run on, and lots of it; either fossil fuels or The Dreaded Alternative. Gas, which is clean but in uncertain supply, or coal, which is plentiful – really, seriously plentiful – but not very clean, are the fossil fuels of choice.

The Dreaded Alternative is plentiful enough, and even relatively cheap, but its cleanliness – or potential uncleanliness – send shivers up the spines of a people who like to consider ourselves environmentally sensitive and aware.

It is somewhat strange, then, that we should have no qualms about flooding huge tracts of South Island wilderness and submerging entire towns, as an alternative to burning a bit of coal. Oh, the conundrum. What's it to be? Do we burn coal and make smoke? Do we flood towns and wilderlands, destroying rivers in the process? Do we go without electricity?

Do we wring our hands, close our eyes, and let the last southern river schemes go ahead, knowing it will only allow a few years grace? Then what?

What will happen in three years, in another dry autumn? Will southern militants blow up the Cook Strait cable as they have threatened, the first time Nelson or Greymouth or Dunedin has power cuts and Auckland doesn't?

Everyone knows that power goes south under the Cook Strait as well as north; but this is for reasons of network maintenance, not because of a shortfall in generating capacity relative to demand in the south.

If push came to shove, we could always phone up the US Navy and have them come park a nuclear powered warship in the Waitemata, for a few months over winter. Plugged into the grid, such a vessel could easily power most of the North Island – the average nuclear aircraft carrier, cruiser, or submarine is capable of pumping enough juice to supply a city of two million people. But, as a nation, we have a problem with this solution too, it would seem. We don't like the idea of nuclear fission, and a good many of New Zealand's ostensibly green-motivated power consumers, when scratched, don't appear to like the Americans very much either. Quite why this should be escapes this writer; America speaks English, spends dollars, drinks cold beer, goes to the football and celebrates Christmas. They are not an alien people. Oh, and they did just happen to save us the trouble of giving up our country and learning to speak Japanese too, out of nothing other than the goodness of their individual and national hearts.

History may yet see our petulant attitude towards fossil fuels be the undoing of our anti-nuclear, anti-American sentiments. Our national inaction may see such a reality forced upon us.

Since Government seems incapable of providing a solution, here is one suggestion.

New Zealand needs to invest, immediately and meaningfully, in the research, development, and installation, of as much wind, solar, micro-hydro, and other clean renewable sources of electricity as possible. We must also bite the bullet and build a few more coal fired power stations – now, not in three years time.

Failure to acknowledge the problem facing us, and tackle it in a mature fashion, could, in a few short years, see New Zealand come face to face with a whole new meaning for the term "Nuclear Winter".

Investigate, October 2003

Water of Life

My bore pump died the other week. Urban dwellers may not appreciate the significance of this; but for those of us who live in the boonies, the simple matter of water coming out of the taps without a second thought, isn't something which can be taken for granted. Don't get me wrong, I live in the country by choice, and I embrace the relative privations thereof. The very fact that I have a source of pure, cold, crystal clear water, just ten feet from my back door, is more than enough compensation for not being able to walk to the shops. And the fact that it's unfiltered, un-fluoridated, un-chlorinated, and all mine, to my way of thinking is far better than paying a thousand bucks extra a year in rates, for the privilege of living in town, where the water is metered, treated, and tastes like every one of the seven sets of kidneys through which it has passed, on the way back to the council bore field or reservoir.

All of which is well and good, until the pump dies. Fortunately, I also have a well (into which the bore pump delivers) capable of holding a week or so's worth of water, from which the house supply feeds, through a separate pressure system with a second pump. (Townies may also not appreciate that we hicks from the sticks can discuss our water supplies in infinite detail, for hours on end; it's a bit like the fascination city folk have with rubbish collections or parking problems or gridlock, all of which is Greek to us.)

The pump company guys did a sterling job, I give them real credit for that. They came out straight after the weekend, looked at the old pump, marvelled that such a museum piece could still have been operating, quoted some figures from NASA as to how much it would cost to repair, and went away again. Over the next few days, in between helping out a couple of my neighbours who happened to be in direr straits, they brought in a crane to remove the old piston pump and case pipe, blew out the bore casing with compressed air, and dropped a submersible loan pump down the hole so we could refill the well.

The sludge they blew out from forty feet down probably had enough gold dust in it to pay for a new pump; I may yet dig up, sieve, and pan the lawn where it landed. After all, the Earnscleugh does sit on an as-yet-un-mined goldfield, and the old tailings, from the 1800s, are only a few kilometres away.

The upshot is that we now have a brand-spanking new submersible pump, and a flow test which tells us that there is a whole lot more water in our bore than the old piston pump was ever capable of extracting. So the silver lining is that my good lady wife can have a proper garden this year, and a real lawn as well, even in the summer when it's 40 degrees and the town is on water rationing.

The one thing I'm really not looking forward to is the bill....but the whole process did get me to thinking.

We do tend to use water with little in the way of afterthought, even those of us who have pumps and wells lurking at the backs of our minds; like air, money, and sex, water only becomes important when we're not getting any.

Farmers are probably the exception to this rule, their very lifestyle and livelihood being dependent on irrigation and stock water, their daily routine dedicated to ensuring that the supply continues.

In a previous life, I worked for a small company building drum pumps. They were based on an adaptation of a design created by a classic Kiwi inventor; an eccentric expat Brit, former serviceman, Post Office technician, and largely self-taught engineer, his pumps were intended to provide low-cost, low maintenance, well water for remote African villages. They defied many of the known laws of hydrodynamics, but they worked anyway. His test tower, simulating a deep well installation, was built into a treehouse, atop a large oak tree overhanging a high bank on his hillside section in Thames. It had a plastic 44-gallon drum at the bottom, connected via a garden hose to a bucket at the top, and ran off an old washing machine motor. The data and results produced by this Heath Robinson contraption and its unorthodox creator (Jones the Pump, as he was known locally) outscored many obtained by some of the world's leading pump testing facilities, from whom he received much correspondence, and the occasional incredulous visit.

But I digress. The point is that most of the world does not share our abundance of clean fresh water. While we launder, bathe, flush, irrigate our crops and frolic in our swimming pools, with little regard to the continuity of supply of the liquid gold which allows this, all too many of our fellow humans must travel long distances, carry water pots on their heads, make do with muddy tepid water holes, or haul buckets by hand from rusty, aging wells – unless they happen to be amongst the lucky few to have been supplied with a shiny new white PVC bore lifter, crafted by a grey-haired, likeable, odd-ball pioneer from far away New Zealand.

Plentiful clean water, probably more than any other advantage, has facilitated the development of our affluent and progressive Western societies. Livestock, crops, food production, industry, hygiene; all depend on fresh water, and nowadays, lots of it.

And therein lies the danger. We have something which is of value, and which others most certainly want. The circling vultures are twofold. The world's supply of fresh water is limited, and demands upon it are growing all the time. Earth's human population has doubled these past thirty years, from around three billion to more than six billion. Livestock numbers have increased exponentially, at the same time that forest lands have been cleared to make way both for grazing and for human habitation – forests which used to provide both a transpiration source, and a filter, for the very fresh water upon which those same people and their animals depend. New industries, irrigation, and growing domestic demand, all impact on what is becoming a critically short and threatened resource. Within our lifetimes, it is entirely possible that human conflict may arise from the need to secure access to this most vital of commodities, just as past wars have raged over everything from spices and opium, to land, minerals, and that other liquid gold, oil. Once unorthodox solutions to the global fresh water crisis have found new validity in recent times; twenty-five years ago at least, by this writer's recollection, more than one wealthy Arab state enquired about purchasing shiploads of fresh water from this country. British water companies have suggested towing icebergs south from the Arctic, and melting them to provide drinking water for the cities of Western Europe. It is those very water companies who constitute the second, more insidious, and perhaps most dangerous of the two vultures.

As with oil, gas, electricity, telecommunications, and a raft of other tangibles, the Corporate world has recognised the need and demand for water, and more importantly, the profit to be made from it. More and more, this essential of life, this basic human right, is falling under the ownership and control of a small number of ever-growing trans-national companies. Rates paid for metered water in the cities and towns of the developed world are finding their way back, not to the communities and local authorities who required and built the water reticulation infrastructures, but into the coffers of the water companies to whom the maintenance and operation of such networks is contracted.

If ever there was a perfect example of the pure evil of profit before people, of inhuman global corporate greed, allowed by the ineptitude, incompetence, corruption, and blind adherence to flawed dogma of Governments, it may be found in the privatisation of water.

Only this week as I write, a retired Texas oil baron has been in the news, projecting to earn, over the next thirty years, at least a billion dollars from his $75 million investment in US water companies. All credit to this man, whose name I have never heard before and don't pretend to remember, for turning a good old-fashioned capitalist profit; what rankles is the unspoken reality that along with his water companies and contracts, he has purchased the right to shut off the supply of water – life itself – to those who don't, or can't manage, to pay the fees.

In New Zealand, we have an ironclad promise from Government (yeah, right) ensuring that ownership of water resources – if not the distribution of same – will remain forever vested in the public. Call me cynical if you will, but I have no doubt whatsoever that some future regime will seek to sell off this lifeblood of the nation just as they have done with all but the knives and forks of the family silver; I am equally sure that they will try to find a way to tax me on the stuff I pump up from under my back lawn.

A wise man once said, many years ago, that there would come a time when a bottle of water would cost more than a bottle of wine. As is common with many visionaries, everyone thought he was mad, and predictably, history now appears to be lining up to prove him right. By that early reckoning, a barrel of water is also well on the way to becoming more expensive than a barrel of oil, and perhaps a great deal harder to obtain. A litre of bottled water will already cost you twice as much as a litre of petrol, with both, somewhat ironically, purchased from the same service station.

So what can we do about it? As always, the answer lies at the ballot box. We must elect Governments who will provide for the adequate defence of our nation, so that others will not simply come and take our water; Governments who will enact laws to protect our basic human needs, and our rights to the essentials of life, against the machinations of corporate avarice.

And we must be ever vigilant, because given half a chance, they'll be charging us for fresh air and sunshine as well. In the meantime, so long as my new pump keeps running, I'll be alright – but I do worry about everyone else.

Investigate, September 2006

Per Ardua ad Astra

To reach for the skies, to strive for the heavens, by effort to achieve the great heights; the Latin motto of the Royal Air Force, and the Royal New Zealand Air Force alike, has many translations. Literally taken it means "through adversity to the stars", which to this writer's mind makes it as fine as any a candidate for a new motto for the City of Christchurch. We will rebuild. Our City will rise again, like a Phoenix from the dust and the ashes, brighter, bolder, stronger. This Otago boy has observed a steely resolve at the core of the Cantabrian character these past couple of years, and we will remake the Garden City with steel in its heart, where once there was brick and mortar. San Francisco came back, Napier came back, Christchurch will come back. Of that there is no question.

I was at work when the quake hit. I had just left the building, a modern two-storey concrete tilt-slab in Riccarton, and sat in my truck, when the shaking started. The next 15 seconds comprised the most violent earthquake your scribe has ever experienced. Before the cellphone networks overloaded, I managed to ascertain that my own home and family north of Rangiora were safe and well. I wish that the same could be said for all my fellow citizens. This time, however, it was not to be.

I have no grounds to complain. There are a few more cracks where we didn't have them before, a slump in the lounge floor, and I've had to secure the tank stand – which is now almost at the point of no return – with cargo strops tied back to a couple of warratahs hastily driven in just over the fence in the neighbour's top paddock. So it's another claim to the EQC, and a few more sleepless nights, though with a fifteen-month-old baby I wasn't sleeping much anyway. But no-one near or dear to me was killed or injured, my house is intact, and we have power and water and a functioning toilet.

It is heartbreaking to view the destruction wreaked on the grand icons of this most fair of cities. The streets are filled with rubble and silt, the once elegant visages of the buildings of yesteryear torn away, leaving the homes and offices of a brutalized population gaping and open to the elements. There is a raw, shocked air to the city; a sense of violation as much as of loss. Cars lie smashed where the ruins fell on them, and amongst it all, the bodies of many of the fallen are still entombed within the detritus of this shattered metropolis. There is anger. This genteel city, this gentle island, this passive nation, did not deserve this brutal and unprovoked assault. It stings. I am incensed.

And so we will rebuild. The calm, graceful authority of Canterbury's capital came not from the fine architecture and wide leafy streets crafted by the Province's founders, but from the drive, confidence, and sheer grit of her people.

The familiar façade of Christchurch will rise again, granite and limestone, tall spires, sweeping arches, and soaring columns; this time, however, bound and braced and rooted with steel. The ship will be made stronger to weather the storm which we hope and pray will never come again.

Muggins was better prepared for this quake than for the last one, thanks largely to the warning shot and wake-up call which the last one embodied. We have a bottled water supply in several places, first aid kits in the house and vehicles, emergency food and baby supplies packed for a rapid departure if necessary, torches and batteries, a wee transistor radio. Probably still not quite everything we need, but getting there.

The nation, on the other hand, was no better prepared, and it is largely down to luck that the response was as swift and effective as it has been. We were paradoxically lucky that the clean-up from the September quake was already underway, because that meant the city was already full of diggers to move rubble and search for survivors. We were lucky that a convention of foreign doctors and another convention of foreign earthquake engineers were also in town, both courtesy of the same quake. We were lucky that a multi-national military exercise was underway in the South Island at the time, that there were 1,000 more soldiers than normal at Burnham Camp, that the *HMNZS Canterbury* was in port at Lyttleton, and that the harbour was flat calm, because the *Canterbury* can't load or unload in any other conditions (which is a story in itself, and one about which I have griped before).

We were lucky that the Singaporeans had two C-130 Hercules here along with their troops for the aforementioned exercise, and that the Australians were happy to lend us another two, because our one functioning aircraft would have struggled to keep up with the demand all on its own. And we were lucky that the Aussies were also willing and able to lend us 300 Police Officers, because despite years of focus on traffic revenue collection, we still, somehow, inexplicably, do not have enough cops in this country.

We are lucky indeed that thousands of students were willing and able to volunteer their services for the massive clean-up effort. This writer for one does not believe that the way to repay their selfless civic-minded generosity, is by taking away their interest-free loans.

We are truly fortunate that we have good friends around the world, that so many nations were so quick to send USAR teams and other rescue specialists. I have no quibble with that. We'd be amongst the first to do the same for them, and in all likelihood, sometime in the not-too-distant future, we probably will. But when New Zealand has to go begging and borrowing for basic things like policemen and aeroplanes and portaloos, then people, we have a problem with priorities.

We were, and are, ill-prepared at best, and we need to do better, and quickly; because we still haven't had the Big One, and the only certainty about that, is that every earthquake to hit this country which isn't the Big One, brings the Big One one quake closer.

It could strike anywhere, anytime. Wellington remains the favourite target, but it could be Christchurch again. Or the Hawke's Bay. Or Tauranga, or Queenstown, or in fact anywhere, maybe even Auckland. The Darfield quake was on a previously unknown fault line; the truth is that we simply don't know exactly what lurks beneath these Shaky Isles.

We cannot stop the earth from moving, but we can, as a nation, prepare ourselves for the aftermath. For this writer's money, the time has come for New Zealand to bring back Compulsory Military Training, and to ready and equip our population for all and any of the worst of possible eventualities. A couple of hundred thousand fit young citizens, trained and equipped, with vehicles and helicopters and generators and camp toilets, might just make all the difference. I'm tired of listening to Government bean-counters lying to us that there isn't enough money for Defence. There's always enough for pay rises for politicians, and new Ministerial limos, and bailing out dodgy finance companies. The defence of the nation, against threats both natural and man-made, has to be more important than any of those. We need to do this and we must, and now, because it is the only thing which makes military, economic, and social sense, for a nation with a small population such as ours.

We can rise through this adversity to reach the stars – but only if we work together, and only if we are prepared. And next time, we might not be quite so lucky.

Investigate, April 2011

Go Forth and Multiply

"There is no finer investment for any community," Winston Churchill once said, "than putting milk into babies."

The Great Man was right, of course, in more ways than we may appreciate in New Zealand today. The Empire was built on the back of the manpower available to the Royal Navy, at the time when Britannia ruled the waves. The Colonies themselves, this country included, grew from the wellspring of surplus life which overflowed from the burgeoning population of the British Isles. From Imperial

Rome to the United States of America, from the Ottoman Empire to the Polynesian migrations of the Pacific, from the westward spread of the Celts to the rise of China, every great surge of human expansion and exploration has stemmed from the generations which rise as a result of booms in birth rates, these being themselves in response to access to better food sources, more resources, land, and industry, which in turn allow for increased birth rates. It is a self-replenishing cycle which both repeats and feeds on itself.

Families need new babies in order that they may continue to live, grow, and flourish. So too do societies, nations, and civilisations. In fact they need new babies not only to go forward, but indeed to stay in one place; because in human population terms, it isn't possible to merely tread water without actually going backwards.

Western civilisation today is in serious danger of doing just that. The hedonistic materialism of our modern lifestyles, combined with – and partly to blame for – our falling birth rate, means that the populations of the developed world are quite simply not replacing themselves. Many Western countries are in a state of terminal decline, and within two generations, some will be past the point of no return.

Simple mathematics means that even to maintain stability, any natural population of a species – *homo sapiens* being no exception – must maintain a birth rate of more than two live offspring per female, just to ensure that, allowing for natural attrition (and the fact that males are not able to carry young), the generation to follow it is able to continue.

Japan and Russia are already on the slippery slope towards depopulation, and many of the nations of Europe are statistically growing only because the birth rates amongst their small populations of ethnically non-indigenous migrants are exponentially greater than those of their host peoples. France and Spain, two of the old colonial powerhouses of Europe, are growing solely because of immigration from their old African and South American colonies, and Portugal and the Netherlands are barely breaking even. Italy, Germany, Sweden, as well as many of the nations of the old eastern bloc, are in a similar position.

New Zealand is actually – if only just – keeping the population decline wolf from the door, with a live birth rate of 2.13 children per woman; considerably higher than that of the Australians, who are nearing dire straits at less than 1.90 and are offering cash payments to parents who opt to have additional children. Canada is already lost, trailing at around 1.5, and the United States is only managing to keep pace with good old New Zealand thanks to the fecundity of her migrants – legal and not – from South and Central America. Curiously, Godzone's new flower of youth is not, as one might expect, primarily the product of our seemingly unstoppable flood of immigrants and supposed refugees, or the unwed mothers of the baby-factory ghettos of South Auckland; no, it's Otago and Southland who are leading the charge, and on top of that, most of the new mothers are married or living in happy stability with the fathers of their children. Many of them are also people who have chosen, for various reasons, to wait until they are late in their thirties and even into their forties before having families. There may indeed be hope for the future yet.

Why is any of this important? Because not only are the populations of the world's wealthier and longer-established nations shrinking or slowing, they are aging as well, and this should be sounding alarm bells for us. Europe and Japan are canaries in the mineshaft for nations such as New Zealand. Advances in medical treatment mean that people are living longer even as they choose to have fewer children. In the not-too-distant future, unless we do something about it now, we will be faced with the reality that there are not enough young and working people to both provide, and care for, what is going to be an unprecedentedly large older generation. When the retirees outnumber the workers, we are all in trouble.

The blunt truth is that all societies need new young folk, and if we're not breeding enough of them ourselves, we will have to import them from somewhere else; and the elephant in the room is that those people from somewhere else may not share our values and perceptions any more than they share our culture or history. When the United States is mostly Mexican, it will still be the United States, but it won't be the US that we know now. When France, and Germany, and even Britain, have Muslim majorities – and in France's case that could be as soon as 2050 – will they still be the nations we have grown up with, in anything but name? The prospect of Sharia Law being dispensed from the Palaise Bourbon, the Bundestag, or the Halls of Westminster, would suggest not.

We are a nation descended from migrants, and we will always need a measure of immigration; not, in this writer's view, to the point that we lose the very beauty and appeal of what is our empty land, or as an excuse for failing to train and employ our own people, but for the skills and expertise that we do not possess ourselves, and for those who truly share our vision and character. Your favourite commentator, as I have mentioned before, is the son of migrants. My fiancée is originally English and our baby daughter is a dual national; and that path, I make no apology for asserting, is the best way for this country to avert our looming population decline – along, of course, with taking the measures necessary to encourage expats to return home. A million New Zealand-born citizens now live overseas, which is a sad indictment on the failure of successive Governments to build the kind of nation and economy where their talents can secure fair reward, and where the entire country can reap the benefits of their input. It is a travesty because every home-grown New Zealander we lose overseas has to be replaced, all too often by second-rate cast-offs from the third world, or from nations who struggle to speak our language, let alone appreciate and adopt our values. Kiwis crossing the Tasman bolt straight into Australian society without even needing a conversion kit, and when they go, they take their education, their drive, and their culture with them. These are qualities and investments which are irreplaceable.

In generations past, when wars were frequent and infant mortality was high, large families were common. Last century, and even after the Second World War, having four or six kids was not unusual. Through the sixties and seventies the bar was lowered, to three, and then to the rather odd modern standard of 2.4.

Once upon a time, we had things like Family Benefits in this country, and we did put milk into our babies, dished out free at school every day. What happened?

I say this, to my generation and to the one immediately behind me; if you haven't done so already, get shackled, get settled, and then get down and breed. New Zealand needs your babies more than ever before.

Investigate, June 2011

Chapter Fifteen

One People, One Country

"The Swiss have used referenda for better than 150 years without the sky falling in, and their peaceful and affluent democracy is testament to the effectiveness of having the People keep a direct rein on the politicians"
— Prosser, Investigate, December 2008

Who wears the Crown?

On the 6th of February 1840 an historic document was signed, between a group of Chiefs of certain of the Maori tribes of the northern island of a land which some of them knew as Aotearoa, and the representative of the Queen of England – the British Crown.

This document, the Treaty of Waitangi, brought together two peoples as one, and laid the foundation for the new British colony which would, in the fullness of time, become the independent nation of New Zealand.

In the 163 years since that historic signing, much has happened and a great deal has changed in this fledgling nation beneath the Southern Cross. Over the last seven or eight generations the two peoples truly have become one, and the new nation has been forged from their amalgamation, vision, and endeavour.

Today, we have pride in our identity as New Zealanders; we no longer regard ourselves as being British, or colonials. Those great many New Zealanders with Maori as part of their ancestral makeup take pride in this also, and for many, it is an intertwined pride, parallel with, and inseparable from, the sense of pride and identity they feel as Kiwis.

Yet divisions still exist within our young society; New Zealand has a way to go before it becomes the racially homogenous and harmonious paradise envisioned by some a century and a half ago.

For some, being Maori can be a cause for enmity as much as pride. For others, being white, or Pakeha, or European, can mean the same. Even the defining terms, Maori and non-Maori – and its various alternatives – serve to illustrate the discomfort which many New Zealanders feel with respect to the obvious separation that still exists between the descendants of the original Treaty signatories.

The greatest difficulty facing New Zealand today in dealing with the problems that still surround the issues of race and the Treaty, is that neither of the original peoples who signed it exist anymore.

Like it or not, we have become a blended nation. Full-blooded Maoridom is gone, consigned forever to the pages of history. And whether we realise it or not, the peoples of the British Crown, insofar as the modern New Zealand is concerned, are gone too. Britain still exists, to be sure, but those British migrants who settle here today do not represent the Crown of 160 years ago. That time and that society, like the environment and the way of life which existed with it, are likewise now eternally lost in the unrecoverable past.

Identifying with one's Maori lineage is a matter of choice for those who have it, as it is their choice to identify with any other part of their makeup. The same applies to those with an ancestry from England, Wales, Scotland, Ireland, Yugoslavia, the Netherlands, and a hundred and one other countries whose people came to settle here. Many New Zealanders enjoy the option of identifying with many such lineages.

Identifying with one's Maori lineage is a simple process. Either a person has it or they do not, and if they do, this is usually, though by no means always, apparent from their appearance. The language is official, and New Zealand society incorporates and displays a great deal in the way of Maoritanga. There is ample scope for the expression of identity within the modern evolution of this living culture.

Identifying with the Crown is by no means as straightforward. Very few New Zealanders, recent British migrants included, would class themselves as being representative of a colonial monarchy from a long time ago in a galaxy far, far away. We take pride in our past, and our fondness for Britain and for the Crown is enduring. But for many New Zealanders it is a very long time indeed since the perception of being British was replaced with a desire to identify proudly as New Zealanders first, and anything else second.

Many of today's Kiwis never had a connection with the British Crown, their families having migrated here from continental Europe, Asia, and lately, the Americas and even African countries. Many others, notably the Scots and the Irish, and to a slightly lesser extent the Welsh, historically felt little love or loyalty towards what was generally perceived as an "English" Crown.

Even those of English descent, who still comprise by far the majority of this country's present population, do not regard their loyalty to the Queen as taking precedence over their sense of national identity, nor do they see themselves as her representatives.

And yet a great many of today's "non-Maori" New Zealanders have come to feel that representation of the Crown has been thrust upon them, though this has not been sought or approved, nor is it in many cases able to be qualified let alone quantified.

A concerted campaign of social engineering on the part of Government in recent years has hijacked the original intention of the Treaty, and redefined it in terms which are at odds with those intended by the signatories.[7]

Where the Treaty intended to make all the Peoples of New Zealand one people, so the social engineers of the New Left have remade them as "partners." The separateness and division which the Treaty sought to dissolve have been restored, enshrined in law and convention, and the harmonious and homogenous nation so keenly desired 163 years ago has been denied by an alternative vision, a New Zealand of legislated polarisation, and of increasing acrimony and bitterness.

How is "The Crown" defined today, and who is supposed to represent it? Arguably, the "Crown" is the New Zealand Government, but we are all, Maori and non-Maori alike, represented by that

---

7 For an accurate 1860 reportage of why Maori chiefs really signed the Treaty, see "Voices From The Past", Investigate, August 2004, http://www.thebriefingroom.com/archives/2007/07/voices_from_the.html

Government; we all pay its taxes, and we are all subject to its laws.

If "Maori" and "The Crown" are still to be separate, then how is it to be decided, and by whom, precisely who is who?

Are those people with Maori ancestry to be regarded as the tangata whenua, and those without it, The Crown?

What of those New Zealanders whose ancestry includes both Maori and European? Are they to be classed as one or the other, and denied some part of their birthright? What of the Dutch, the Yugoslavians, the Chinese? Are they automatically deemed "Crown", by virtue of being non-Maori? Where does that leave those New Zealanders whose lineage includes Dutch, Yugoslavian, or Chinese – as well as Maori?

In a perfect world, for clarification, we could seek the opinions of those New Zealanders whose ancestry is pure Maori; but alas, and alas for the agenda of the brainwashers, manipulators, apologists and control freaks of the left, there is no longer any such thing.

We are who we are, and we are one people, irrespective of how dearly some in Government would prefer us to be two.

The continued push for division is unmandated, unwarranted, undesirable, unnecessary, unsustainable, and ridiculous. New Zealanders did not fight long and hard to see apartheid torn down in another country not so far from here, only to have it foisted on us in another guise.

The current debate over ownership of the seabed and foreshore highlights this division. Am I to be denied access to the beaches because I do not have Maori ancestry? Are those with Maori ancestry to leave a portion of themselves – the non Maori bit – at home they go to the beach?

The provision for the Queen's Chain was intended to ensure access to the coastline for all New Zealanders. Not just British; not just Maori; not just the wealthy, the landed, the influential. It was for all.

We have all enjoyed the rights and freedoms of the Common Law of Britain, and we all enjoy the privileges and advantages this country has to offer. We all follow the rugby, we all perform the haka, we all celebrate Christmas, and we all enjoy a barbeque as much as a hangi. We have all contributed to what this country has become, and we are all New Zealanders in it.

I am not the Crown, any more than my neighbour down the road is some kind of noble savage suffering under colonial oppression. We are not partners under some misrepresented and long irrelevant treaty; we are citizens both, free and equal.

The Treaty of Waitangi, as it was created, cannot be said to exist today any more than can the two now-disappeared peoples who signed it.

It is time that the Treaty was given the pride of place it deserves in our National Museum; time that the stranglehold of its ever-lengthening and ever mutating tentacles was removed from the law and fabric of New Zealand society.

It is time that it was replaced by a written Constitution, to enshrine our rights and freedoms, and to accomplish for all the peoples of New Zealand that which the Treaty intended; to make us One.

Investigate, September 2003

Independence Day

Another Waitangi Day has come and gone, and with it, once again, has come protest, controversy, and debate as to its relevance, and indeed, its appropriateness as New Zealand's National Day. Now that the hooplah has died down for another year, perhaps it is time to reflect on that appropriateness.

Some people claim that the Treaty of Waitangi is New Zealand's founding document, that it serves as our de facto Constitution, or, in the modern interpretation, that it constitutes a partnership between Maori and the Crown.

Others contend that the Treaty is divisive, imprecisely translated, too narrow in its purpose and intent, and too simplistic to serve as the constitutional basis for a modern nation. Debate continues over discrepancies between not only the English and Maori versions of the text, but between the various translations from one form to the other, and indeed back again. In addition, there continue to be doubts as to whether the English version of the Treaty as it was signed on the day was, in fact, true to the final draft as intended by Governor Hobson and translated by the Reverend Henry Williams and his son Edward; it may have been altered, unbeknown to Hobson, by last-minute editing on the part of James Busby. The unaltered version, now known as the Littlewood Treaty, which was lost for many years and is still discredited by some Treaty historians, may in fact be the true and correct English text of Te Tiriti.[8]

Whatever history may finally record with regard to these questions, it is certain that, in recent years, Waitangi has come to symbolise protest, conflict, and separation, more so than harmony, unity, or any sense of partnership. The Treaty itself is perhaps somewhat contentious as the choice of a starting point for the birth of New Zealand. It was not accepted by a significant number of Maori tribes, never ratified by the British Government, and had no legal recognition in New Zealand until 1975, the year after February 6th was first made a national public holiday.

October 6th could serve New Zealand as Discovery Day, as it was on this date in 1769 that Nicholas Young first sighted the coastline near the southern end of Poverty Bay, from the masthead of the *Endeavour*. Still further back in time, and perhaps of even greater significance, on December 13th 1642, Abel Tasman first laid eyes on "a great land, uplifted high" from the deck of the *Heemskerck*, and New Zealand's modern history began.

There are other days on the calendar which mark milestones in this country's history, of perhaps greater significance, and in the south, certainly of greater relevance than the Treaty of Waitangi, which, contrary to popular presumption, never applied to the South Island, and nor did Lieutenant-Governor William Hobson, or his superior, Governor George Gipps of New South Wales, intend that it should.

In explaining the ramifications of the Treaty to the assembled Chiefs at Waitangi on February 5th 1840, the day before the signing, Hobson stated that acceptance of its terms "must be deemed a full and clear recognition of the sovereign-rights of Her Majesty over the northern parts of this land ...." This explains why he signed the treaty as "Consul and Lieutenant Governor" since the cession concerned the northern territory only. (http://www.teara.govt.nz/1966/W/WaitangiTreatyOf/Preliminaries/en).

---

8 See *Investigate*, January 2004, http://www.investigatemagazine.com/jan4treaty.htm

The northern part of New Zealand was already an independent country, recognised by the British, by virtue of the Declaration of Independence of the Confederation of United Tribes, signed on October 28th, 1835, and which the Treaty over-rode. This northern part comprised Northland, the greater Auckland area, and the Hauraki district, and the declaration was recognised by the British Resident, James Busby, who both encouraged its creation, and helped to draft it.

While it can be argued that Busby, as a Consul with no real power, was acting outside his authority in recognising the Declaration of Independence, some thirteen Northern Chiefs had petitioned King William IV for protection – from the French, the Americans, the growing lawlessness of existing British settlers, and indeed each other – as far back as 1831, and the Declaration was formally acknowledged by the Crown in 1836.

The Treaty of Waitangi did not establish grounds for British authority over New Zealand, as this had already been proclaimed in January 1840 – on the 19th, by Gipps in Sydney, and on the 30th, by Hobson himself at Kororareka. Rather, it allowed for peaceful government, the orderly transfer of lands, and the protection of everyone's rights and assets. The January proclamations were a deliberate measure to impose British authority on the settlers of the New Zealand Company at Port Nicholson, now Wellington, who were attempting to set up an independent administration, and a pseudo-British colony outside the rule of the British Crown. Although there was little enthusiasm within the British Government generally, and the Colonial Office in particular, for the acquisition of yet another colonial territory, New Zealand was regarded as being at least a British possession, and a protectorate of sorts.

After the signing at Waitangi, copies of the Treaty were sent throughout the North Island, finding some Chiefs who would sign it and some who would not; but the reality was that British rule would be implemented, by force if necessary, irrespective of regional or tribal acceptance of the Treaty. This had been the intention of the British since December 1837, when they had decided, albeit reluctantly, to intervene in New Zealand to ensure that colonisation was regulated.

Te Arawa and Ngati Tuwharetoa refused to sign the Treaty. To this day, Tuhoe do not recognise its validity. By no means all the Chiefs of the Waikato were convinced by arguments in favour of a Treaty with the British, and the Kingitanga movement, founded in 1858, which included the powerful and populous Tainui Confederation, was seen by many as being in direct opposition to the authority of a British Crown which they simply did not accept. Indeed when conscription to military service was imposed on Waikato/Tainui in 1917, the Maori King, Te Rata, refused to enforce it.

In April 1840, Major Thomas Bunbury brought the Treaty to the South Island, where he experienced difficulty in finding many Maori at all, let alone significant numbers who even wanted to claim Chieftainship, or whose claim to such could be verified, and who could thus be offered the opportunity to sign.

On 21st May 1840, even before Bunbury had returned to the Bay of Islands, Hobson declared British sovereignty over the whole of New Zealand; of the North by virtue of both proclamation and the Treaty, and of the South by virtue of discovery. The Maori population of the South Island was so small and so sparse that the island was declared *Terra Nullis*, a land without people, and Hobson annexed both it, and Stewart Island, on the basis of Cook's 1769 declaration of possession.

Bunbury, unaware of Hobson's actions, issued his own declarations, for Stewart Island and the South Island, on June 5th and 17th respectively.

However, neither this annexation, nor the Treaty or proclamations, were the basis for the establishment of a new and separate colony named New Zealand; rather, they constituted the addition of the New Zealand territories to the colony of New South Wales, through which Britain would govern these islands for another year.

Other powers continued to harbour designs on New Zealand. On August 10th 1840, the Royal Navy warship *HMS Britomart*, despatched by Hobson, reached Akaroa only five days ahead of the French frigate *L'Aube* – which would have arrived first, had it not spent four of those days anchored off the point waiting for the arrival of the converted whaler *Compte de Paris* and her complement of 57 eager French colonists – thus averting the establishment of a French colony on Bank's Peninsula, and ensuring that the whole of New Zealand remained British and therefore English-speaking.

On the 1ˢᵗ of July 1841 New Zealand was made an independent colony separate from New South Wales, and we gained self-governance with the British Government's passing of the Constitution Act 1852, on June 30ᵗʰ of that year.

Flag Day could be said to be either March 24ᵗʰ or June 12ᵗʰ, the respective days in 1902 when King Edward approved the current New Zealand Ensign, and when the design was gazetted.

New Zealand's status was elevated from colony, to that of dominion with full self-Government on Dominion Day, September 26ᵗʰ 1907, following the Royal proclamation of September 9ᵗʰ. Forty years later, this country became a fully independent nation, when we finally ratified the 1931 Statute of Westminster, taking legal responsibility for our own defence and foreign policy. It is perhaps this date, November 25ᵗʰ 1947, which may serve New Zealand best, as a National Day, a day of unity, and of pride in our Independence.

Anzac Day, April 25ᵗʰ, has been suggested as an alternative New Zealand Day more than once, and it is certainly revered by all; but it is a precious day with meaning and memories which need to stand on their own, and besides, we share it with Australia.

The final link between New Zealand and our history of British governance ended with the New Zealand Parliament's passing of the Constitution Act 1986 – on December 13ᵗʰ, the same day, fittingly, that Tasman first sighted these islands – when the British Parliament ceased to have the power to pass legislation for New Zealand on our behalf and at our request.

The history of this country is long and colourful, and contains many dates of great importance in the shaping of a modern democracy, from what was once little more than a lawless and vice-ridden whaling outpost.

Perhaps it is time for us to choose one of them, and create a New Zealand Day which is inclusive and relevant as we go forward into the 21ˢᵗ century, and which leaves behind the bitterness and division of the past.

Since 1840 great changes have swept this country. Maori and Pakeha have become inextricably linked and intertwined through marriage and the development of a unique culture. New migrants have arrived and assimilated, many of them having few links to the Imperial Britain of the past; and technology and the passing of time have melded us into a modern society, ever further removed from our various pioneering origins.

For this writer's money, the Day for our Nation should be November 25th, our existing yet sadly unsung Independence Day. It is a day which represents what we have all become – not something which many of us never were, and to which none of us can ever go back.

Investigate, February 2007

Introduced Species

The Cat came in the other morning, deposited a recently deceased bird on the mat in front of the fireplace, and proceeded to eat.

I have long since given up attempting to dissuade Him from consuming His kill indoors; but I felt that some statement affirming my position as Master of the House was called for nonetheless.

"I do hope that isn't a native," I said sternly, an eyebrow raised over the top of the Sunday paper.

He paused (pawsed?) momentarily. "No idea," He said. "It's very tasty, though."

"Well, see to it that you don't catch native birds in future," I instructed. "They're protected, you know."

"Not from me," He replied with a smirk. "Anyway," He continued after a moment, "how do you tell the difference? I wouldn't know a native if I fell over one, which, being sure-footed and graceful, I'm not likely to."

"Native species are the ones that were here before us," I informed Him. "They have no natural defence against introduced predators such as Yourself, so they are afforded the protection of the Law."

"Very magnanimous of you, I must say," He remarked, "given that you are an introduced species yourself."

"That's as maybe," I told Him. "But I – We – do know what's best for them, you know."

"I'm sure they appreciate it, and I'm sure they forgive you for your introduced pests and diseases, your roads and railways, your gin traps and your 1080 poison, and all the other things you've done for them," remarked The Cat.

"Never mind being clever," said I, feeling somewhat flustered. "Just leave the native species alone in the future, OK?"

"I'm not allowed to touch them?" said he.

"Nope."

"Not even in self-defence?"

I lowered my Star-Times. "You're stretching things a bit here," I replied. "What native species could possibly be a threat to you?"

"How about dogs?" he asked, poker-faced.

Got you, I thought. "We don't have any native dogs in this country," I informed Him. "Our only native mammals are two species of bat, neither of which is any bigger than a large moth, and certainly no threat to an accomplished predator such as yourself."

"What about Maori dogs?" came the quick-fire response. "You know, the Kuri?"

"Aha, but they're not native," said I, just a little too quickly. "The Maori brought them with them when they came here."

"But you call the Maori natives, so don't their dogs have to be native too?" He inquired.

"I don't," I said.

"Your society does," said The Cat.

"Well, they were here before us, but that still doesn't make them native," I replied.

"The Maori, or the dogs?"

"You know perfectly well I'm talking about the dogs."

"Sounds like a convenient double standard to me," He said sarcastically.

"Anyway, there are no pure ones left. They've all interbred with the dogs who came after," I told him.

"So does that mean the new ones have become native, then?" The Cat inquired.

"Well, I don't know," I said. "I suppose, for some of them, the ones with native dog in their ancestry, they could be called native."

"How much native dog would they need to qualify?" asked my feline companion, giving the back of a paw a quick wash.

"I don't think it's about percentages," I replied. "I think it's about whether or not you identify with that part of your makeup."

"And the ones who identify as being native, they have special rights and protections, and I'm not allowed to pick on them?"

"No, I think all dogs are equal under the law," I said. "Just leave the birds alone."

"Because they need more in the way of protection, or because they're more native? Are there degrees of nativeness, then?"

"No, not at all," I reassured Him, and repeated my earlier assertion: "Native species are the ones who were here before we arrived, and the rest of us are introduced."

"But I was born here," remarked The Cat, "and so were you. We didn't arrive from anywhere."

"That's true," said I, "but we weren't the first here, you see. So those who were here first are the natives."

"So," drawled Felis Domesticus, "let me get this straight. In order to be a native you just have to be here before someone else. And then you have special rights and protections, and so forth."

"I'm sure it doesn't work that way," I insisted, though admittedly, he did appear to have a point.

"So as far as the neighbour's cat is concerned, I'm a native?"

"How on earth do you arrive at that conclusion?" I asked Him.

"They brought their cat with them from England," He replied. "And I was already here. One of us has to be more native than the other, surely."

"The distinction doesn't seem to have affected your relationship with her," I remarked a little cynically.

He stretched, and jumped up onto the sofa. "It's entirely consensual, I assure you," He said with a purr.

Presently He spoke again, though it was clear that He was drifting towards sleep. "What about rats, then?" He asked.

"I know what you're going to say," I said. "The Kiore falls in the same boat as the Kuri, a rat is a rat, they're all introduced, and they're all pests. So yes, they're fair game."

"Here's one for you," He said, eyes closed. "If a Tui, or a Bellbird, were to be bred in a foreign zoo, and then brought here and released, would it still be a native, and would I be allowed to eat it?"

"I'm not going there," said I. "We're all of us introduced, apart from the birds and the bats and a few lizards, and you're to leave them alone, alright?"

"No special privileges unless you're one of the above?"

I ignored His jibe. "I'll clear away the rest of that starling for you, shall I?"

"Thank you," replied The Cat, as he re-entered the Dreamtime.

Investigate, February 2003

Vive la Revolution

I have become a Republican. It's for all the wrong reasons, and I'm not entirely comfortable about it, but there you go.

Essentially I'm a Monarchist at heart. So why the change? Fundamentally, I suppose, because in realistic terms, the Monarchy as it is executed in New Zealand has ceased to have relevance.

The shift, for me, has come about as a result of the retrospective legislation, the Appropriation (Parliamentary Expenditure Validation) Bill, which legalises the now-carried-out theft of money from the public purse and its misappropriation by political parties.

Howls of outrage from ordinary New Zealanders, at this blatant railroading of the democratic process, have resulted in a rapidly-growing online petition to the Governor-General, entreating His Excellency to withhold the Royal Assent from the Bill, thus preventing it from becoming law.

Naturally, no-one expects Mr Satyanand to do any such thing; but as I write, just on 41,000 people have signed the petition, in just over four days – surely a record for our historically placid and dispassionate electorate. Yours Truly is amongst them, signing in as disgruntled citizen and voter No. 3029.

Sometime later this week, the Bill will flit across the Governor General's desk, receive the Vice-Regal seal of approval, and pass into the statute books as a sad and sorry blot on New Zealand's legislative history.

As the only Constitutional check in between minority Government and the People, the Governor General has a vital, irreplaceable role in the maintenance of New Zealand's democracy. When the individual bearing the Office of the Governor General fails in the execution of his or her duty, democracy and the moral right of law and governance fail with them.

It is a doubly sorry performance on the part of the Queen's Representative because, no matter how it is dressed up, in signing the Bill, the Governor General, himself a former Judge, will be saying that it is perfectly legal to steal, or at least that it can be made to be so.

This is where I have a problem. The issue of retrospective legislation to validate theft is a clear-cut case of right versus wrong. Part of the foundation of our society itself is a clear delineation between the two. We assume that people will know what is right from what is wrong, we endeavour to teach our children this very basic lesson, and we base our laws and their consequences on this simple principle. It's wrong to steal, and it's wrong to lie, and we expect pre-school children to understand these truths and live by them.

There has been, in recent weeks, a great deal of what can only be described as male bovine excrement spouted about this issue, from the very corridors of power which are supposed to house the moral foundation of the nation. None of it changes the very simple facts. Politicians have stolen, and politicians have lied, and now politicians have changed the law to make it OK that they did these things. And our Head of State is about to let them get away with it. And we can't do anything about it, because we can't do anything about him – apart from this petition, which, as we all know very well, he is convention-bound to ignore.

To my simple rural way of thinking, it's pretty much black-and-white; political parties were told, well in advance of the election, how much could be spent, when it could be spent, what it could be spent on, and where these funds were allowed to come from.

They all knew the rules. However, all bar Jim Anderton claim not to have understood these rules. Personally I just plain don't believe them.

Perhaps Jim saw a different copy; or maybe he's the only one who wasn't lying.

They broke the rules, knowingly, deliberately, cynically.

They overspent what was allowed to be spent, and some of them stole from funds which they knew they weren›t allowed to use, in so doing.

There was no confusion over the rules. They just nicked the money, plain and simple.

And they got caught.

They thought the Auditor General would back down. He didn›t.

What may have happened in the past is irrelevant. What they may have got away with in previous elections doesn't count. This time they were told, this time they knew, this time they did it anyway. The burglar, the rapist, the speeding or drunken driver, cannot claim immunity from prosecution on the grounds that they haven't been caught before.

Retrospective legislation is not, as Parliament's Speaker, Margaret Wilson, and certain apologist commentators would have us believe, the only way in which the «unlawfulness can be remedied» – in the real world, may I inform Ms Wilson, this is achieved by somebody going to jail.

Of course the Governor General is not going to refuse Assent. Nobody believes for a minute that he will. That›s why he›s there; to be a politically appointed tame rubber stamp. But that he, a former Judge, can allow a law to be passed which legalises theft, indicates that the corruption of both his office, and the Government, is now complete.

That politicians should be corrupted to the degree that they would choose to follow such a course of action in the first place, is distasteful. That they should then attempt to justify their actions with lies, is reprehensible. That such lies should be given the validation of a law which reaches back into the past is abhorrent, and in itself, opens a Pandora's box which I fear may only be closed again by the very strongest of ethical fortitude and leadership, the like of which our country does not currently visibly possess. That the legislation could have been stopped were it not for the abstention of the Greens and the Maori Party is nauseating, and their collective inaction indicates a moral cowardice which gives the lie to their previous, and now subsequent, proclamations of integrity. Of the positions taken by Winston Peters and Peter Dunne, little remains to be said which their actions have not already illustrated clearly. To think that once we held them both in high regard, as protectors of truth, honesty, and the rights of the common man....well, I can only shake my head.

In almost any other jurisdiction, such a brazen and publicly derogatory piece of lawmaking, carried out with such arrogant disdain and disregard for the principles of democratic rule, would struggle to pass muster, simply because the body of Government attempting to bring it about would itself be answerable to one or more separate levels of interrogation and inspection, each of them answerable themselves to the will of the people via the ballot box, or a written Constitution, or both.

Because our single-tier Government has neither, Constitutional integrity rests with the personal fortitude of the holder of the Office of the Sovereign's Representative. By convention, the Governor General does not exercise his or her Reserve Powers against the dictates of Government or the resolutions of Parliament, but it must be remembered that the same convention of honest and ethical behaviour is all which prevents the Government from stooping to corrupt or unconscionable practices in the first place.

I would contend that in creating this piece of cowardly, dishonest, and insidious, retrospective legislation, and passing it under urgency, with the support, or the complicity, of those who stood to either profit from it or to be exonerated by it, the Government has departed from this convention. When the Governor General spinelessly allows this Bill to become law, the usurpation of our Parliamentary democracy will also be complete.

One man, and one man only, has stood against the tide of corrupted thought and illegal action which has begun creeping through the machinery of government in New Zealand, and that man is the Auditor General, Kevin Brady.

So what can we do about it? In the past, I have suggested that the Queen's Representative be someone who was above and beyond politics, who held the interests of the nation as paramount, and who was able to carry out the role of Statesperson, fairly, impartially, and with the courage to sack the Government of the Day, should such action prove necessary. I have suggested the Maori monarch as a suitable contender for this role. Maoridom, however, appear singularly disinterested in this idea. So be it. I can move on from there.

There has also been some suggestion that we as a nation should elect our Governor General by universal ballot. Yes, maybe; but only if the holder of the Office is empowered with both the desire and the legal right to behave as I have described – and if they do, it begs the question, have we then moved on from the concept of Monarchy altogether?

Certainly, we have arrived at a point in our nation's development where it has become necessary for the Prime Minister to be elected directly by the whole country. The office has already become that of Executive President by default, and it is time we recognised that truth, and took steps to regulate the unbridled power which this situation has come to provide to its holder.

It may be better, I would contend, to abandon pretence, and establish a new and unarguable hierarchy of Governance; a multi-tiered Assembly of the People, with each part answerable to the others; a combination of national and regional Government, an Upper House, a Supreme Court wherein Judges are elected by the People, and all of it regulated ultimately by a written Constitution.

And, of course, for this new Republic – or perhaps, Confederation of Republics – a President; someone elected by the People, answerable to the People, able to be recalled by the People, and above all, with both the authority and the balls to dismiss the Government if the latter should transgress the letter of the Constitution or the spirit of democracy.

Such a President will need to be a person of proven moral conviction and dedicated courageous application, steadfast in the face of corruption and unswerving in their respect for, and their desire to uphold, the law of the land; someone who believes that the conventions of the past are more important than the arrogance of those who would seek to disregard them.

May I be the first to propose Kevin Brady as a contender for the job.

Investigate, November 2006

Our Word is Law

The election is just over a week away as I sit and type. By the time this edition hits the news stands it will be all over bar the shouting; and bar the crying and screaming, the recriminations, the taunts and jeers – and that's only what will be happening in the media, even before the playful scamps we elect to represent us are let loose in their poorly supervised Wellington kindergarten.

I have my own predictions as to the outcome, of course, and preferences; I'll let you know how close I got next month, but in some ways that isn't really the most important thing right now.

What bugs me most – at least this month – about the electoral process, is not that the individuals who comprise society have so little influence over the final outcome, but that we have no influence at all over what happens after that. We have one chance and one chance only, every three years, to haul on the reins of the nation, to apply a well-aimed riding crop to the comfortable and corpulent rump of Government. After polling day, we are ejected from the saddle again, and the will of the people parts company from the riderless nag of the State's direction.

Since 1996 it has become fashionable to blame MMP for the fact that politicians of all hues appear incapable of doing as they are told by the people who employ them. This is nonsense, of course; politicians were ignoring the wishes of the nation long before we changed the voting system. And MMP, while far from perfect, is still better than the farce of First-Past-The-Post which preceded it. MMP at least makes an attempt at pretending to be representative democracy in action, which FPP never did.

The problem with MMP is not that it requires Governments to

be cobbled together out of disparate Parties with diverging agendas. That is in fact one of its strengths, and the consensus policy-making which it is meant to impose on the nation's lawmakers would be a great step towards the aforementioned representative democracy.

Your favourite commentator is cynical enough to believe that MMP was foisted upon us in its present form purely because it is, in fact, the worst of the Proportional Representation voting methods; the powers that be, I would suggest, believed we would tire of it in short order, and demand a return to the simple minority-dictatorship offered by FPP.

We haven't, but neither have we as a nation learned how to use MMP to best effect yet, either. It still delivers an FPP Parliament, largely because we expect it to. We still speak of its potential outcomes in terms of National Government or Labour Government, rather than consensus coalition. We still expect the largest minority Party to form the core of any Government, and its Leader to become the Prime Minister. In Europe's more mature democracies, conversely, coalitions where the smaller Party gets to fill the Top Job, and the larger one controls the purse strings, are commonplace. Here we fret about tails wagging dogs, and cling to the antiquated and somewhat bizarre notion that one Party or another has some kind of divine right to govern, even when better than 60% of the electorate didn't vote for them.

MMP could certainly be improved. Constituency MPs could be elected by Preference or STV, rather than the undemocratic plurality system we employ now. Candidates could be required to stand for an electorate seat, or be on the Party list, but not both, which would remove the paradoxical situation of Party hacks making it into Parliament on the list, despite having been rejected by their constituency voters – though this may be a somewhat mute point, because once again, under plurality voting in the electorates, a candidate can "win" a seat even when a clear and overwhelming majority of voters wanted someone else entirely.

The threshold for Parties to gain seats in the house could be lowered from 5% as we and the Germans set it, to 3% as it is in Bolivia, or even 1% if we wanted to ensure that Parliament gained a sizeable contingent of real nutters to keep the establishment honest. I rather like the 1% idea. All sorts of Independents could find voice and influence in the house, just as an independent candidate in an electorate seat may do today – and who's to say that the fringe dwellers shouldn't be able to send someone to Wellington just because they're spread over the entire country, rather than all living in the same place? An independent MP can currently gain a seat in the House of Representatives by winning a simple plurality vote under the FPP system in a single constituency, with the support of as few as 15,000 people – or around 0.5% of the total number of people on the electoral roll. Why should the bar for representation be set at ten times that figure for a similarly independent-minded group of people, simply because they don't all live in a single electorate?

We would, of course, have a Parliament littered with nutcases and extremists (if indeed we don't anyway), but by the same token, the "big" Parties would be forced to accommodate the desires and demands of such folk, instead of ignoring them just as they do the majority of ordinary New Zealanders at present.

We shy away from such possibilities because we are, as a nation, rather hung up on the idea of stability. We don't like the idea that Governments may topple at a moment's notice, to be replaced with something unknown. In this writer's opinion, such concern is misplaced. Instability in Government can be a good thing – not ideal as far as the politicians themselves are concerned, but not necessarily bad for the economy either. Italy is a case in point. Despite having had 62 Governments since the Second World War, Italy's standard of living remains near the top of the OECD.

But I am digressing. MMP is a dog, and it needs to go. What most definitely doesn't need to happen, however, is that we be returned to FPP. That was never democracy, and it never worked. Its promoters and supporters need to take themselves out for a cold shower and a good slapping. STV, Preferential Voting, 1-2-3 PV, almost anything would be better. But not what we had before. That was just ridiculous.

And there are other changes necessary. A written Constitution to limit the powers of Government goes without saying. Our unicameral Assembly affords far too great a degree of unbridled power to far too few people, specifically the Cabinet, and in particular, the Prime Minister. Unless we are to recreate the second chamber, the Upper House which New Zealand had for a hundred years until 1951, the office of Prime Minister needs to be a position elected by the people, directly and universally. Giving absolute executive power to a single individual, placed in their role by a small and unaccountable group of invisible Party insiders, and justified by the self-fulfilling lie that voter support for a given Party translates to tacit support for that choice, with no other constitutional checks or balances, is simply insane. If New Zealand's Prime Minister is to exercise the powers of an Executive President, then the person holding that office needs to be mandated directly by the People.

Further, the person holding that office should be, indeed must be, accountable to the People at all times throughout their tenure, and not, as is presently the case, only once every three years, or alternatively, as the aforementioned group of invisible and unaccountable insiders see fit.

Arnold Schwarzenegger became Governor of California via a process known as Recall. Under this system, a dishonest or ineffective politician may be removed from office at any time during their elected term, by way of a special vote on the back of a petition initiated by a minimum necessary number of registered voters.

Our Prime Minister, and members of the Cabinet, need to have a similar Sword of Damocles hanging over them; they need to know that if they don't perform, conform, behave properly, and do as We The People tell them, that they'll be out on their ears, not maybe in three years time, but maybe next month. That should keep the bastards honest.

But perhaps the single most powerful and important tool which needs to be made available to the New Zealand voter is the mechanism of Binding Citizens' Initiated Referenda.

The Swiss have used referenda for better than 150 years without the sky falling in, and their peaceful and affluent democracy is testament to the effectiveness of having the People keep a direct rein on the politicians.

Naysayers in our own Halls of Power are wont to criticise the use of binding referenda on the basis that it makes continuity of governance difficult, or even that the People themselves don't want to be running off to the polls every five minutes. Indeed we don't, but by the same token, if the Government of the Day would only take it upon itself to actually listen to the mood of the nation, and do as the People desire, there would be no need for referenda.

BCIR in New Zealand would mean a very different shape to the policy and direction of Government. We would still have an Air Force. Our dogs would have remained un-microchipped. It is quite conceivable that we might countenance nuclear power via referendum. And Section 59 of the Crimes Act would still be there on the Books, where 80% of New Zealanders still want it to be. That we are to be grudgingly allowed a plebiscite on the completely unwanted anti-smacking legislation is something of a pyrrhic victory, given that the result – which we already know will overwhelmingly reject it – will not be binding on the Government, who will use all manner of lies and subterfuge to avoid taking heed of the wishes of the People.

Whoever makes up the next New Zealand Government, which-ever collection of strange bedfellows and expedient friends, there is something that they all need to learn and understand, and it is this; we the People are growing tired of being ignored. This is our democracy, and our word is the Law. We send people to Wellington to represent us, not to lead, and certainly not to follow their own flights of fancy at the expense of our express wishes.

The challenge for the next Parliament is not to overcome the foibles of MMP whilst blaming it for their own shortcomings. It is to give the People the tools they need to ensure that democracy actually works, regardless of whichever voting system we choose to employ.

Investigate, December 2008

Terms of Reference

In 1676 Nathaniel Bacon, a tobacco farmer from the upper reaches of the James River in Virginia, led a rebellion against the colonial regime of King Charles I's Governor, Sir William Berkeley.

Berkeley, a favourite of the King, had failed repeatedly to deliver on a promise to provide protection to the colonists from attacks by local Indians. The colonists, their patience expired, went to the capital and extracted a commission from the Colonial Assembly to deal with the Natives themselves, at the point of 400 muskets. Further frustrated by inaction on the part of the Governor, the rebels, led by Bacon – who happened to be the Governor's wife's cousin – marched on Jamestown in force, sacked the capital and burned it to the ground, and drove Berkeley and his forces out of town and across the river before looting his house.

Bacon's Rebellion petered out when Bacon died of malaria on October 26th, with the Governor returning to power, hanging some two dozen former rebels, and seizing their property. But things ended badly for Berkeley as well, removed from office and recalled to England by Charles II, who was less than impressed by his Vice-Regal's behaviour. The disgraced Berkeley died in May of the following year, as history recalls, "a half a world away from the place which had become his home."

460-ish years earlier, the forebears of both sides of the aforementioned quarrel had been involved in another stoush wherein the ruling authority was compelled to acquiesce to the wishes of a group of disgruntled subjects, on pain of death. Muskets being less in vogue in 1215 than they were to prove in the centuries to come, it was instead by the pointy end of a sword that the Barons gave King John the choice of signing the Magna Carta, or else. Since "or else" involved being dead, John wisely agreed, and the foundation for our modern Common Law was laid.

History shows us time and again that this is all too often the way; those in power will simply not listen to the will of the people, until and unless someone is faced with actual violence or at least the very real threat of it. It is a rare revolution indeed which is entirely bloodless.

In civilised parts of the world, of course, we have a different way of looking at things; we use referenda to inform our political masters of our various opinions, and elections to enforce such sentiment upon them. The Swiss are past masters of this system. Since 1847,

Swiss voters have enjoyed the power of pure democracy to advise and control their representatives, going to the polls about twice a year to direct, instruct, or over-rule the Government on everything from simple local matters to major constitutional issues.

Conservative in their implementation of Direct Democracy as they are in almost everything else, the Swiss have passed or approved only around a tenth of the questions and initiatives put before them, which goes some way towards dampening the arguments of those opponents to plebiscite democracy who claim that enforced accountability to the electorate makes governance impossible.

So why do we not have Binding Referenda in New Zealand? Why is it, I ask, that such questions as we are permitted to confront our Parliamentarians with, may be belittled, usurped, or plain ignored, whilst Government continues with nary a nod to the populace which elected it and which pays for it?

Good question. Perhaps the answer is that, to date, no Government in this fair land has ever been confronted with the serious possibility of having to face either a sharp blade or the barrel of a gun. That's probably our fault. I mean we talk big, but we're a wee bit spineless when it comes to holding a Bowie knife up to authority's nostril, and saying, "No."

Why not, I find myself compelled to ask? We own them, after all; they work for us; we pay their wages, we set the rules, we send them to Wellington to represent our views, our interests, our wishes. We are actually in charge. Neither Government, nor Parliament, nor any of their various officials or minions, has any authority which we do not expressly afford them, nor do they have any power or let beyond that which We The People proclaim or reserve for ourselves. The Police – in spite of their own protestations to the contrary – do not have any greater authority of arrest or prosecution than that available to the general public, although their daily exercise of it has been smoothed by regulation; the Inland Revenue may not take that which we do not authorise, and at the end of the day, no act of legislation which does not pass the muster of general public approval and consent, may be said to have any recognizable lawful authority. The essence of Governmental power is that regardless of any terms in which its legality may be couched, its foundation is wholly and solely contained within the consensus of public opinion and the willing compliance of the people.

We send our representatives to Parliament every three years, and we expect them to spend the intervening periods adhering to our rules, abiding by our wishes, and following our instructions. We send them with fairly clear Terms of Reference, but we do not follow these up with any kind of system of accountability. More fool us.

The Anti-Smacking referendum is a case in point. It will be almost all over bar the shouting by the time this issue goes to print, but that doesn't really matter. The Prime Minister has already said that he intends to ignore the result, regardless of what that may be. Your favourite commentator is not normally a betting man, but this time I think I'll go out on a limb and predict an 80% rejection of Sue Bradford's overwhelmingly hated Bill. What gives John Key any kind of authority or right to disregard such a clearly stated declaration of the nation's will?

Key does say that he will change the law if it doesn't appear to be working. How magnanimous of him. He seems unconcerned by the fact that no-one wanted it in the first place. I don't know about anyone else, but this writer finds such utter gall infuriating almost to the point of sedition – which, perhaps fortunately, isn't a crime in New Zealand anymore.

The whole business "smacks" particularly, because almost the whole sorry mess which is Parliament was, and is, in on the deal. All but eight of our "representatives" voted to abolish Section 59 of the Crimes Act, despite the fact that eight out of ten New Zealanders wanted it retained. No-one wanted the law changed, no-one wanted the "compromise" deal stitched up by Helen Clark and John Key, late at night in a back room, and no-one gave these politicians permission to go ahead and do it anyway. Not content with blatantly ignoring the instructions of their employers, the same Parliamentarians who foisted this thing on us have sought to disrupt the referendum against it, calling the process unnecessary, the wording misleading, and the exercise a waste of money.

Well for my money, the only excuse anyone could have for finding the question misleading is that they're plain thick. Since most politicians are, by definition, possessed of at least enough cunning to enable themselves to get elected in the first place, their only excuse must be that they're lying.

And if democracy at $3 per voter is a waste of money, to whom should we send the nine million dollar bill? Sue Bradford, for authoring the law change to begin with? Helen Clark, for refusing to hold the referendum at the same time as the election, when it would have cost nothing? John Key, for declaring that he will ignore the result? How about the National Party, for failing to recognize that the 2008 election itself was a de facto referendum on anti-smacking and the Nanny State generally? Personally I think we should split the cost 113 ways, and send every MP who voted for the Bradford Bill an invoice for $79,646.01, because we didn't want it, and we said so very clearly at the time.

And if the process itself is unnecessary, why do we even bother to have elections? No, the answer does not lie down that road. The truth is that we need better rules to go with our electoral processes, unarguable and mandatory regulation to bind politicians, and systems to make them immediately and completely accountable for their actions.

If the Prime Minister is to be vested with the apparent authority to unilaterally decide and declare what will and what will not be law, then the Prime Minister needs to be elected by a direct ballot of the people, not appointed to the Office by default, as a result of becoming the Leader of any given political Party.

That person, and every other Minister and Member of the House, needs to be able to be recalled from office by a plebiscite on the back of a successful petition, at any time during their tenure, if their behaviour should make such action necessary. The same should apply to Judges, Police Commissioners, and Department Heads; all those who interpret the laws of the land and who exercise power over the People, must be ultimately and swiftly accountable to the People.

And referenda, initiated by the citizenry, absolutely must become irrevocably binding on the Government. Of all the mechanisms which we as a society put in place to ensure fair representation and good governance, this is perhaps the most important of all. It has become glaringly apparent that those who regard themselves as our lords and masters have little interest in voluntarily adopting the practice of democracy along with the theory; and so its adoption must be made involuntary upon them.

This is important because it must be recognized, in reality and in law, that the convention by which the public choose to obey the dictates of Government, rests upon an equal acceptance by Government, that the consent of the People is the sole basis of the Government's power, and the sole foundation of the legitimacy of Statute; this and nothing else. We have a right to be listened to by the Government, we have a right to be heard by the Government, and we have a right to be obeyed by the Government. And if they will not listen and obey on the basis of an instruction delivered via the ballot box, then they risk, by consequence, discovering that we also retain the ultimate right to resort to the musket and the sword.

Investigate, September 2009

He Iwi Tahi Tatou

The call for separate Maori seats on the proposed Auckland Supercity Council, and its predictable rejection by the National Government, is one of the odder quirks of New Zealand's unique racial and electoral makeup. That we have them at all in the nation's Parliament is an oddity in itself, a relic of our history which saw the Maori seats created on a temporary basis – originally intended to be no longer than five years – way back in 1867. In those early days of representative democracy in the brave new colony, voting rights were restricted to men – and to men who owned property, at that. Since most Maori land was owned communally, few Maori qualified, and the Maori seats were created to ensure that the Natives, in fair accordance with the rights and privileges afforded them under the Treaty of Waitangi, would have access to some form of accountable representation, at least until they could learn to behave like good individual capitalists and take up land titles in their own right.

Since then of course many things have changed; women got the vote as well, in 1893 – though the right to stand for Parliament had to wait until 1919 – Maori did indeed take rather splendidly to capitalism, trading independently with the Australian colonies just as they had done with the visiting sealers and whalers of the preceding centuries; and the Treaty was rewritten, in meaning if not in actual words, time and again as its changing interpretation suited various interests of the day. This process remains, as we know, a work in progress.

The seats, however, did not go the way of Victorian social conventions or pure Maori bloodlines, fading irrevocably into the past; instead, they remained, as a reminder perhaps that not everyone was happy with Lieutenant Governor Hobson's proclamation that "We are now one people" – or even with the other interpretation of those famous words, that being "our people are now together." Indeed the preservation of the Maori seats is a clear indication that many, for various reasons, would like us to still be very separate.

This writer doesn't really understand why Maori appear to want to keep the Maori seats in Parliament, or the Maori electoral roll. Personally I think the concept of racial separatism is a disempowering one, restricting those who choose to identify with it, to never being anything more than a voice on the fringes of policy making. Maori, who comprise 15% of New Zealand's population, could have a far stronger influence over the direction of the nation if they were to vote together within the mainstream – but then that, I think is the key to the matter. Maori don't vote all together as one, just like they don't do anything else all together as one. Pre-European Maori were never one single homogenous group, let alone nation, and post-Colonial Maori are every bit as diverse and free thinking as any other component element of this melting pot we call New Zealand. In the MMP environment, it could be argued that Maori don't need separate seats in order to ensure representation; but the reality is that, despite the MMP environment, most Maori don't even appear to be interested in separate representation, at least not on racial grounds. For most Maori, the choice of who gets the tick in the polling booth is about pragmatism, philosophy, economics, and personality, same as it is for most everyone else. Maybe that's why only 45% of eligible Maori voters choose to enrol on the Maori roll, and why the Maori Party only attracts 1.5% of the popular vote.

The creation of the Maori seats has been described by some commentators as a cynical mechanism to contain and control Maori electoral influence, at a time when Maori greatly outnumbered the settler population. Personally I think that's an uncharitable assessment; I believe the early Colonial Government did genuinely want the spirit of British rights to extend to all those peoples to whom the Treaty had granted them, though I also think it is fair to say that the seats were probably preserved by vested interests long after their intended purpose had been served, for precisely the reason hitherto mentioned.

In the same manner, I believe that the supposed sanctity of the Maori seats today is promoted by similar vested interests, but this time it is those who seek to benefit from their own guaranteed inclusion on the gravy train which is politics generally. I don't doubt that there are some who have represented Maori constituencies, whose genuine motivation was and is to serve their people; but at the same time, I think that too often, ordinary Maori are held back and held down by a system which entrenches the culture of the past, and which by its very nature espouses separateness, and thereby inequality and its inevitable accompanying sense of injustice.

I hear the likes of Willie Jackson and John Tamihere talking about this sort of thing on the radio, and the irony is hilarious. Willie would probably label me an arch-racist for suggesting that Maori don't need separate electoral representation, despite the fact that I could happily vote for JT if that was an option for me. The thing is, y'see, that me and people like me are not racists – and neither are the vast majority of Maori. I'd be happy to vote for JT because he's a good straight-up-and-down Kiwi bloke, and he tells it like it is. But I'd never vote for Willie because he's too much of a leftie pinko for my liking, and that's about as simple as it gets. I couldn't give a wet slap what colour a man is. It's all about the person and their philosophy. Likewise I wouldn't vote for Barack Obama, but I'd jump at the chance to give Ron Mark the big tick if he ever makes a comeback. There you have it, from the mouth of a self-confessed redneck; us right-wing whities don't vote on racial grounds, and I don't believe most modern Maori do either. Democracy has moved on from that sort of thinking.

But separate Maori seats in Auckland aren't about democracy, and they aren't about ensuring a voice for the downtrodden brown underclass. They're about tribalism, and an attempt to preserve the myth of the Treaty being a "partnership" – a term coined, to this writer's recollection, by Michael Cullen in a speech back in the nineties, though I could be wildly wrong about that.

Wherever the concept came from, it is a fact that no version of the Treaty, in either language, contains or even suggests the word "partner." Interestingly however, only the late Sir Hugh Kawharu's translation, back to English from the signed Maori text, states that Maori will receive the duties of citizenship (actually subject hood, back then, given that there were no citizens as such – everyone was a subject, and did as the Monarch commanded) along with the rights and privileges also conferred; an acceptance of which could have long since put paid to the current and ongoing bickering about whether or not the signatories really meant for the Queen to be in charge afterwards.

But I digress. I caught up with an old mate from school recently. He's a very brown chap with a very white name, and I have known him since the primers, but he never went past the 5th form and we lost touch, as happens all too often. Thanks to the Internet, he popped up again a few weeks back, living in Sydney where he's been for the last twenty years or so. Currently he owns two companies and employs thirty-eight people. Not bad for a Maori boy who never got School C, eh.

He could never, in his own words, have attained the heights in New Zealand that he has risen to in Australia; his family wouldn't have let him. He would, by his own assessment, have remained the under-achiever his culture demanded, and probably ended up in trouble with the law along with it. If urban Maori today, in any Supercity-to-be, need special representation, then I would venture it is more likely to be useful if it is delivered via the likes of John Tamihere and his hands-on practical approach to modern socioeconomic concerns, than by the special reservation of some elitist tribal appointment which is stuck in the past and distanced from mainstream reality.

And that poses questions in itself; would the proposed seats be open to any Maori candidate, or would they be reserved for the mana whenua tribes, and if so, why aren't they being promoted as such? Would a Ngati Whatua or Tainui Councilor be there to represent all Maori in Auckland, and if so, why couldn't anyone else do that? Will they be allowed to represent the interests, views, and wishes of non-Maori as well? Are we really so different as human beings, that issues concerning roads and rates and rubbish, pose different problems for people depending on their ethnicity?

In truth I don't really mind what Auckland ends up doing, because I don't live there and it doesn't affect me, other than in the sense that, Governments being what they are, whatever gets foisted on Auckland will almost certainly be foisted on the rest of us too...that and the fact that I was born a Westie, and I really wouldn't like to see the place go down the gurgler. And I'm not against self-determination *per se*, for those who want it, at least not on a regionalised basis; if Tuhoe really want to create their own Republic in the Ureweras, I say good on them and good luck, and it's no secret to anyone that I'm a supporter of self-government for the South Island. But if Auckland is to be united as one Supercity – and I'm yet to be persuaded that that's necessarily a good idea – then it needs to be a union of all its peoples, and if the Treaty – or apartheid, come to that – have taught us anything, it's that two systems for one place simply don't work.

Maori language, history, and culture, are special and important. But they're not **more** special or important than anyone else's language, history, or culture, and I think this is a truth of which Treaty revisionists and the promoters of elitist tribalism need reminding. Separate seats on the Supercity Council won't help modern Maori with the problems which confront them, but they will further the bitterness and division which increasingly afflicts our fractured nation. If we truly desire to be One People, this is not the way to achieve it.

Investigate, October 2009

A Moral Vacuum

It was British philosopher and statesman Edmund Burke who coined the immortal and oft-quoted phrase, "The only thing necessary for the triumph of evil is for good men to do nothing."

Burke's now somewhat clichéd observation was intended as a warning, but in many instances, it is apparent that that warning has not been heeded.

There is an evil afflicting modern New Zealand society, and we as a nation are doing little if anything about it.

The creeping evil which is spreading through this country is the stealthy corruption of our national moral fibre, brought about by the steady and systemic failure of individuals, and of the institutions of which they are part, to correctly use their free choice to do what is right, in situations where decisions of right and wrong are involved.

Our national institutions and the structures of our society are rotting from the top down, and We, the People, are doing nothing to stop it. Government, Industry, organised religion, the establishments of Education, non-Governmental organisations, international bodies, and even some sporting and cultural structures, are affected by this malaise.

I am not referring to any moral conundrum of the type decried from the pulpit, or railed against by evangelists. I am talking about the simple departure from the unspoken acceptance of the requirement – the duty, even – of every person, to speak the truth, keep their word, and do the right thing, as they know it to be.

From the highest levels of Government we see this spreading darkness. Cabinet Ministers, a Prime Minister even, caught lying, and worse; double dipping, drink-driving, falsifying tax returns, falsifying election expenses, forgery, cheating on housing expenses, and advocating sodomy with beer bottles, amongst other things. Yet rather than resign immediately from the nation's Parliament, these individuals attempt to justify their actions, and worse still, they receive a measure of outward support from their parties and superiors in this attempted justification.

These actions do not go unnoticed in society, and they set an example more powerful than a thousand policy speeches could ever hope to achieve. And we allow this evil to prevail, by doing nothing about it.

The same Government uses its Parliamentary majority – which is not a numerical majority of the electorate, and can in no way be regarded as a mandate – to railroad through social engineering policies such as the Civil Unions Bill, the disbandment of the Air Force, and the ban on smoking in pubs; changes for which there is no public desire, and much disquiet and contention. In any previous generation, Government and its individual members would have felt duty-bound to respond, and to acquiesce, to the wishes of the silent majority of the population; today, they do whatever they please, simply because they know they can. When and why did this change come about, and why do we, the people, permit it?

Other shifts are taking place in the corridors of power. Restructuring of the public sector, driven by dogma and ideology, has seen the departure of the cream of a once-proud Civil Service; an institution steeped in tradition, apolitical, dedicated to the nation, and whose members were considered incorruptible, now replaced by a corporate structure driven by the profit motive.

We the People have supported this change, by not preventing it at the ballot box.

The Chief of our Defence Forces, previously chosen by peer review – in line with two hundred years of British tradition – may now be a political appointment. This insidious change removes us from the process followed by the likes of Britain, Canada, Australia, and the United States, and into the company of such nations as Chile, Argentina, Zimbabwe and Indonesia. The traditional, apolitical, allegiance of the military – and indeed the Police – to the Sovereign, and thereby the nation, is now within the grasp of the Government of the Day. And We the People have likewise failed to prevent it.

Alongside this degeneration of Governmental standards of behaviour, has been a parallel faltering on the part of Big Business and mainstream religion.

From the scams of Mr Asia, and the speculators of the '87 crash, to the Winebox and the parasites of privatisation, New Zealand business has fled from the age-old ethics of established industry like rats leaving a sinking ship; and once again, in our united silence, we ordinary New Zealanders have failed to stop it from happening.

And scarcely a day goes by without yet another report of sexual abuse against young people in the care of one religious order or another. With every one of these attacks against the very fabric of the decent society, we are seeing an erosion of the time-honoured and respectful way in which our nation was built, and with it, the loss of more and more of what we once liked to call "Family Values".

Family Values....we all grew up under them, so did our parents and grandparents. Where are they now? Why is our generation failing those who will come after us, those for whom we are responsible? What's changed?

In part, I would guess, increased communication, via TV, the internet, and so on, has revealed to more and more people the previously hidden truth of the increasingly corrupt nature of national governments and big business. And people do follow examples.

Partly, also, it is the deliberately anti-family activities, of deliberately anti-family organisations such as the United Nations, in corrupting the new generation into thinking that the family is bad, and should be replaced by some international institution.

And just for the record, I do happen to think that there is a Great Conspiracy, and I do happen to think that the UN is pure evil supported only by utter fools, and is an integral part of it.

Partly, also, endemic corruption within the established churches, who are supposed to provide some sort of ethical guy rope to society, is more and more being exposed by the same increased communication as has illuminated Government and business. In the past, though such corruption has almost always been present, it has also been hidden, and people have had more of a motivation to follow the example held up before them, rather than the unseen truth of the institution promoting it.

Partly, the cult of self; the relentless march of self-gratification allowed by advancing technology, and promoted by the profit motive of capitalism.

But mostly, I think, it has come about through the abrogation of responsibility.

There was a time when a man's word was his bond, when a deal was set in stone with a handshake. People had honour then. Now, we have lawyers and contracts and lawsuits and countersuits. Why?

Young men will not take responsibility for the children they have fathered. Why not? Because society allows them to abrogate that responsibility, by setting them the example that there is a way out, just as there is a way out of a contract, and a way out of honouring your word.

Mankind – western civilisation if you prefer – has become decadent and corrupt, and we are in danger of going to hell in a handcart, just as many societies have done before us.

If there is a way to stop this, and it may not be too late, then I believe it will not come from Governments, or any of the "established" Churches, or Corporations, or International Organisations, or any other corrupted institution.

It will come from the hearts and minds of individuals; ordinary decent people who want the best for the generations who are to follow us.

The politicisation of education, the march of political correctness, the unrequested and downright dangerous pacification of a nation and its new generation, and the tacit approval of a host of other sins through the complicity of non-action, is the responsibility of every ordinary New Zealander. We must not rest in silence while our nation is stolen from around us. We owe it to our forebears, and to the generations who will follow, to claim responsibility for the nation which has been forged in our name, and to refill the moral vacuum which has been created through our collective inaction in the face of an insidious evil.

Take responsibility for your word, thought, and action, in your own life; if we all do this, it must follow, that the direction of mankind and his societies will do the same.

I believe in capitalism, I support the profit motive, I welcome technology. But I believe also that we have a greater responsibility; that sometimes we must put our personal interests as secondary to those of the people who depend on us, our children and families.

We all know right from wrong; we must all make the personal

choice to do the right, and take responsibility for that, even when it involves suffering or going without.

We must regain the lost legacy of our immediate ancestral past, and re-attain the moral fortitude to live with honour.

And thus we may see the return of "Family Values", and of the decent society, which currently appears to be inexplicably lost, in a fog of selfishness, shallowness, and cynical legalese.

Perhaps this will not be such a bad thing.

Investigate, February 2005

OTHER BOOKS FROM HOWLING AT THE MOON PUBLISHING

The Critics On *Breaking Silence*

"*Breaking Silence* is not on my recommended read list. I firmly believe it is *compulsory* reading for anyone over 18." – Andrew Stone, *Albany Buzz* business magazine

"The book has real value" – Larry Williams, Newstalk ZB

"I found it an incredibly surprising book, and a very relevant book, and a very important book". – Anna Smart, Newstalk ZB

"I had no particular views on the case before this book came out but I have to say it's a powerful read. An influential read, one might say...All those people who poured out their invective when it became known the book was about to hit the book shops really should just read it for themselves. It may not be quite what they think." – Helen Hill, *The Marlborough Express*

"*Breaking Silence* is a chilling narrative and the most important I have read. Adults may need to read the story to gain any understanding. Younger people should read in it a warning: that it is the way we make decisions early on that may determine the course of our life and the lives of those entrusted to our care." – Pat Veltkamp Smith, *Southland Times*

The Critics On *The Inside Story*

"Undeniably...when Wishart hits he hits big. *Arthur Allan Thomas: The Inside Story* is a book two generations of New Zealanders have waited for...With his thorough analysis of the evidence and his generous use of first-person accounts it's a stellar piece of journalism..." – *Southland Times*

"Wishart has a brand new prime suspect and he lays out his case in this fascinating and highly readable book. Wishart is painstaking in his investigation, and his interviews with the man at the centre of the case, Arthur Thomas, offer a remarkable insight into one of New Zealand's most memorable characters. " – Kerre Woodham, Newstalk ZB

"Through the book Wishart lays the ground for his claim that Johnston was actually the murderer and by his position on the inquiry team and proximity to Hutton, was able to influence an outcome which saw Thomas convicted twice of a double murder. Wishart's conclusions are disturbingly possible in my view. – former Det. Insp. Ross Meurant, *NZ Herald*

BREAKING SILENCE

THE KAHUI CASE

MACSYNA KING AND
THE REAL STORY OF THE
MURDER OF HER TWINS

IAN WISHART
#1 bestselling author

Arthur Allan Thomas:
THE INSIDE STORY

CREWE MURDERS: NEW EVIDENCE

Jailed for a crime he didn't commit,
now for the first time in 40 years,
he tells his incredible story as
we name a new prime suspect

Ian Wishart
#1 bestselling author

Lawyers, Guns & Money

Ian Wishart

A true story of horses & fairies, bankers & thieves...

"It's the closest thing to a John Grisham novel, but it's the real thing"

The
Paradise
CONSPIRACY

Ian Wishart

From the shady cover of a tropical tax haven, they hatched a billion dollar plan to raid the treasuries of the world, robbing the poor to give to the rich

THE HUNT

A KIWI MUM, HER KIDNAPPED BABIES, AND A 30 YEAR WORLDWIDE SEARCH

IAN WISHART & GEORGE LONDON

AIR CON

seriously

THE INCONVENIENT TRUTH
ABOUT GLOBAL WARMING

IAN WISHART   #1 BESTSELLING AUTHOR